W9-DHN-935

Beating the Grünfeld

Beating the Grünfeld

ANATOLY KARPOV

Translated by John Sugden

An Owl Book
Henry Holt and Company
New York

Henry Holt and Company, Inc.
Publishers since 1866
115 West 18th Street
New York, New York 10011

Henry Holt® is a registered trademark
of Henry Holt and Company, Inc.

Copyright © 1992 by Anatoly Karpov
All rights reserved.

First published in the United States in 1993 by
Henry Holt and Company, Inc.
Originally published in Great Britain in 1992 by
B. T. Batsford Ltd.

Library of Congress Catalog Card Number: 92-56735

ISBN 0-8050-2632-0 (An Owl Book: pbk.)

First American Edition—1993

Printed in the United Kingdom
All first editions are printed on acid-free paper.∞

10 9 8 7 6 5 4 3 2 1

Adviser: R. D. Keene, GM, OBE
Technical Editor: Andrew Kinsman

Contents

Preface

I have to admit that the title of this book has an air of sales-talk about it, as similar titles generally do. Anyone trying to think up a recipe for beating this or that opening will scarcely succeed, and the Grünfeld Defence is no exception. But seriously: to chessplayers whose repertoire includes the Grünfeld, the author imagines that the present work will be of considerable interest and use. Hence it is indeed quite possible that the book will help many readers to score wins – with Black if they are adherents of the Grünfeld, and with White if they are looking for a way to combat this defence.

The book consists of a collection of games (or fragments of games) which reflect the contemporary state of Grünfeld theory. It is constructed around twenty-five paradigms of play by connoisseurs of this opening (like many authors I have a weakness for round figures), but the total number of examples is about ten times higher! The notes to each of the twenty-five principal games constitute a thorough discussion of the currently popular variations. As a result, all the most fashionable systems occurring in grandmaster practice in the last few years have found their way into the book. The selected games are not arranged chronologically but grouped according to themes. For this reason, the freshest examples – those from the recently concluded duel for the world chess crown, which incidentally are the most fully annotated – do not form the culmination of the book, but are placed in the middle of it .... .

This book is written in the same format as the four-volume work probably already familiar to the reader: *The Open Game (Semi-Open Game / Closed Openings / Semi-Closed Openings) in Action*. That is to say, the scores of all the principal games are given in full, and in analysing the opening the reader will mostly be able to study its relation to the middlegame or even the endgame. In some games, the later stages are of independent interest and consequently receive fairly detailed notes. The informal layout of material has permitted the author to select contemporary games according to his own discretion (in contrast, say, to an opening monograph, where you also have to include systems that have not been used in practice for a long time).

Whereas the four-volume work just mentioned covers the development of theory in the period 1984–7 (the last-but-one World Championship cycle), all the principal Grünfeld games in the present book are from the later period 1988–90, including the most recent World Championship match.

In my encounters with Gary Kasparov, the Grünfeld Defence has figured prominently. In our last three matches the most varied systems were tried out, and in our preparations we utilised all the most important theoretical material. As a result of these matches, the theory was in turn substantially enriched. Many ideas employed for the first time by Kasparov and myself have seen an onrush of further developments. Suitable examples of this are included in the book, while practical sources prior to 1988 are incorporated in the notes to the principal games.

I should mention that I usually play the white side of the Grünfeld while Kasparov plays Black, and that both of us strive for victory (not only when playing each other). Such is the nature of this sharp and uncompromising opening, in which playing for the draw is inimical to both sides – although, to be sure, our fierce contests have often ended peacefully. For those who like statistics, let me give my overall score against the Grünfeld in each of these matches. London/Leningrad 1986: +3 =6. Seville 1987: +2 −1 =7. New York/Lyon 1990: +1 =3. As you can see, we have played almost an entire World Championship match of Grünfelds – with a definite plus score in my favour. If you like, you may conclude from this that I *have* unearthed the secret of *Beating the Grünfeld* ... .

Obviously it is not only the World Champion and ex-champion who repeatedly contest this popular opening. It belongs to the repertoire of many prominent players. Suffice it to mention such names as Vassily Ivanchuk, Boris Gelfand and Jan Timman. Some of the valuable discoveries by these super-grandmasters will be found in this book.

In the course of working on the text, I have utilised a great many sources (*Informator*, books and magazines), and this is reflected in the sheer quantity of references to games by masters and grandmasters. In the majority of cases where a variation or individual move is of major significance, its originator is mentioned.

In conclusion, I must thank Soviet Master Evgeny Gik, my co-author in many books, for his help in preparing the manuscript.

Anatoly Karpov

1 Seville Variation

Game No. 1
Kuzmin–Henkin
Moscow 1989

1	d4	♘f6
2	c4	g6
3	♘c3	d5
4	cd	♘xd5
5	e4	♘xc3
6	bc	♗g7
7	♗c4	c5
8	♘e2	♘c6
9	♗e3	0–0
10	0–0	♗g4

The game has followed the main system of the Grünfeld. I would just remind the reader that in the event of 10 ... cd 11 cd ♘a5 12 ♗d3 ♗e6 13 d5, theory states that White obtains a dangerous attack for the exchange.

11	f3	♘a5 *(1)*

But now Black can answer 12 ♗d3 with 12 … cd 13 cd ♗e6, and the exchange sacrifice (14 d5) is less dangerous to him, since in several lines he has an important queen check on b6 (the details can be found in any reference work on the Grünfeld). However, in this situation White's exchange sacrifice is by no means forced. We shall later acquaint ourselves with a recent game with 14 ♖c1 instead (Game No. 6, Yusupov–Kasparov).

	12	♗xf7+

So International Master Kuzmin, one of my seconds, has decided to participate in the theoretical debate launched by Kasparov and myself in Seville. After that 1987 match, Kasparov stated that the plan chosen by White with 12 ♗xf7+ was unpromising. But to judge from the way the play went in the five games in question, it cannot be said that Black easily solved his opening problems. And in the post-match duel to which we shall presently turn (Game No. 2), he was thoroughly routed.

The pawn structure that now arises gives White every reason to count on the initiative, besides which he has an extra pawn. But then again, the position is highly dynamic and may very well suit the taste of the player of the black pieces.

Anyway, interest in this variation has not died down in three years, and numerous games enriching its theory have been played. Most of them will be mentioned in this book, over the first five main games. Of course, to some extent it will also be necessary to refer back to the Seville games.

12	…	♖xf7
13	fg	♖xf1+
14	♔xf1	

Let me emphasise that the main feature of the position is not the extra pawn; the freedom of Black's game compensates for this minor deficit. White's basic plan is to block up the enemy bishop on g7, by means of the pawn chain c3/d4/e5/g5/h4. Black will rely on tactical devices to enable his bishop to escape onto the h6–c1 diagonal.

14	…	♕d6 *(2)*

This queen sortie occurred in three games in the Seville match and two of our later encounters. It has also been played in many other games in recent years. Let us nonetheless mention some alternatives.

In the ninth game in Seville, Kasparov preferred **14 … cd** 15 cd

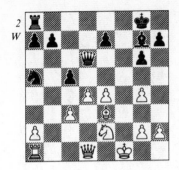

♕b6, and after 16 ♔g1 ♕e6 17 ♕d3! I returned the pawn while keeping all my positional trumps. The offshoots arising from 14 ... cd 15 cd will be examined in detail in Game No. 5 (apart from 15 ... ♕b6, the moves 15 ... ♕d7 and 15 ... e5 have been seen).

The Seville match was not yet over when the new move **14 ... ♕d7** occurred in a game Chernin–Gavrikov, Lvov 1987. That game proceeded: **15 dc** ♖f8+ (15 ... ♕xg4 16 ♘f4!) 16 ♔g1 ♕xg4 17 ♘f4 (17 ♕d3 ♘c6 18 h3 is not bad either) 17 ... ♕xd1+ (but not 17 ... ♖xf4? 18 ♗xf4 ♕xf4, on account of 19 ♕d8+) 18 ♖xd1 ♗xc3 19 ♘d5 (White gains nothing from 19 ♘e6 ♖c8 20 ♖d7 ♔f7 21 ♘g5+ ♔e8 22 ♖d3 ♗b4, or in this line 21 ♗g5? ♗f6! 22 ♗xf6 ♔xe6) 19 ... ♗f6 20 ♗h6 (the advantage is with White, but Black manages to hold on) 20 ... ♖e8 (but not 20 ... ♖f7 21 ♘xf6+ ♖xf6 22 e5 ♖f5 23 g4, and White wins) 21 ♘xf6+ ef 22 ♖d7 ♖xe4 23 ♖g7+ ♔h8 24 ♖c7 ♔g8 25 ♖g7+ (25 ♗d2 ♘c6 26 ♖xb7 ♖e7) 25 ... ♔h8 26 ♖c7 ♔g8 27 ♖g7+ ♔h8 28 ♖c7, draw. Gutman suggests 20 g4! ♖e8 21 ♖b1 a6 22 ♔f2, followed by ♔e2 and ♗d2, with the initiative.

In answer to 14 ... ♕d7, a more logical move seems to be **15 g5** *(3)*, as played in Karpov–Gavrikov, European Speed Chess Championship, Spain 1988.

Despite the 'non-serious' nature of the contest, the game is of considerable interest: **15 ... ♕e6** 16 e5! ♕c4! 17 ♔g1 ♖d8 18 ♕e1 ♘c6 19 ♗f2 a6 (wouldn't 19 ... b5!? have been better?) 20 a4 ♘a5 21 h4 ♗f8 22 dc! ♘b3 23 ♖b1! (more precise than 23 ♖d1 ♖xd1 24 ♕xd1 ♘xc5) 23 ... e6 (but now 23 ... ♘xc5 loses to 24 ♖b4 ♕d5 25 ♖d4) 24 c6! bc 25 ♘d4 ♘xd4 26 cd ♕xa4 27 ♕c3 (White has an obvious endgame advantage) 27 ... ♖c8 28 h5! gh 29 ♕h3 ♖e8 30 ♕xh5 ♖e7 (30 ... ♕c2 31 ♖b7) 31 g6 ♕c2 32

gh+ ☖xh7 33 ♕g4+ ♔h8 34 ☖f1 ♕f5 (34 ... ♕d3 35 ♗h4!) 35 ♕xf5 ef 36 ♗e3 ☖h5 37 g4! ☖h3 38 ☖xf5 ☖xe3 39 ☖xf8+ ♔g7 40 ☖f4! (the rook ending is won for White) 40 ... a5 41 ♔f2 ☖b3 42 ☖f6 ☖d3 (42 ... ☖c3 43 ♔e2 a4 44 ♔d2 etc.) 43 ☖d6 a4 44 ♔e2 ☖g3 45 ☖xc6 ☖xg4 46 ♔d3 47 ☖a6 ♔f7 48 ♔c4 ☖g3 49 d5 1–0.

From diagram 3, a game Gligorić–Popović, Yugoslavia 1988, continued differently: **15 ... ☖d8** 16 ♔g1 e6 (an evident improvement is 16 ... cd 17 cd ♔h8 18 ♕d3 ♘c6 19 ☖d1 ♘xd4 20 ♘xd4 e5) 17 ☖b1 ♘c4 (17 ... cd 18 cd ♘c6 19 d5 ed 20 ed ♕xd5 21 ♕xd5 ☖xd5 22 ☖xb7 is good for White) 18 ♗f2 b5 19 ♕d3 a6 (White can now obtain the better game with 20 h4 ♘e5 21 ♕h3, but Gligorić prefers to move his other rook's pawn) 20 a4 ♘e5 21 ♕c2 (now 21 ♕h3 ♘c6 22 ab ab would lead to unclear play – but not 21 ... ba 22 de a3 23 ♗e1! etc.) 21 ... ♘g4! 22 e5 ba (Gligorić gives the variation 22 ... ♘xf2! 23 ♔xf2 b4! 24 dc ♗xe5!, and Black has no problems) 23 ♗g3 ♕c6 24 ♕a2 ♘e3 25 ♘f4 (White has a slight edge in the endgame, but it isn't enough for victory) 25 ... ♘d5 26 ♘xd5 ♕xd5 27 ♕xa4 cd 28 cd ♕xd4+ 29 ♕xd4 ☖xd4 30 ☖b6 ♔f7 31 ☖xa6 ☖d5 32 ☖a7+ ♔g8 33 h4 ♗xe5 34 ♗xe5 ☖xe5 35 ☖e7 ☖e4 36 g3 ☖e1+ 37 ♔f2 ☖e5 38 ♔f3 ☖e1 39 ♔f4 ☖e2 ½–½.

Perhaps an even sounder answer to 14 ... ♕d7 is **15 h3**. This occurred in Yusupov–Popović, Belgrade 1989. There followed 15 ... ♘c4 16 ♗f2 cd 17 cd e5 18 de ♘d2+ 19 ♔e1 ♗xe5? (according to Yusupov, unclear play results from 19 ... ♗h6 20 ♕c2 ☖c8 21 ♕b2 ♘xe4 22 ♕b3+) 20 ☖c1 ☖d8 21 ♕c2!, and in the endgame White made no mistake in exploiting his extra pawn.

In addition to 14 ... cd, 14 ... ♕d6 and 14 ... ♕d7, Black has one other option: **14 ... ♛c8**. This move was tried out in Portisch–Korchnoi, Reykjavik 1988. After **15 ♛a4?!** Black obtained an active game with 15 ... cd 16 cd ♘c4 17 ♗f4 a6 18 g5 b5 19 ♛b3 e5 20 de ♛c6. At this point, instead of 21 ♖d1, White should have preferred 21 ♛d3!? ♘xe5 22 ♛d5+ ♛xd5 23 ed b4, with about equal chances (but not 23 ... ♘d3 24 ♖d1 ♘xf4 25 ♘xf4 ♖f8 26 g3 ♗e5 27 d6 ♗xf4 28 gf ♖xf4+ 29 ♚e2, with initiative for White). Korchnoi answered 21 ♖d1 with 21 ... ♖f8!, whereupon Portisch played 22 ♖d5, overlooking the blow 22 ... ♛xd5!. After 23 ed ♘d2+ 24 ♚e1 ♘xb3 25 ab ♖d8, Black gained a decisive endgame advantage – though it took him fifty more moves to achieve the win!

Evidently White should react to 14 ... ♛c8 in the same way as if the queen had gone to d7, with **15 h3** or **15 g5**. Seirawan–Kudrin, USA Ch. 1989, went 14 ... cd 15 cd ♛c8 16 g5, when the black queen utilised its possession of the c-file with 16 ... ♛c4. However, after 17 ♚g1 ♖d8 18 ♛e1 ♘c6 19 e5 e6 20 ♛f2 ♘b4 21 ♘f4 ♖c8 22 ♖f1, it became clear that the raid with the queen had achieved nothing and the white centre was invulnerable. In the endgame after 22 ... ♘d3 23 ♘xd3 ♛xd3 24 ♛f7+ ♚h8 25 ♗f2, White had a material and positional plus, which he duly converted to a win.

15   e5

In the 11th match game in Seville, I chose 15 ♚g1. For the current state of theory on that move, see the notes to Game No. 4, where the completely new 15 ♛a4!? will also be discussed.

15   ...   ♛d5 *(4)*

15 ... ♛e6 has also been seen. After **16 g5** ♘c4 (16 ... ♛c4 17 ♚g1 transposes into Karpov–Gavrikov, where play resolved itself clearly in White's favour), White has to avoid the trap 17 ♛d3? ♛f5+! which costs him a piece; but even with 17 ♗f2 ♖f8 18 ♚g1 ♛f7 19 ♛e1 ♘a3 20 ♖c1 ♛xa2, he achieves nothing.

A game Makarov–Hodko, USSR 1988, went **16 h3** ♘c4 17 ♛d3 ♖d8 18 ♛e4! (18 ♘f4 ♛a6!) 18 ... ♛c6 19 ♛xc6 ♘xe3+ 20 ♚f2 ♘xg4+ 21 hg bc 22 ♖b1 cd 23 cd c5 24 ♚e3! cd+ (24 ... ♖d5 25 ♚e4 e6 26 ♖b5 ♗f8 27 ♖a5 is bad for Black) 25 ♘xd4 ♖d5 26 ♘c6. At this point, in Makarov's view, Black should have played 26 ... ♖c5; after 27 ♖b8+ ♗f8 28 ♖c8 ♚g7, White has no more than a slight edge.

Quite a good reply to 15 ... ♛e6 seems to be **16 ♘f4 ♛c4+** 17

♕e2! ♖f8 18 ♕xc4+ ♘xc4 19 ♔e2, with the better ending for White. One other possibility, **16 ♔g1**, was tried in Hansen–Ferčec, Aosta 1989. Black restored the material balance, but after 16 ... ♕xg4 17 ♕d3 ♕e6 18 ♗g5! ♖f8 19 h3 cd 20 cd ♗xe5 21 de ♕xe5 22 ♗c1! ♕xa1 23 ♕d5+ e6 24 ♕xa5 ♖c8 25 ♕d2 b5 (doubtless a more accurate line was 25 ... ♕b1 26 ♔h2 ♕c2 27 ♕e3 ♕xa2 28 ♘c3 ♕b3 29 ♗d2, with a minimal plus for White) 26 a3, his position was fairly difficult.

4
W

16   ♗f2

In this case 16 ♘f4 is weak, since the queen gets to e4. A game Lichak–Asrian, Leningrad 1990, went 16 ... ♖f8 17 ♔g1 ♕e4 18 ♕f3 ♕xf3 19 gf ♗h6 20 ♘d5 ♗xe3+ 21 ♘xe3 cd 22 cd ♘c6 23 ♖b1 b6 24 ♔g2 ♘xd4, and Black had an endgame advantage.

16   ...   ♖f8

So far, the play coincides with game 5 in Seville. In the 7th match game, the black rook preferred to go to d8, forcing the white queen off the central file. In later games, 16 ... ♖d8 completely replaced the transfer of the rook to f8; we shall go into details in the notes to the next game in this book.

17   g5 *(5)*

A valuable novelty. The game in which this position first arose (number 5 in Seville) continued 17 ♔g1 ♗h6 18 h4 ♕f7 19 ♗g3 ♗e3+ 20 ♔h2 ♕c4! 21 ♖b1 (21 dc is met by 21 ... ♕xg4, with a good game) 21 ... b6 22 ♖b2 (but here 22 dc is sounder) 22 ... ♕d5! 23 ♕d3 ♘c4 24 ♖b1 b5, and the sharp duel should have ended in a draw (although a blunder by Kasparov eventually enabled me to win). However, 24 ... g5 would have given Black good winning chances.

With 17 g5, White achieves his principal aim of shutting off the opposing bishop. Admittedly his king is dangerously placed opposite the black rook, but this is just a temporary problem.

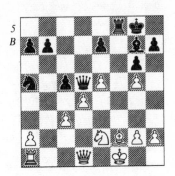

| 17   ...   ♕f7 |

Gutman gives the variation 17 ... ♕e4 (or 17 ... ♘c4 18 ♔g1 ♕e4 19 ♘g3 ♕f4 20 ♕e2 b5 21 ♘e4, with the better game for White) 18 ♘g1! ♘c4 19 ♘f3 ♘e3+ 20 ♗xe3 ♕xe3 21 ♕b3+ ♔h8 22 ♖e1!, and Black's position is not to be envied. 22 ... ♖xf3+ may look inviting, but after 23 gf ♕xf3+ 24 ♔g1 ♕g4+ 25 ♔f2 ♕h4+ 26 ♔e2 ♕g4+ 27 ♔d2 ♕xg5+ 28 ♔c2, there is no perpetual.

| 18   ♕e1   h6 |

In reply to 18 ... ♕f5, Henkin gives these variations:
(a) **19 h4**, and now:
(a1) 19 ... ♕g4 20 ♔g1 h6 (or 20 ... ♘c4 21 ♘g3! ♕xh4 22 ♘e4, with a distinct plus) 21 gh ♗xh6 22 ♘g3! cd 23 cd ♕xh4 24 ♘f5! ♕g5 25 ♘xh6+ ♕xh6 26 ♕xa5, and wins.
(a2) 19 ... h6 20 gh ♗xh6 21 ♘g3, with a clear advantage.
(a3) 19 ... ♕e4 20 ♔g1 cd 21 cd ♘c4 22 ♖c1! (but not 22 g3? ♗xe5 23 de ♘xe5) 22 ... ♘e3 23 ♘f4!, and if 23 ... ♖xf4 24 ♗xe3 ♖xh4 25 ♖c8+, White has a considerable initiative.
(b) Another playable line is 19 ♘g3 ♕xg5 20 ♘e4 ♕f4 21 ♔g1 cd 22 cd ♘c6 23 ♖b1! with the advantage.

In a game Kuzmin–Malishauskas, USSR 1989, Black played a new move, **18 ... ♘c4** (18 ... ♘c6 is also possible). There followed **19 ♘g3 ♘b2 20 ♘e4 ♘d3 21 ♕e3** (21 ♕e2 ♘f4!) **21 ... ♘xf2 22**

♘xf2 (Kuzmin recommends 22 ... ♕c4+, without the exchange in the centre; after 23 ♔g1 ♖d8, Black has the initiative) 23 cd ♕c4+ 24 ♔g1 ♖d8 25 ♕b3 ♕xb3 26 ab ♖xd4 27 ♖xa7 ♗xe5 ½–½ (Black would lose after 27 ... ♖b4 28 ♘d3 ♖ × b3 29 ♖a8+ ♔f7 30 e6+!). A much stronger answer to 18 ... ♘c4 is **19 ♘g1!** followed by 20 ♘f3.

	19	**gh**

Stronger than 19 ♘g3 hg 20 ♘e4 cd 21 cd ♕f5.

	19	**...**	**♗xh6**
	20	**♔g1**	**♘c4**

An inadequate alternative is 20 ... ♗d2 21 ♕xd2 ♕xf2+ 22 ♔h1 ♔g7 23 ♕d3 ♘c6 24 ♖d1.

	21	**♘g3!**	**♗d2**

Otherwise White is a clear pawn up. The bishop move to d2 would also have been a good reply to 21 ♗h4.

	22	**♕e2**	**♗xc3**
	23	**♖f1!**	

23 e6? ♕xf2+ 24 ♕xf2 ♖xf2 would lose for White.

	23	**...**	**♕e6**

If **23 ... cd**, then 24 e6! is immediately decisive. On **23 ... ♘d2?**, White has 24 ♖d1 cd (24 ... ♕xa2 25 ♘e4!, or 24 ... ♕f4 25 dc!) 25 ♖xd2 ♗xd2 26 ♕xd2 d3 27 ♗xa7.

	24	**dc!**	**♗xe5**
	25	**♖e1**	**♕d5**

25 ... ♕f7 or 25 ... ♖f4 would be safer.

	26	**♖d1**	

If 26 ♕g4 (26 ♘e4 ♗d4!), Black has 26 ... ♖xf2! when Henkin's analysis goes: 27 ♕xg6+ ♔f8 28 ♔xf2 (28 ♕h6+ ♗g7) 28 ... ♗d4+! (28 ... ♕d4+ 29 ♔f1 ♘e3+ 30 ♖xe3) 29 ♔f1 ♘e3+ 30 ♖xe3 (but not 30 ♔e2 ♕xg2+ 31 ♔d3 ♕c2+) 30 ... ♗xe3 31 ♕f5+ ♕xf5 32 ♘xf5 ♗xc5, and Black seizes the initiative.

	26	**...**	**♖xf2**

After 26 ... ♕e6 or 26 ... ♕f7, Black could still offer resistance, but now the game ends at once.

	27	**♖xd5**	**♖xe2**
	28	**♘xe2**	**♔f7**
	29	**c6!**	**b6**
	30	**♖xe5!**	

1–0

Game No. 2
Karpov–Kasparov
Belfort 1988

1 d4 ♘f6 2 c4 g6 3 ♘c3 d5 4 cd ♘xd5 5 e4 ♘xc3 6 bc ♗g7 7 ♗c4 c5 8 ♘e2 ♘c6 9 ♗e3 0–0 10 0–0 ♗g4 11 f3 ♘a5 12 ♗xf7+ ♖xf7 13 fg ♖xf1+ 14 ♔xf1 ♕d6 15 e5 ♕d5
16 ♗f2 ♖d8

After the 7th game in Seville, in which Kasparov played this move for the first time, the rook manoeuvre to d8 became standard practice in this position. On d1 the queen was quite conveniently placed, but now the threat of 17 ... ♗xe5 compels it to leave its post. White gains nothing from **17 ♘f4 ♕c4+** (17 ... ♕f7 18 ♘h3!) 18 ♕d3 ♕xd3+ 19 ♘xd3 cd 20 cd ♘c6 21 ♘c5 ♘xd4 22 ♘xb7 ♖d5 23 ♖e1 ♖xe5 24 ♖xe5 ♗xe5 25 ♘d8 a6, with equality.

There are three ways for the queen to vacate the d-file: along the d1–a4 diagonal (to a4 or c2), or with **17 ♕e1**. We examine **17 ♕a4** in the present game, and **17 ♕c2** in Game No. 3. But first, let us recall how the Seville game proceeded: **17 ♕e1 ♕e4 18 g5 ♕f5!** 19 h4 ♘c4 (he should have put pressure on the centre with 19 ... ♘c6 20 ♔g1 ♕e4, leading to sharp play) 20 ♔g1 ♕g4 (20 ... b5 was more precise, as after White's next move, the black knight will feel uncomfortable) 21 a4 h6 22 ♖a2! hg 23 ♕b1! (White thus succeeds in exploiting the weakness of the a2–g8 diagonal) 23 ... gh 24 ♕b3 ♕e6 25 ♘f4 ♕f7 26 ♘xg6 ♕xg6 (I shall refrain from further comment until we reach one particular critical position; this book is not the place for exhaustive notes on the Seville games, they are no doubt well known to the reader already) 27 ♕xc4+ ♔h8 28 ♖b2! cd 29 cd ♕g4 30 ♕f7! ♖xd4 31 ♗xd4 ♕xd4+ 32 ♖f2 ♕xe5 33 ♖f5 ♕e1+ 34 ♖f1 ♕e5 35 ♔h1? (although we are quite a long way out of the opening, it is appropriate to take stock of the situation. With 35 ♕f4!, White should come out on top: 35 ... ♕xf4 36 ♖xf4 ♗f6 37 ♖c4 ♔g7 38 ♖c7 b6 39 ♔f1, with a won ending) 35 ... b6 36 ♕f4 ♕h5 (a withdrawal that was impossible a move earlier. If now 37 ♕b8+ ♔h7 38 ♕xa7, the white queen is far from the scene of action, and after 38 ... ♕e2 Black has enough initiative to draw. But White has another way to exploit the awkward position of the black queen on the rook's file 37 ♕f5? (at this point, 37 ♖f3! ♗f6 38 ♕b8+ ♔g7 39 ♕xa7 ♕c5 40 ♕a6 was decisive) 37 ... ♕e2 38 ♖c1? (here was White's third successive opportunity to win this

game. He should have checked first – 38 ♕c8+ ♔h7 – and only
then played 39 ♖c1, threatening ♕c2+. If 39 ... ♕h5, then 40
♕c2+ ♔h8 41 ♕d1! etc.). The game lasted another 40 moves,
but all my efforts to overcome my opponent were in vain. Although
Black was on the brink of defeat more than once in this game, we
have seen that the opening was not to blame. After 17 ♕e1, Black
had the means to obtain a perfectly reasonable position.

17   ♕a4 (6)

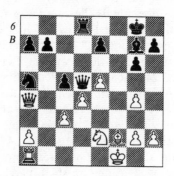

Now after the reply 17 ... b6, my queen would withdraw to c2.
You might ask what point there is in provoking a useful move of
Black's b-pawn instead of placing the queen on c2 at once. The
explanation is that in some variations (after Black's ... ♕c4, for
example) White can play ♕e4, gaining a valuable tempo by
attacking the knight which would by now have returned to c6.
So 17 ♕a4 has its plus side. But I will not offer a categorical
verdict as to where the queen feels more comfortable, although I
have tried both possibilities in my games.

17   ...   b6

In the event of **17 ... ♘c6 18 ♕b3 c4 19 ♕xb7**, White has the
better game.

After **17 ... ♘c4 18 ♘f4 ♕f7 19 g3 ♘d2+ 20 ♔g2 ♘e4 21 ♕c2
♘xf2 22 ♕xf2** White would again have a plus, but at move 20
Black has the powerful **20 ... g5!**, pointed out by Gutman.
He suggested that White should play **18 g5!** himself, with the
continuation **18 ... ♖f8 19 ♔g1 ♕f7 20 ♗g3 ♘e3 21 ♗f4 ♘d5
22 ♖f1**. Black's initiative has been neutralised and his bishop
imprisoned, which is to say that the opening contest is settled.

After **17 ...** ♖**f8** 18 ♔g1 ♕f7 19 ♗h4! ♘c4 20 ♕b3, the bishop is again unable to break out and free itself: 20 ... ♗h6 21 g5! ♗xg5 22 ♗xg5 ♕f2+ 23 ♔h1 ♕xe2 24 h3, with a substantial advantage to White.

18   ♕c2

There is nothing more for the queen to do on a4.

18   ...   ♖f8

After this, the black pieces come under pressure. Evidently **18 ... ♖c8** *(7)* was more exact, trying to obtain counterplay along the c-file.

7
W

From diagram 7, here are some important recent examples:

Tisdall–Thorsteins, Reykjavik 1989, went **19 dc** bc (19 ... ♖f8? 20 cb ♘c4 21 ♔g1) 20 ♖d1 ♕xe5 21 ♕a4 ♖f8 22 ♖d3 c4 23 ♖f3 ♕d5 24 ♖xf8+ ♔xf8 25 ♗xa7 ♘c6 26 h3 ♕e4 27 ♕b5! and White had a considerable plus. However, 20 ... ♕c4! is more accurate: 21 ♗g3 ♕xg4 22 h3, with chances for both sides.

Lputian–Dzhandzhgava, Simferopol 1988, went **19 ♕d1 ♖d8 20 ♕c1** (20 ♕c2 repeats moves) 20 ... ♖f8 (the position that has now arisen is the same as in my game with Kasparov, except that the white queen is on c1. The difference is not too important, but ...) 21 h3 (this is a serious inaccuracy. Correct moves are 21 ♔g1 and 21 g5) 21 ... ♕f7 22 ♕e1 ♗h6 23 ♘g3 ♘c4 24 e6 ♕g7 25 ♘e4 ♗e3 26 ♕e2 b5 27 ♔g1 ♗xf2+ 28 ♘xf2 cd (Black has won his pawn back and seized the initiative; the game doesn't last much longer) 29 cd ♕xd4 30 ♖c1 g5 31 ♖c2 ♘e3 32 ♖d2 ♕a1+ 33 ♘d1 ♖f1+ 34 ♔h2 ♕e5+ 35 g3 ♕e4 36 ♖d8+ ♔g7 37 ♕b2+ ♔h6 0–1.

In Douven–Ilincić, Alma-Ata 1989, after 19 ♕d1 ♖d8, White played **20 ♕e1**, an improvement on the previous example. There followed 20 ... ♘c4 (a more precise method was 20 ... cd 21 cd ♗h6 22 ♔g1, and only then 22 ... ♘c4) 21 g5 ♕e4 22 ♔g1 ♕g4 23 ♘g3 cd 24 cd ♕xg5 25 ♕b4 ♖c8 26 ♘e4 ♕f4 27 ♕xe7 ♔h8 28 ♕e6 ♖f8 29 ♕xc4 ♕xe4 30 ♖e1, with a clear advantage.

19 ♘f4 is well answered by 19 ... ♕f7 or 19 ... ♕c4+ 20 ♕d3 ♗h6. Another inadequate line is **19 ♕d2** ♖f8 20 ♕g5 ♕f7 21 ♕h4 ♗h6! (but not 21 ... ♘c4? because of 22 g5!, as in Schneider–Ljubojević, Pernik 1988) 22 ♔g1 ♘c4!, and the initiative is with Black. At move 20, the unfortunate 20 ♔g1? led to a quick loss in Schulz–Filipović, Korimofen 1989: 20 ... ♗xe5 21 ♖d1 ♗xh2+!

It only remains to add that **18 ... ♕c4** would be met by 19 ♕e4 with favourable consolidation, for instance: 19 ... ♖f8 20 ♔g1! ♗h6 21 ♗h4!. Notice one peculiarity of the position resulting from 17 ... b6: Black now constantly has to reckon with the exchange d4xc5.

19 ♔g1 ♕c4

The bishop cannot now break out onto the open board: 19 ... ♗h6 20 h4 ♕f7 21 ♘g3, or 19 ... ♘c4 20 h4.

20 ♕d2!

White continues with his plan of restricting the bishop's mobility. After 20 ♕e4, he would have to reckon with 20 ... ♗h6 and especially with 20 ... ♘c6!?, threatening to capture on e5; naturally, 21 ♕xc6 ♕xe2 cannot arouse White's enthusiasm.

20 ... ♕e6

20 ... ♕f7 is not good, since after 21 ♘g3 everything fits together for White: his knight is transferred to e4, and his queen to e2. Nor does 20 ... ♗h6 21 ♕xh6 ♕xe2 rid black of his worries, on account of 22 ♕e3 ♕xg4 23 dc bc (23 ... ♘c4 24 ♕d4) 24 ♕xc5.

21 h3 ♘c4
22 ♕g5! *(8)*

A critical moment. In addition to ♘e2–f4, White will now be threatening ♗f2–h4 in some variations.

22 ... h6

22 ... ♗f6 is no good, if only because of 23 ef (23 ♘f4 is also strong) 23 ... ef 24 ♘f4.

23 ♕c1 ♕f7

To obtain counterplay Black had to opt for 23 ... b5, intending

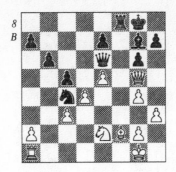

(for example) 24 ♘f4 ♕f7 25 ♘d3 b4!? – even though 25 ♗g3 maintains a plus for White. 23 ... ♕d5 would not work in view of 24 ♕c2!, while after 23 ... h5 the queen would return to g5.

24 ♗g3   g5

This move was roundly condemned by the commentators. But I do not recall that any serious alternative was suggested to give Black counterplay. **24 ... ♕d5** (for example) has been recommended, but then **25 ♘f4 ♕e4 26 ♘e6** would put Black in a very dangerous position. There are three variations – let us look at them:

(a) **26 ... ♖c8 27 ♕b1! ♕e3+ 28 ♗f2 ♕xc3+ 29 ♕xg6 ♕xa1+ 30 ♔h2**, with unavoidable mate.

(b) **26 ... ♘e3 27 ♕d2 cd 28 cd ♖c8 29 ♖e1 ♖c2 30 ♖xe3 ♕c6 31 d5**, and Black is lost. He could have tried driving the queen to e2, with 27 ... ♘c4 28 ♕e1 ♘e3 29 ♕e2 cd. Then 30 cd ♖c8 would give Black strong counterplay, but 30 ♘xf8 ♗xf8 (30 ... d3 31 ♕f2) 31 ♕f3! ♕d3 32 cd ♕xd4 33 ♖e1 clears up the situation completely – since 33 ... ♘c2+ 34 ♗f2 ♘xe1 is refuted by the intermediate 35 ♕b3+.

(c) **26 ... cd 27 ♘xf8 ♘e3 28 ♕d2 dc 29 ♕e2 ♗xf8 30 ♕f3**, with a big advantage.

25 ♕c2   ♕d5
26 ♗f2   b5
27 ♘g3   ♖f7

Forced. If 27 ... b4, then 28 ♘f5 is unpleasant, while 28 ... ♖f7 is met by 29 e6 ♕xe6 ♖e1 ♕d7 31 cb.

28 ♖e1

If White had wanted, he could have put a stop to Black's queenside counterplay with 28 ♖c1.

28	...	b4
29	♕g6	♚f8

29 ... bc loses immediately to 30 ♘f5 ♚f8 31 e6 ♖xf5 32 gf ♘d6 33 dc.

30	♘e4

30 ♘f5 is also strong: 30 ... e6 31 ♘xh6 ♖f4 32 ♕xg5, or 32 ♕h7.

30	...	♖xf2

The exchange sacrifice is incapable of improving matters. All it demands from White is a modicum of accuracy.

31	♚xf2	bc
32	♕f5+	♚g8
33	♕c8+	♚h7
34	♕xc5	♕f7+
35	♚g1	c2
36	♘g3	♗f8
37	♘f5	♚g8
39	♖c1	

1–0

Black's pieces on the kingside never succeeded in breaking free. As this game was played in the World Cup in the French town of Belfort, someone jokingly called 17 ♕a4 the Belfort variation ... .

I might add that this game was declared the best game played in the first half of 1988 (*Informator*, vol. 45). Also, it proved to be our last decisive encounter until the following (already our fifth) World Championship match.

Game No. 3
Karpov–Timman
Rotterdam 1989

1 d4 ♘f6 2 c4 g6 3 ♘c3 d5 4 cd ♘xd5 5 e4 ♘xc3 6 bc ♗g7 7 ♗c4 c5 8 ♘e2 ♘c6 9 ♗e3 0–0 10 0–0 ♗g4 11 f3 ♘a5 12 ♗xf7+ ♖xf7 13 fg ♖xf1+ 14 ♚xf1 ♕d6 15 e5 ♕d5 16 ♗f2 ♖d8

In the fifth game in Seville, Kasparov chose 16 ... ♖f8 (see Game No. 1). As we know, the rook move to d8 was first employed in the 7th game of the match.

17	♕c2

In the first game with this line, I chose 17 ♕e1 (see Game No.

2); in Belfort 1988, I preferred 17 ♕a4 (Game No. 2).

<blockquote>17 ... ♛c4</blockquote>

In Grünberg–Ilinčić, Prague 1989, an equal game resulted from 17 ... ♖c8 18 ♘f4 ♛f7 19 ♕e4 ♝h6 20 g3 ♖f8 21 ♔g2 ♝xf4 22 gf ♕xf4 23 ♕xf4 ♖xf4 24 ♔g3 ♖f8.

<blockquote>18 ♕b2</blockquote>

But not 18 g5? on account of 18 ... cd. If 18 ♕e4, then 18 ... ♖d5!, threatening 19 ... ♖xe5, is quite good for Black.

<blockquote>18 ... ♝h6</blockquote>

In Ljubojević–Timman, Linares 1989, Black moved his rook again: **18 ... ♖f8.** There followed **19 ♔g1 ♝h6 20 ♖d1! ♕a4** 21 ♖e1 cd (better was 21 ... ♘c4 22 ♕b3 ♕xb3 23 ab ♘b2) 22 ♘xd4 ♕c4 23 h3 b6 24 ♘f3 ♖d8 25 ♝d4 (25 g5! is also playable) 25 ... ♝f4 26 ♔f2 ♕d5 27 ♕b1 ♘c4 28 ♕e4 ♘b2 29 ♕c2 ♕b5 30 ♖b1 ♘d3+ 31 ♔f1 ♕c4 32 ♕e2 b5 33 ♘e1! ♘xe5 34 ♖xb5 ♕f7! 35 ♔g1 ♘c6 36 ♘f3 ♘xd4 37 cd ♖c8 (but not 37 ... ♝d6 38 ♘g5 ♕f4 39 ♕e6+ ♔g7 40 ♕xe7+ with advantage, or 39 ... ♔f8? 40 ♖f5+ and wins) 38 ♖c5 ♖b8, and the players decided to draw by repetition. It remains to be noted that at move 28, White could have kept the initiative with 28 ♖e2!

After 18 ... ♖f8 19 ♔g1 ♝h6 20 ♖d1, an innovation, **20 ... ♕e6,** was played in L. Hansen–Jasnikowski, Warsaw 1990. (Instead, 20 ... ♕f7 21 ♘g3! ♘c4 22 ♕e2 ♕xf2+ 23 ♕xf2 ♝e3 24 ♘e4! ♖f4 25 ♖d3 is hardly good for Black.) However, after 21 h3 ♘c4 22 ♕xb7 ♝e3 (22 ... ♘e3 23 ♖a1 ♕f7 24 ♝xe3 ♝xe3+ 25 ♔h1 ♕f2 26 ♕b5 cd 27 ♘xd4!) 23 ♝xe3 ♘xe3 24 ♖d3 ♕f7 (or 24 ... ♖f1+ 25 ♔h2 ♘xg4+ 26 hg ♕xg4 27 ♖f3 ♕h5+ 28 ♖h3 ♕xe2 29 ♕xe7 ♖f7 30 ♕xc5 and wins – Hansen) 25 ♕f3! ♕xf3 26 gf ♖xf3 27 dc! White had a clear endgame advantage.

<blockquote>19 h4 *(9)*</blockquote>

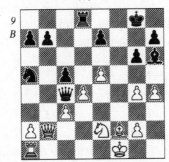

This position first occurred in Karpov–Kasparov, Amsterdam 1988, which proceeded as follows: **19 ... ♕f7 20 ♔g1** ♖f8 21 ♘g3 (21 ♗g3 is met by 21 ... ♗e3+ 22 ♔h2 ♕e6 23 g5 ♕g4) 21 ... ♘c4 22 ♕e2 ♕xf2+! (other continuations lead to advantage for White: 22 ♗d2 23 ♘e4, or 22 ... cd 23 cd ♕xf2+ 24 ♕xf2 ♗e3 25 ♕xe3 ♘xe3 26 ♖c1) 23 ♕xf2 ♗e3 24 ♕xe3 (24 ♔f1? ♖xf2 25 ♖xf2 cd) 24 ... ♘xe3 25 dc ♖c8 (but not 25 ... ♘xg4 26 ♖b1, when White is already better) 26 ♖b1 ♖xc5 27 ♖xb7 ♘xg4 28 ♖b4 (White may also play 28 ♖xe7 ♖xc3 29 ♘f1 ♖a3 30 e6 ♖xa2, which quickly draws) 28 ... h5 29 ♘e4 ♖xe5 30 g3 (30 ♔f1 ♘e3+ 31 ♔e2 ♘d5 32 ♖b8+ is simpler) 30 ... ♔f7 31 ♔g2 ♔e6 32 ♔f3 (a more accurate choice is 32 ♘g5+ ♔f6 33 ♖f4+ ♖f5 34 ♖e4 ♖f2+ 35 ♔g1 ♖xa2 36 ♖f4+ ♔e5 37 ♖e4+ ♔d6 38 ♖e6+ ♔d7 39 ♖xg6, and a draw can be agreed) 32 ... ♔f5!. Black now has slightly the better endgame, not that there is much danger to White. After a further two dozen moves, we agreed a draw.

The question arises whether the strange retreat with the queen to f7 can really solve all Black's problems. It turns out that this is not quite the case. In Vyzhmanavin–Ernst, Stockholm 1990, Black was dealt an annihilating blow, radically altering the assessment of the variation. The game went 19 ... ♕f7 **20 g5!** (White isn't afraid of the pin on his bishop. The main thing is to shut the opposing bishop out of play) 20 ... ♘c4 21 e6! (this is just the intermediate move that constitutes the refutation of Black's defence. White deflects the queen, now allowing his opponent to double on the f-file, and only afterwards picks up the b-pawn) 21 ... ♕f5 22 ♘g3 ♕xe6 23 ♕xb7 ♖f8 24 ♖e1! (now Black can't avoid loss of material) 24 ... ♘e3+ 25 ♔g1 ♖xf2 26 gh cd 27 cd ♖f8 28 ♕b2 ♘c4 29 ♖xe6 1–0.

Perhaps Timman had a foreboding of such misfortunes, and therefore avoided the move that justified itself in Amsterdam (19 ... ♕f7), preferring to occupy the f-file with his rook.

19	**...**	♖f8
20	**g5!**	

The stock manoeuvre; here too it guarantees White a plus.

20	**...**	♕d3
21	**♕b1!**	

Gaining a couple of tempi for bringing the queen to the defence.

A mistake would be 21 gh? ♘c4 22 ♕c1 ♕f5 23 ♕e1 ♘e3+ 24 ♔g1 ♘c2.

21	...	♕e3
22	♕e1	♗g7
23	♔g1	

But not 23 ♘c1? cd and everything is fine for Black, as after 24 ♕xe3de, he wins.

23	...	♕e4 *(10)*

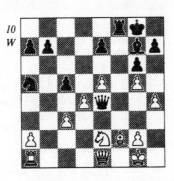

24	♘g3!

White returns the pawn but seizes all the key squares with his pieces. A familiar precept!

24	...	♕xh4
25	♘e4	

25 ♘f5 is also strong: 25 ... ♕xg5 26 ♘xg7 ♕g4 (26 ... ♔xg7 27 ♗h4 ♕g4 28 ♗xe7, etc.) 27 d5 ♔xg7 28 ♗xc5 ♕d7 29 ♕e4, and Black is in a bad way.

25	...	♖xf2

An exchange sacrifice (again not entirely voluntary!) analogous to the one that occurred in Karpov–Kasparov at Belfort. 25 ... ♕g4 does not help either: 26 ♘xc5 b6 27 ♕e4 ♕xg5 28 ♕d5+ ♖f7 29 ♘e6, and White should win.

26	♘xf2	cd
27	♖d1!	d3

On 27 ... ♘c6, I had in mind 28 cd ♘xd4 29 ♕e3 ♘c6 30 ♕b3+ ♔f8 31 ♕xb7 ♕c4 32 ♕c8+ ♔f7 33 ♘g4!. Nor is 27 ... dc 28 ♕xc3 ♘c6 29 ♕b3+ any better for Black.

28	♕e3!	♘c6

28 ... ♘c4 is well answered by 29 ♕d4.

29	♘xd3	♕a4
30	♕f3!	♕a5
31	e6	♘d8
32	♘f4	♗e5
33	♘d5!	♕c5+

If 33 ... ♘xe6, then 34 ♖f1! is decisive.

34	♔h1

1–0

There is no defence against the threats of 35 ♘f6+ and 35 ♖f1.

Game No. 4
Naumkin–Neverov
Moscow 1989

1 d4 ♘f6 2 c4 g6 3 ♘c3 d5 4 cd ♘xd5 5 e4 ♘xc3 6 bc ♗g7 7 ♗c4 c5 8 ♘e2 ♘c6 9 ♗e3 0–0 10 0–0 ♗g4 11 f3 ♘a5 12 ♗xf7+ ♖xf7 13 fg ♖xf1+ 14 ♔xf1 ♕d6

15 ♔g1

In the 5th and 7th match games in Seville I continued 15 e5, and the current state of theory on that line is given in the notes to the first three games of this book. In the 11th match game, however, I played the king to g1 here. White is prepared to return the pawn in order to obtain a sturdy centre. But before going on to a detailed discussion of the prospects for either side, it is worth mentioning one other possibility: **15 ♕a4!?**

This occurred in Zakharov–Henkin, Voronezh 1989, where Black replied 15 ... ♕xh2! *(11)*.

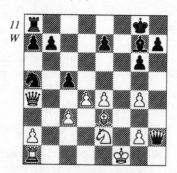

A bold piece sacrifice. Instead, the timid 15 ... b6 16 ♔g1 cd 17 cd ♕e6 18 d5! ♕xg4 19 ♖e1, followed by 20 h3, is in White's favour.

The game proceeded: 16 ♕xa5 ♖f8+ 17 ♔e1 (but not 17 ♗f2? on account of 17 ... ♕h4! 18 g3 ♕h1+ 19 ♘g1 ♕h2, and wins) 17 ... ♕h1+ 18 ♘g1! (on 18 ♗g1?!, Black has the very strong 18 ... ♗h6! 19 ♕xc5 ♕xg2, threatening 20 ... ♕f1 mate) 18 ... ♕xg2 (but here, 18 ... ♗h6 comes too late: 19 ♔d2 ♖f2+ 20 ♔d3 c4+ 21 ♔xc4 ♗xe3 22 ♕d5+ ♔g7 23 ♖e1, with the better endgame chances for White; if he prefers, he can give perpetual check by 23 ♘f3 ♕xa1 24 ♕e4+) 19 ♕b5 ♗h6 (after 19 ... cd 20 cd ♕xe4 21 ♕e2 and 22 ♖d1, White consolidates; but now, a highly unusual distribution of forces comes into being) 20 ♕e2 ♕g3+ 21 ♔d2 ♖f2 22 ♗xh6 ♖xe2+ 23 ♘xe2 ♕h3! 24 ♗e3! ♕xg4 25 ♖f1! h6! (a very strong move according to Henkin, who gives the following variations: 25 ... cd 26 ♗h6! dc+ 27 ♔c1 ♕c8 28 ♘d4, threatening ♘e6 and ♖f8+; 25 ... h5 26 ♘f4, followed by ♖g1; or 25 ... ♔g7 26 ♘f4 g5 27 ♖g1 ♕h4 28 ♖xg5+!. Now the game heads towards a draw) 26 ♗xh6 ♕xe4 27 ♖f8+ ♔h7 28 ♗g5 ♕e6 29 a4 cd 30 cd ♕a2+ 31 ♔e1 ♕xa4 32 ♖f7+ ♔g8 33 ♖xe7 ♕b4+ 34 ♔f2 a5 35 ♗f6 ♕b6! 36 ♗e5 a4 37 ♘f4 ♕b2+ (Black loses after 37 ... ♔f8 38 ♗g7+!, or 37 ... a3 38 ♘e6!) 38 ♔g1! ♕c1+ 39 ♔h2 ♕b2+ 40 ♔g1 ♕b1+ 41 ♔h2 ♕b2+ ½-½.

So the extravagant 15 ♕a4 is not dangerous to Black. It must be acknowledged that 15 e5, which we have already examined, is the most precise; White can move his king if the need arises. Nonetheless, 15 ♔g1 should also be studied.

15 ... ♕e6

In Polajžer–Anka, Dortmund 1988, Black played **15 ... ♖d8**. It isn't clear that the rook on d8 is useful to Black after **16 ♕d3 ♕e6 17 g5!**. However, White replied **16 ♕a4 ♕a6 17 ♖e1 ♕d3 18 ♗f2 ♘c4 19 ♕b5 ♖f8 20 ♕b1 ♕d2 21 ♕b3 b5 22 ♕xb5 ♘e3 23 h3**, and now, in Gutman's view, 23 ... ♗h6! would have given Black a powerful initiative.

16 ♕d3 ♕c4

So far, the play has followed the 11th game in Seville, and the text move is better than the capture on g4, which occurred (with a transposition of moves and the insertion of the pawn exchange on d4) in the 9th match game. In Chernin–Malishauskas, Lvov 1987 (played while the Seville match was still in progress), Black didn't hurry to exchange queens, preferring **16 ... cd 17 cd ♖d8**. After **18 g5 ♘c4 19 ♗f2 b5 20 a4** (20 h3 was worth considering)

20 ... ba 21 ♘f4 ♛f7 22 ♘d5 ♖f8 23 ♗g3 ♘b6 (but not 23 ...
♘b2 24 ♛c3 a3 25 h3, followed by ♗e5, with advantage) 24 h4
(24 ♘xb6 ♛b3!) 24 ... ♘xd5 25 ed ♛xd5, the chances were equal.
Instead of 18 g5 White can play **18 h3**, but after the queen exchange
Black's chances, once again, are no worse: 18 ... ♛c4 19 ♛xc4
♘xc4 20 ♗f2 e5 21 d5 ♗h6 22 h4 (22 a4 ♘d6!) 22 ... ♗d2 23
a4 ♘d6!. Note that variations involving the pawn exchange in the
centre (... c5xd4, c3xd4) will be examined more closely in Game
No. 5.

$$17 \quad \text{♛xc4}$$

It hardly pays White to avoid the queen exchange: 17 ♛d2 cd
18 cd ♛a6! or 17 ... ♛e6.

$$17 \quad ... \quad \text{♘xc4}$$
$$18 \quad \text{♗f2}$$

Yasser Seirawan, who has also incorporated this variation in
his repertoire, twice played **18 ♗g5** *(12)* here. Both games are
worth examining.

Seirawan–Lputian, St John 1988, continued **18 ... h6** 19 ♗xe7
cd (Black can win a piece with 19 ... ♖e8 20 ♗xc5 b6, but after
21 ♗xb6 ab 22 e5, White obtains more than enough pawns for
it. Furthermore, once his king is centralised and the knight jumps
to e4 via g3, the white pawn mass can become highly mobile) 20
cd ♖e8 21 ♖c1 ♘a5 (21 ... ♖xe7 22 ♖xc4 ♖xe4 23 ♔f2 ♖xg4
24 ♖c8+ ♔h7 25 ♖c7 is no better for Black, but 21 ... b5 was
worth considering) 22 ♖c7 ♘c6 23 ♗c5 ♖xe4 24 ♔f2 ♗xd4+
(in the event of 24 ... ♘xd4, Lputian gives 25 ♖xg7+! ♔xg7 26
♗xd4+ ♔f7 27 ♔f3 ♖e6 28 ♗xa7 ♖a6 29 ♗e3 ♖xa2 30
♗xh6 b5 31 ♘c1, with advantage) 25 ♘xd4 ♘xd4 26 ♖xb7 ♘c6

27 h3 ♖a4 28 a3. White has an extra pawn, which he eventually exploited to win (though it took him 30 moves!).

Seirawan–Hort, Lugano 1988, went **18 ... cd** 19 cd e5 20 ♖c1 (20 d5 h6 21 ♗c1 ♞d6 22 ♞g3 ♖c8 23 ♗e3 ♖c3 24 ♔f2 ♗f6! 25 a4 ♗g5 led to equality in Dlugy–Nikoloff, Toronto 1989; Black can also play the immediate 20 ... ♞d6 21 ♞g3 ♖c8 22 ♗e3, with adequate counterplay) 20 ... b5 21 de ♗xe5 22 ♖d1 ♖c8 (22 ... ♖e8 is more accurate and gives equality) 23 ♗f4! ♗g7 24 ♖d5 a6 25 ♔f2 ♖e8 26 ♔f3 ♔f7 27 h4 ♞e5+ 28 ♗xe5 ♖xe5 29 ♖d3 b4 30 ♞f4. Here again, White has an extra pawn, but this time Black managed to hold out.

Interestingly, his loss to Seirawan made such a strong impression on Lputian that he took the first opportunity to play this variation with White. In Lputian–Hansen, Dortmund 1988, Black played (from diagram 12) the immediate **18 ... e5**. There followed **19 d5 b5** (19 ... h6 20 ♗c1 is sounder for Black) **20 ♖b1 ♖b8 21 ♔f2** a5 22 ♞c1 h6 (22 ... ♞a3 23 ♖b3 b4 24 cb cb 25 d6) 23 ♗e3 ♞xe3 (in Lputian's view, 23 ... ♞d6 24 ♔f3 ♖f8+ 25 ♔e2 c4 26 ♔e1 ♞xe4 27 ♖xb5 ♞xc3 28 ♖xa5 ♖d8 would have given equality; but not 23 ... ♖f8+ 24 ♔e2 ♞xe3 25 ♔xe3 ♖f1 26 ♖a1! and 27 ♞b3!) 24 ♔xe3 c4 25 ♞e2 ♗f8 26 ♞g1 ♗c5+ 27 ♔e2 ♗xg1 28 ♖xg1 ♔f7 29 a3 ♔e7 (29 ... b4 would have retained some saving chances) 30 ♖b1, and White won the rook ending. After the game, Lputian explained that at move 21, the correct course was **21 a4!** b4 22 cb cb (or 22 ... ♖xb4 23 ♞c3 ♞d6 24 ♖e1, preparing 25 ♗e7) 23 ♞c1 ♗f8 24 ♞b3 ♞d6 25 ♞d2 b3 26 ♗e3 a6 27 ♔f1! ♖b4 (28 ... b2 29 ♔e2) 28 ♗c5 ♖xa4 29 ♗xd6 ♗xd6 30 ♖xb3, and White has the better chances.

18 ... cd

Black can play 18 ... e5 at once, without opening the c-file. After 19 d5 (19 dc ♖d8 20 g5 ♗f8) 19 ... b6 20 g5 ♖f8, he has a perfectly secure fortress.

19 cd e5

After 19 ... b6 or 19 ... b5, White plays 20 ♖b1! with the better chances.

20 d5 *(13)*

20 ♖c1 ♞d6 21 de ♗xe5 is not dangerous for Black.

20 ... ♞d6

A refinement on the 11th game in Seville. But before going any further, let us recall how that game (which played an important

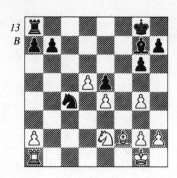

part in the match) proceeded. It might, incidentally, have been worth including it (accompanied as it is by some new annotations) among the 'basic' games in this volume. But we will not break our rule: only games played in 1988 or later are to be specially numbered.

20 ... ♗h6 21 h4 ♗d2 22 ♖d1 ♗a5

If 22 ... b5, White has 23 ♘c1!, heading for b3. Gutman quotes the following analysis by H. Wirthensohn: 23 ... a5 (23 ... ♗xc1 24 ♖xc1 ♘d6 25 ♖e1 a6 26 ♗g3 ♖e8 27 ♔f2) 24 ♘b3 ♗b4 (24 ... ♗c3 25 d6 a4 26 d7 ♖d8 27 ♘c5 ♘b6 28 ♖d6) 25 ♗c5 ♗xc5 26 ♘xc5 ♖c8 (26 ... ♘d6 27 ♘d7 ♘xe4 28 ♘xe5 ♘d6 29 ♖c1) 27 ♘b7 ♖c7 28 d6 ♖d7 29 ♖d5 ♘b6 30 ♘c5, and White is on top.

23 ♖c1 b5

Here 23 ... ♘d6 is no good: 24 ♘g3 ♗b6 25 ♗xb6 ab 26 ♖c7 ♖a4 27 ♖e7 ♘xe4 28 ♘xe4 ♖xe4 29 d6 ♔f8 30 ♖xh7 ♔e8 31 h5, and Black is doomed.

24 ♖c2 ♘d6 25 ♘g3 ♘c4 26 ♘f1 ♘d6 27 ♘g3 ♘c4 28 g5 ♔f7

White has consolidated his advantage. If 28 ... a6 (28 ... ♗b6 29 a4 ♘a3 30 ♖b2 ba 31 ♖a2), there follows 29 ♘f1 ♘d6 30 ♖c6 ♘xe4 31 ♘g3! ♘c3 32 d6! ♔f7 33 d7 ♖d8 34 ♗c5 ♖xd7 35 ♖f6+ ♔g8 36 h5 gh 37 ♘xh5 ♖d8 38 ♖xa6 ♗c7 39 ♘f6+, and Black is in a bad way.

29 ♘f1 ♘d6 30 ♘g3 ♘c4 31 ♔f1 ♔e7

Korchnoi suggested 31 ... ♗b6 32 ♗xb6 ab 33 ♔e2 ♖a4, but a stratagem we have seen before – 32 a4! ♘a3 33 ♖b2 ba 34 ♖a2 – gives White the advantage.

32 ♗c5+ ♔f7 (14)

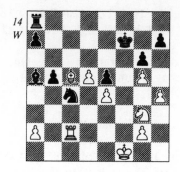

33 ♖f2+

A critical moment in the game. After the obvious 33 ♔e2, Black would scarcely be able to save himself: 33 ... ♗b6 34 a4 ♗xc5 35 ab ♖b8 36 ♔d3! ♖xb5 (36 ... a6 37 ♔xc4 ab+ 38 ♔b3 ♗d6 39 ♖c6 ♔e7 40 ♘e2 ♖a8 41 ♘c3 ♖a3+ 42 ♔b2, or 40 ... b4 41 ♘c1, with a won position) 37 ♔xc4 ♖b7 38 ♘f1 ♗d6 (38 ... a5 39 ♘d2, or 38 ... ♗b4 39 ♘e3) 39 ♘d2, etc.

33 ... ♔g7 34 ♖f6 ♗b6 35 ♖c6??

By retreating his bishop to f2, White would preserve the better chances. Instead of this, I commit a fatal blunder. The sad fact is that the possibility of the black knight jumping to the edge of the board has escaped my attention.

35 ... ♘a5 36 ♗xb6 ♘xc6 37 ♗c7 ♖f8+ 38 ♔e2 ♖f7 39 ♗d6 ♖d7 40 ♗c5 ♘a5 41 ♘f1 ♖c7 42 ♗d6 ♖c2+ 43 ♔d3 ♖xa2 44 ♘e3 ♗f7 45 ♘g4 ♘c4 46 ♘xe5+ ♘xe5 47 ♗xe5 b4 48 ♗f6 b3 49 e5 ♖xg2 50 e6+ ♔f8! 0–1.

Now at last we return to the game Naumkin–Neverov, which, as it happens, was decided very quickly.

21	♘g3	♗h6
22	♗c5	

White proceeds ineffectively and is soon in a difficult position. The immediate 22 h4 was better.

22	...	♘c4
23	h4	♖c8!
24	♗f2	♗f4
25	♘e2	♗d2
26	♖d1	a5!

White's loss of time in moving his bishop about begins to tell: Black creates a passed pawn, which decides the issue.

27 g5 b5 28 ♘g3 b4 29 ♘f1 ♗c3 30 ♘h2 a4 31 d6 b3 32 ab ab 33 ♘g4 b2 34 d7 ♖d8 35 ♖f1 ♔g7 36 ♘f6 ♘d2 37 ♘e8+ ♔f7 0–1

So 12 ♗xf7+ doesn't guarantee victory. One or two inaccuracies, and Black may assume a decisive initiative.

Game No. 5
Seirawan–Popović
Manila 1990

1 d4 ♘f6 2 c4 g6 3 ♘c3 d5 4 cd ♘xd5 5 e4 ♘xc3 6 bc ♗g7 7 ♗c4 c5 8 ♘e2 ♘c6 9 ♗e3 0–0 10 0–0 ♗g4 11 f3 ♘a5 12 ♗xf7+ ♖xf7 13 fg ♖xf1+

14	♔xf1	cd
15	cd *(15)*	

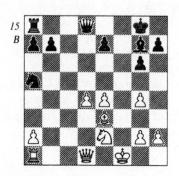

Curiously enough, this precise position arose as long ago as 1955, in the game Spassky–Korchnoi from the 22nd USSR Championship. Play continued: **15 ... ♕d7** 16 h3 ♕e6 17 ♕d3 ♕c4 18 ♕d2 (or 18 ♕xc4 ♘xc4 19 ♗g5 e6 20 ♖d1 b5, and despite White's extra pawn and the queen exchange, the initiative is with Black; Panteleyev–Prakhov, Bulgaria 1970. An improvement was 20 ♖b1!) 18 ... ♕a6! 19 ♕c2 ♘c4 20 ♕b3 ♔h8 21 ♔g1 ♘d2 (21 ... ♖f8 is stronger) 22 ♗xd2 ♕xe2 23 ♗e3, with equal chances. If Black wants, he can force a draw with 23 ... ♖c8 24 ♖f1 ♖c2 25 ♖f2 ♕e1+ 26 ♖f1 ♕e2.

The immediate pawn exchange on d4 at move 14 occurred only once in the Seville match – in the ninth game. Let us take quite a close look at it (recently some new thoughts about it have come to mind!):

15 ... ♛b6 16 ♔g1

With the queen on b6, 16 h3 can be strongly answered by 16
... ♞c4 17 ♗f2 ♛b2! 18 ♔g1 ♖f8 19 ♖b1 ♛xa2 20 ♖xb7 ♗h6!
with the initiative.

16 ... ♛e6

With the white king on g1, the line just mentioned no longer
gives Black anything: 16 ... ♞c4 17 ♗f2 ♛b2 18 ♞f4! ♖f8 19
♞d3.

17 ♛d3!

White returns the pawn while retaining all the positional trumps.
The position had first been seen (it arose by transposition) in
Alfeyevsky–Werner, corr. 1984. That game went 17 ♞g3 ♖d8 18
♖c1 (18 ♖b1 ♗xd4 19 ♗xd4 ♞c6 20 ♞e2 ♞xd4 21 ♞xd4 ♛c4)
18 ... ♛b6 19 ♞e2 ♞c6 20 ♖b1 ♞xd4! 21 ♖xb6 ♞f3+ 22 ♔f2
♖xd1 23 ♖xb7 ♞xh2 24 g4 ♞g4+ 25 ♔f3 ♞h2+, with a peaceful
conclusion by perpetual check.

17 ... ♛xg4

After this, I succeed in obtaining a substantial plus. After 17 ...
♖d8 18 g5 ♞c4 19 ♗f2 b5, the play would transpose into
Chernin–Malishauskas which we have examined before (see page
31). (I should point out that the ideas and variations in Games
1–5 have much in common, while sometimes being distinguished
by small nuances; I hope the reader will not get tangled up in the
'undergrowth'.) Instead of the capture on g4, a better idea is 17
... ♛c4, aiming to exchange off the strongest pieces. This idea was
employed in game 11 of the Seville match, with the difference that
the exchange on d4 took place later (see notes to Game No. 4).
White may avoid the queen exchange by retreating with 18 ♛d2
(exploiting the absence of the pawn from c3 and thus gaining a
tempo). After 18 ... ♛a6 19 ♛c2 ♞c4 (19 ... ♛c4 is well answered
by 20 ♖c1! – emphasising once again that the removal of the c-
pawns is favourable to White) 20 ♗f2 ♗f8 (20 ... ♗h6 21 h4)
21 g5, and Black's position is devoid of counterplay.

18 ♖f1 ♖c8

The alternative 18 ... ♖f8 is worse: 19 ♖xf8+ ♗xf8 20 d5 b6
21 ♞d4!

19 h3! ♛d7 20 d5 ♞c4 21 ♗d4

More precise than 21 ♞d4 ♞xe3 22 ♛xe3 ♖c4 23 ♞e6 ♛xe6
24 de ♗d4 25 ♛xd4 ♖xd4 26 ♖f7 ♖xe4 27 ♖xe7 b5, with
equality; but 21 ♗xa7 b6 22 ♗b8!? was worth considering.

21 ... e5

If 21 ... ♘e5, then 22 ♗xe5 ♗xe5 23 ♘d4 ♗xd4+ 24 ♕xd4 b6 25 e5 ♕c7 26 ♕g4! is not bad for White.

22 de ♕xe6 23 ♗xg7 ♔xg7 24 ♘f4 ♕d6 25 ♕c3+ (16)

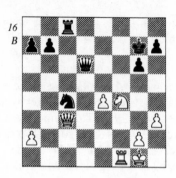

25 ... ♔h6

The only move. There would be a striking finish after 25 ... ♕e5 26 ♘e6+! ♔g8 (26 ... ♔h6 27 ♕c1+ g5 28 ♖f5) 27 ♕xc4! ♖xc4 28 ♖f8 mate. Another line that fails is 25 ... ♔g8 26 ♘d5 ♘b6 27 ♘f6+ ♔h8 28 ♕b2 ♕c5+ 29 ♔h2 ♕c3 30 ♘e8! ♘d7 (30 ... ♔g8 31 ♕b5 ♖c5 32 ♘f6+!) 31 ♕xc3 ♖xc3 32 ♖f7 ♖d3 ·(32 ... ♖c8 33 ♘d6) 33 e5 ♔g8 34 e6, and White wins.

26 ♘d5?

Black's king is in quite a dangerous position, and White should have tried to approach it from the other direction with 26 ♘d3! The threat of ♘d3–f2–g4+ is then fairly serious (26 ... ♘b6 27 ♕d2+ ♔g7 28 ♕b2+ ♔g8 29 ♕b3+ ♔h8 30 ♖f7, with a winning position).

26 ... ♕e5 27 ♕d3

White could have maintained the tension with 27 ♕e1. Many annotators recommended 27 ♕b4 instead, but this is not dangerous for Black: 27 ... ♕xe4! 28 ♘f6 a5! 29 ♕b5 (29 ♕c3 ♕e3+, or 29 ♕a4 ♕d4+ 30 ♔h1 ♖f8 31 ♘g4+ ♔g7, with advantage to Black) 29 ... ♕d4+ 30 ♖f2 (in the event of 30 ♔h1 ♘e3 31 ♕xb7 ♘xf1 32 ♘g4+, the black king fearlessly marches forward: 32 ... ♔g5 33 ♕e7+ ♔f4 34 ♕f7+ ♔g3 35 ♕xf1 h5 36 ♕f3+ ♔h4 37 g3+ ♔xh3 38 ♘f2+ ♕xf2! 39 ♕xf2 ♖c1+, and wins) 30 ... ♕a1+ 31 ♖f1 ♕d4+ 32 ♖f2 ♕a1+, and the contest could end in perpetual check.

27 ... ♔g7 28 ♘f6 ♛d6 29 ♕c3 ♛e5 30 ♕d3 ♕d6 31 ♕c3 ♛e5 32 ♕b3 ♖c7 33 ♕d3 ♖f7 34 ♕xc4 ♖xf6 35 ♖d1 b5

The position is drawn, but Black is playing somewhat recklessly. A simpler method is 35 ... ♖e6 36 ♖d7+ ♖e7 37 ♖xe7+ ♕xe7 38 ♕d4+ ♔f7 39 ♕xa7 ♕xe4.

36 ♖d7+ ♔h6 37 ♕e2 ♕c5+ 38 ♔h2 ♛e5+ 39 g3 ♛c3 40 ♔g2 ♕c4 41 ♕e3+ g5 42 ♖d2 ♕f1+ 43 ♔h2 ♕f3

The sealed move. Once again, just as happened in game 7 of the match, I persistently sought winning chances after resumption, and reached an endgame a pawn up – but alas, a drawn result was unavoidable. We will follow this interesting game to the end.

44 ♕d4 ♖e6 45 e5 ♕f5 46 ♖e2 a5 47 ♕d5 b4 48 ♕xa5 ♕d3 49 ♖g2 ♕d4 50 ♕a8 ♕xe5 51 ♕f8+ ♔g6 52 ♕xb4 h5 53 h4 gh 54 ♕xh4 ♖d6 55 ♕c4 ♖d4 56 ♕c6+ ♔g7 57 ♕b7+ ♔h6 58 ♕c6+ ♔g7 59 ♖c2 ♖h4+ 60 ♔g2 ♕e4+ 61 ♕xe4 ♖xe4 62 ♖c7+ ♔g6 63 ♖a7 ♖e3 64 ♔h3 ♖c3 65 ♖a8 ♖c4 66 a4 ♔g5 67 a5 ♖a4 68 a6 ♔h6 69 ♔g2 ♖a3 70 ♔f2 ♔g7 ½–½.

15 ... e5!?

This move had first occurred in the game Kir. Georgiev–Ivanchuk, Reggio Emilia 1989/90.

16 d5

The natural reaction – White creates a passed pawn. Despite the pawn extra, the endgame arising from **16 de ♗xe5 17 ♕xd8+ ♖xd8** holds no danger for Black. Seirawan–H. Olafsson, Reykjavik 1990, continued 18 ♖c1 ♘c6 19 g3 ♖d3 20 ♗f4 ♗d4 21 ♘xd4 ♖xd4 22 ♖b1 ♖b4 23 ♖xb4 ♘xb4 24 a4 ♘c6 25 ♔e2 a6 26 ♗d2 b5 27 ab ab 28 ♗c3 ♔f7 29 ♔e3 ♔e6. Subsequently Black tried to make something of his passed b-pawn, but without success, and a draw was agreed after another 25 moves.

Nor does White do any better with **16 ♖c1 ♕d7 17 de ♕xd1+ 18 ♖xd1 ♘c4 19 ♗f2 ♗xe5 20 ♖d7 b6 21 ♗d4 ♗xd4 22 ♘xd4 ♘d2+ 23 ♔e2 ♘xe4 24 ♘c6 a5 25 ♖b7 ♘c3+ 26 ♔d2 ♘xa2 27 ♖xb6 ♘b4**, and the game is level; Schüssler–Kudrin, Saint-Martin 1990.

16	...	♘c4
17	♗f2	♕f6
18	♔g1	♖f8
19	♕e1	

The position is unclear after **19 ♗xa7 b6**, or **19 ♗c5 ♖c8 20 ♗xa7 b6**.

19 ... ♗h6

Threatening ... ♗d2.

20 ♘g3 ♛a6

20 ... ♛xf2+ would be over-hasty: 21 ♛xf2 ♗e3 22 ♛xe3, followed by ♖c1.

21 ♔h1

The threat was ...♖xf2, for example: 21 ♛e2 ♖xf2! 22 ♔xf2 ♗e3+; while if 21 ♘f1, then 21 ... ♘b2! is decisive.

21 ... ♛a4

21 ... ♛a3 is also worth trying.

22 ♗g1! *(17)*

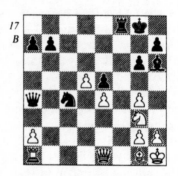

The white queen's problems can be solved later. In Georgiev–Ivanchuk, White played **22 ♛e2**, and there followed: **22 ... b6** 23 h4 ♗f4 24 ♘f1 (24 g5 ♘d6 25 ♖e1 was more precise) 24 ... ♘d6 25 ♖e1 ♖c8 26 g3 ♖c2 27 ♛f3 ♛xa2 28 ♔g1 ♗h6 29 g5 ♗g7 30 ♘e3 ♖c7 31 ♘g4 ♖f7 32 ♛e3 ♛c2 33 h5 ♘c4 34 ♛c1 ♛xc1 35 ♖xc1 gh 36 ♖xc4 hg 37 ♖c8+ ♗f8 38 ♗e1! (Ivanchuk gives 38 ♔f1! b5 39 ♔e2 b4 40 ♗c5 a5 41 ♖a8 b3 42 ♔d2, with a great deal of play left; or 38 ... ♔g7 39 ♔e2 b5 40 ♖a8) 38 ... ♔g7 39 ♗c3 ♗d6! 40 ♖c6 ♗c5+ 41 ♔g2 ♖f2+ 42 ♔h1 ♗d4 43 ♗b4 ♖f7! 44 ♖e6 ♖b7! 45 ♖c6 a5 46 d6? (Ivanchuk considers this the decisive mistake, although even after the more stubborn 46 ♗a3 b5 47 d6 ♖f7! 48 ♖c7 ♗b6 49 ♖c6 ♗d8 50 ♗b2 ♖d7 51 ♗xe5+ ♔f7, Black has a clear plus; not however 47 ... ♗b6?? 48 ♖xb6!) 46 ... ab! 47 ♖c7+ ♔f8 48 ♖xb7 b3 49 ♖b8+ ♔f7 50 d7 b2 51 ♖f8+ ♔e6 52 d8♘+ ♔e7 53 ♖f1 ♔xd8, and White soon resigned.

One other game is worth mentioning. In Naumkin–Mirallès, Voskresensk 1990, Black answered 22 ♕e2 with **22 ... ♗g5**, and only after 23 ♘f1 did he play 23 ... b6. (He could have brought about simplifications with the bold 23 ... ♘d6! 24 ♗c5 ♘xe4! 25 ♗xf8 ♕d4 26 ♗c5! ♕xa1 27 ♕xe4 ♕xf1+ 30 ♗g1 ♗d8, threatening ... ♗b6.) Naumkin now seized the initiative: 24 h4 ♗e7 25 g5 ♗c5 (25 ... ♘d6 26 ♘d2) 26 ♗g3 ♘d6 27 ♘d2 ♗d4 28 ♖c1! ♕xa2 29 ♖c6! ♖d8? (it was better to take the central pawn: 29 ... ♘xe4 30 ♕xe4 ♕xd2 31 ♖xg6+ hg 32 ♕xg6+ ♔h8 33 ♕h6+, with a draw; sharp play would result from 31 ♔h2 ♕e3 32 ♕g4!?) 30 ♔h2! a5 (Naumkin gives these variations: 30 ... ♕a1 31 ♘f3, or 30 ... ♘xe4 31 ♕xe4 ♕xd2 32 ♖xg6+ hg 33 ♕xg6+ ♔f8 34 ♕f6+ ♔e8 35 ♕e6+ ♔f8 36 g6 ♗g1+ 37 ♔xg1 ♕xd5 38 ♕f6+, with a substantial advantage to White) 31 h5 ♕a1 32 ♘f3 gh (nor can he save himself with 32 ... ♕b2 33 ♘xd4 ♕xd4 34 ♕g4 ♕xe4 35 ♕e6+ ♘f7 36 ♖c8!) 33 ♘xd4 ♕xd4 34 ♕xh5 ♘e8 35 g6 1–0.

22 ... b6

Before playing the knight on d6, it is essential to cover the c5-square.

23 ♕c3 ♖f7

23 ... ♘d6 is premature because of 24 ♕xe5 ♗g7 25 ♕e6+.

24 ♖b1 ♗d2

24 ... ♕xa2 is bad on account of 25 ♖b4, and the pawn on e5 falls. Seirawan recommends 24 ... ♘d2 25 ♖b4 ♕d1 26 ♕xe5 ♗e3 27 ♕e8+ with a draw, but instead White can maintain the pressure with 25 ♖e1.

25 ♕d3

After 25 ♕b3ʹ ♕xb3 26 ab ♘d6, White's extra pawn is of no significance.

25 ... ♕xa2

25 ... ♗h6 (25 ... ♗f4 26 ♘e2 and ♘c3) is answered by 26 a3, and the a-pawn is invulnerable: 26 ... ♘xa3 27 ♖a1.

26 d6! ♘xd6

The only move. On 26 ... ♖d7, Seirawan gives 27 ♕d5+ ♔g7 28 ♖f1! (28 ♕e6 ♖xd6 29 ♕e7+ ♔g8 30 ♖f1 ♗f4) 28 ... ♗f4 29 ♖xf4! ef 30 ♗d4+ ♔h6 31 g5 mate. (*Editor's note* – it appears that Black can escape with 30 ... ♔f8. Therefore White should prefer Stohl's 30 ♘f5+!! gf (30 ... ♔f8 31 ♘h6 ♔g7 32 g5!) 31 ♗d4+ ♔f8 32 ♕xf5+ ♔g8 33 ♕g5+, forcing mate).

27	♕xd6	♕xb1
28	♕xd2	a5

28 ... ♕b5 29 h3 ♕d7 30 ♕c3 ♕c7 31 ♕b3 is more tenacious, although White's chances are still better.

29	♕d8+	♔g7
30	♕g5	h6

White threatened the deadly 31 ♘f5+.

31	♕xe5+	♔h7
32	h3!	♖d7

White was intending to bring his bishop into play after 33 ♔h2. But now the denouement comes instantly.

33	♘h5!

1–0

The debate about the 12 ♗xf7+ variation still continues.

2 Exchange Variation with 7 ♗c4 – other systems

Game No. 6
Yusupov–Kasparov
USSR Ch 1988

**1 d4 ♘f6 2 c4 g6 3 ♘c3 d5 4 cd ♘xd5 5 e4 ♘xc3 6 bc ♗g7 7
♗c4 c5 8 ♘e2 ♘c6 9 ♗e3 0–0 10 0–0 ♗g4 11 f3 ♘a5**
12   ♗d3

12 ♗xf7+ attained wide popularity after the World Championship match in Seville, but capturing on f7 is, of course, not obligatory – the bishop may retreat instead. It is most securely placed on d3, although occasionally 12 ♗d5 is also seen.

12   ...   cd
13   cd   ♗e6
14   ♖c1 *(18)*

The once fashionable Sokolsky attack, 14 d5 ♗xa1 15 ♕xa1 f6, has now practically fallen into disuse. Black is the exchange up and can extricate himself without too much difficulty.

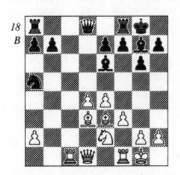

14   ...   ♗xa2
15   ♕a4

This is more precise than 15 d5 at once.

15	...	♗e6
16	d5	♗d7
17	♕b4 *(19)*	

An alternative is **17 ♕a3**, whereupon, apart from the more conventional 17 ... e6, Black has **17 ... b5!?**. After **18 ♖fd1**, the reply **18 ... ♖b8** is rather slow, for example: 19 ♕b4 a6 20 ♘d4 ♖e8 21 ♗e2 ♗e5 22 ♖a1! ♗c7 23 ♘e6! ♗d6 24 ♕xd6! fe 25 ♕e5 1–0; Piskov–Lputian, Belgrade 1988. In Ilić–Ferčec, Kladovo 1989, Black introduced the important innovation **18 ... b4!**, giving the pawn back but obtaining adequate counterplay: 19 ♕xb4 ♖b8 20 ♕e1 ♘b3 21 ♖b1 a5 22 ♗c2, and now 22 ... a4 is logical, with a complicated game.

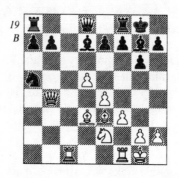

In this diagram we have a standard position in contemporary practice. Black can now choose between 17 ... e6 (the game continuation) and 17 ... b6. Before going any further, let us examine the latter.

17 ... b6

Safer than 17 ... b5, for example: 18 ♖fd1 ♗e5 19 ♗c5 ♘b7 20 ♗xe7 ♕b6+ 21 ♔h1 a5 22 ♕d2 ♖fc8 23 f4 ♗g7? (the bishop should have been placed on d6) 24 e5 b4 25 ♗c4 b3 26 ♗a3! with a won position for White; Balashov–Sibarević, Lugano 1988.

18 f4

Or 18 ♗a6 ♗c8 19 ♗b5 a6 20 ♗d3 b5 21 f4 e5! 22 ♗c5 ♖e8 23 ♗d6 ♕b6+ 24 ♗c5 (24 ♔h1 ♗g4! 25 ♗c7 ♕e3) 24 ... ♕d8 25 ♗d6, with a draw; Savchenko–Lputian, Tallinn 1988.

18 ... e5

Stronger than **18 ... e6** (18 ... ♖c8 19 ♘c3 ♘b7 20 ♗a6 ♖c7 21 e5 ♘c5 22 ♗c4 ♕b8 23 ♕a3! ♖cc8 24 ♖fd1 ♖fd8 25 ♗xc5!

and Black is in serious trouble; Vyzhmanavin–Ivanchuk, Tashkent
1987) **19 d6 e5** 20 f5 ♖c8 21 ♘c3 ♗c6 22 ♘b5 ♕d7 23 f6! with
a clear plus; Balashov–Hansen, Malmö 1987/8. However, after **19
... ♘c6** 20 ♕b3 e5! 21 f5 ♖c8 22 ♘c3 ♘d4 23 ♗xd4 ed 24 ♘d5
♖xc1 25 ♘e7+ ♔h8 26 ♖xc1 gf 27 ef ♗f6, Black has everything
in order; Dolmatov–Gavrikov, Kiev 1986.

19 ♖f2

In Vaiser–Gavrikov, Tallinn 1988, Black seized the initiative
after **19 f5?!** ♖e8 **20** ♗a6? ♗f8 21 ♕c3 b5. At move 20, White
should have played **20 d6** ♗f8 21 ♗c4 ♘xc4 22 ♕xc4 ♕f6 23 fg
(23 ♘c3? ♖ec8 24 gf ♖xc4! 25 gh+ ♔xh7 26 ♖xf6 ♗e6 27 ♘b5
♖xe4, with advantage to Black; Heinig–Gauglitz, Berlin 1988) 23
... ♕xg6 24 ♖f3 ♕e6, with complex play (Gauglitz).

19 ... ♖c8 20 ♖cf1 ♕c7

It is hard to give a preference to either side.

17 ... e6

This position occurrred as far back as 1954, in the game Geller–
Liliental from the 21st USSR Championship. Play continued **18
de** ♗xe6 19 ♖fd1 b6 20 ♗a6 ♕h4 21 ♘d4, and now by means
of 21 ... ♗c8 22 ♗b5 ♗e5 23 g3 ♕f6 24 f4 ♗d6 25 ♕a4 ♗g4
Black could have kept his extra pawn with a sound position.

Nor does **18 d6** give White anything, for example: 18 ... ♘c6
19 ♕xb7 ♖b8 20 ♕c7 ♖b3! 21 ♖fd1 ♘e5 with the initiative;
Razuvayev–Lputian, Sochi 1987.

In the same Soviet Championship as the game we are annotating
(1988), Belyavsky–Kasparov continued as follows: **18 ♘c3 ed** (18
... b6 is also interesting: 19 f4 ed 20 ♘xd5 ♗e6 21 ♖fd1 ♗xd5
22 ♗b5 ♕f6 23 ♖xd5 ♖ac8 24 ♖xc8 ♖xc8 25 e5 ♕e6 26 ♕e4
♗f8 27 ♗d7 ♖c4 28 ♕d3 ♕e7 29 e6, with approximate equality;
Naumkin–Krasenkov, Vilnius 1988) **19 ed** (Black similarly has a
good game after 19 ♘xd5 ♗e6 20 ♖fd1 ♗xd5 etc.) **19 ... ♖e8**
(19 ... b6 is also playable: 20 ♘e4 ♖e8 21 ♗d4 ♘b3 22 ♗xg7
♘xc1 23 ♕d4 ♖xe4! 24 fe ♘xd3 25 ♗h6 f6, with a good game;
Utemov–Obodchuk, USSR 1988) **20 ♗f2 ♗f8** 21 ♕b2 (after 21
♕f4 g5! 22 ♕g3 ♘b3 23 ♖b1 ♘c5 24 ♗c2 f5! Black would seize
the initiative, so White is not justified in playing for a win here)
21 ... ♗g7 22 ♕b4 ♗f8 23 ♕b2 ½-½.

The next two examples are identical with Belyavsky–Kasparov
up to move 20.

Yusupov–Timman, Rotterdam 1988, continued sharply with **20**

... ♗e5 21 ♘e4 ♗f5 22 ♗b5 ♖f8 23 ♗c5 b6! (not 23 ... ♗xe4? 24 fe ♕h4 25 g3 ♗xg3 26 ♖c2! and White has an obvious plus) 24 ♗xf8 ♕xf8 25 ♕xf8+ ♔xf8 26 ♖fe1! (after 26 ♖fd1? the exchange on e4 *is* good for Black: 26 ... ♗xe4 27 fe ♔e7) 26 ... ♘b3 27 ♖cd1 ♘d4 28 ♗a6 ♘c2 29 ♖e2 ♘d4 30 ♖ee1 ♘c2 31 ♖e2 ♘d4 ½–½.

One other game by Yusupov likewise ended in a quick draw: **20 ... b5!** 21 ♖fd1 (or 21 ♘e4 ♘b7 22 ♗xb5 a5 23 ♕a4 ♗xb5 24 ♕xb5 ♘d6, with equality; Naumkin–Mokry, Nemestovo 1987) 21 ... ♘c4 22 ♗xc4 a5 23 ♕b3 bc 24 ♕xc4 ♖c8 25 ♕d3 ½–½; Yusupov–Smejkal, Munich 1988.

18 ♖fd1

It seems to me that a very strong move here is 18 ♘d4, but it doesn't appear to have occurred in practice yet.

18	...	ed
19	ed	♖e8
20	♗f2	b5!

This looks like a serious weakening, but Black secures for his knight (via c4) the shortest route to the centre, where the main action is going to take place.

21	♘d4	♘c4
22	♘c6	

By exchanging the troublesome knight on c4, White would restore the material balance but could hardly count on an advantage: 22 ♗xc4 a5 23 ♕c5 bc 24 ♕xc4 a4. Yusupov endeavours to extract the maximum from the position.

22	...	♗xc6
23	dc	♘b2! *(20)*

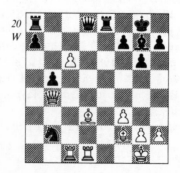

24   &xb5!

White would lose after the hasty 24 c7? ♕xd3 25 ♖xd3 ♘xd3 26 c8(♕) ♖axc8 27 ♖xc8 ♖xc8 and 28 ... ♖c1+.

24   ...   ♘xd1

25   c7   ♕d5!

It looks as if both sides are playing to win. As Kasparov has pointed out, a draw would result from 25 ... ♕c8 26 &xe8 ♘xf2! (26 ... ♘c3? 27 ♖e1! ♕xc7 28 ♖e7) 27 ♕e7 ♘h3+ 28 gh ♕xe8 29 ♕xe8+ ♖xe8 30 c8(♕) &d4+ 31 ♔g2 ♖xc8 32 ♖xc8+ ♔g7.

26   &xe8

The ingenious **26 &c6** is answered by the calm 26 ... ♕e6 27 &xe8 ♘xf2, and now 28 ♕b8 would lose to 28 ... ♕e3!. On the other hand, **26 ♕c4** ♕xc4 27 ♖xc4 ♘xf2 28 &xe8 ♘h3+ 29 ♔f1 ♖xe8 30 c8(♕) ♖xc8 31 ♖xc8+ &f8 32 gh ♔g7 leads to a draw.

26   ...   ♘xf2

27   c8(♕)

27 &c6 would be met by 27 ... ♘h3+. Two other variations also lead to drawn endgames: 27 &xf7+ ♔xf7 28 ♕f4+ ♔e7 29 c8(♕) ♖xc8 30 ♖xc8 ♘h3+ 31 gh ♕d1+, or 27 ♕c4 ♘h3+ 28 ♔f1 ♕xc4+ 29 ♖xc4 ♖xe8 etc., as in the note to White's 26th move.

27   ...   ♖xc8

28   ♖xc8   ♘h3+! (21)

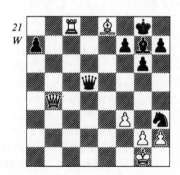

The knight has sped right the way across the board to get its king out of trouble.

29   gh

29 ♔f1?? loses to 29 ... ♕d3+ 30 ♔e1 ♕e3+ 31 ♔d1 ♘f2+ 32 ♔c2 ♕d3+ 33 ♔c1 ♕d1 mate.

$$\begin{array}{lll} 29 & \dots & \text{\wdl1+} \\ 30 & \text{\textcircled{g}2!} \end{array}$$

And now, 30 &f2?? is answered by 30 ... &d4+ 31 &g3 &g1+ 32 &f4 &e3+ 33 &g3 &g5 mate.

$$\begin{array}{lll} 30 & \dots & \text{We2+} \\ 31 & \text{\textcircled{g}1} \end{array}$$

½–½

There is no escaping the perpetual check: 31 &g3 &e5+ 32 f4 (32 &g4? f5+) 32 ... &e3+ 33 &g2 &e2+ 34 &g1 &d1+ 35 &g2 &e2+.

Game No. 7
Polugayevsky–Kudrin
New York 1989

1 d4 &f6 2 c4 g6 3 &c3 d5 4 cd &xd5 5 e4 &xc3 6 bc &g7 7 &c4 c5 8 &e2 &c6 9 &e3 0–0

10 &c1 *(22)*

In the present game we are still dealing with the main system (Exchange Variation) of the Grünfeld, but turn our attention to a line in which White postpones castling by one move, resulting in play of a wholly different character.

In passing, we should also mention the innovation 10 &b1!?, employed in Korchnoi–Kasparov, Reykjavik 1988. There followed: 10 ... &a5 11 &d3 cd 12 cd b6 13 0–0 (immediate kingside activity with 13 h4 could come up against counterplay with obscure consequences: 13 ... e5 14 d5 f5 15 h5 f4 etc.) 13 ... e6 14 &a4 (14 &d2 &b7 15 h4 &c8 16 &fc1 &d7 17 h5 &xc1+ 18 &xc1 &c8 leads to equality) 14 ... &b7 15 &fd1 &c8 16 &d2 &c6 17 &c3 &h4! 18 &e1 &fd8 19 f3 &e7 20 &b5?! (in Kasparov's view 20 &f2 is better, leading to equality after 20 ... &a5, but then Black also has 20 ... &h6!?) 20 ... a6! 21 &xa6 &xa6 22 &xa6 &xd4 (the initiative is with Black, but after 23 &xd4 &xd4+ 24 &h1, or 24 &xd4 &c5 25 &f2, White has adequate defensive resources; instead, he commits the decisive error) 23 &f2? &a8! 24 &d3 (24 &c4 b5) 24 ... &a3, winning the queen and with it the game (25 &xd4 &xd3 etc.).

10 ... cd

The more placid **10 ... &d7** is also payable. In Vyzhmanavin–Mikhalchishin, Moscow 1989, there followed: **11 0–0 &c8 12 &d2 &a5 13 d5 &e5 14 &b3 c4?! 15 &c2 e6 16 &b1! b6 17 f4 &g4**

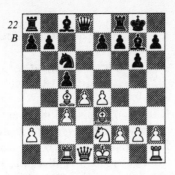

22
B

18 de fe 19 e5! and White gained a clear plus. At move 14, Black introduced a valuable novelty in Shirov–Epishin, Daugavpils 1989: **14 ... e6!** 15 f4 ♘g4 16 c4 (16 de ♗xe6 17 ♗xe6 fe 18 ♗f2 ♖cd8 19 ♕c2 ♘xf2 20 ♖xf2 ♕a6, with the better prospects owing to the threat of ... ♕c4) 16 ... ♕xd2 17 ♗xd2 ed 18 cd ♗b5 19 ♗c4 ♗xc4 20 ♖xc4 b5 21 ♖c2 ♘f6 22 ♘g3 (in Shirov's opinion White could have maintained equality with 22 ♘c3 b4 23 e5 bc 24 ef cd 25 fg ♔xg7 26 ♖xd2, or 24 ... ♗xf6 25 ♗xc3) 22 ... ♖fe8! 23 d6 ♘d7! and the initiative passed to Black.

11	**cd**	**♕a5+**
12	**♔f1**	**♗d7**

An inferior choice is **12 ... ♖d8** 13 h4 h5 14 ♕b3 e6 15 d5 ♘e5 16 de ♘xc4 17 ef+ ♔h7 18 ♕xc4 ♗g4 19 f3 ♖ac8 20 ♕b3 ♖xc1+ 21 ♗xc1 ♗e6 22 ♕xe6 ♖d1+ 23 ♔f2 ♖xh1 24 ♕d6! ♕xa2 25 ♕e7!. However, **12 ... ♕a3!?** deserves attention. This novelty occurred in Savchenko–Dimov, Varna 1989. After 13 ♕b3 ♕xb3 14 ♗xb3 ♖d8 15 d5 ♘a5 16 ♗a4 e6 17 ♗g5 f6 18 ♗f4 e5 19 ♗d2 b6, the game is about level.

13   h4 (23)

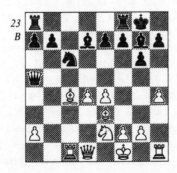

23
B

13 ...   ♖ac8

In the diagram position Black has various options. Let us look at them.

The blocking move **13 ... h5** is inadequate; Polugayevsky gives 14 ♘f4 ♔h7 15 e5!? ♖ac8 16 ♗d3 ♔g8 17 e6! fe 18 ♖c5! with powerful threats.

Polugayevsky–Korchnoi, Haninge 1988, went **13 ... e5** 14 d5, and Black gave up a pawn to no avail: 14 ... ♘d4 (14 ... ♘e7 is safer) 15 ♘xd4 ed 16 ♗xd4 ♗xd4 17 ♕xd4 ♖ac8 18 ♔e2! (but not 18 ♔g1? on account of 18 ... b5!). Black has no compensation for the pawn, and the game ended quickly: 18 ... ♖fe8 19 f3 ♖xc4 20 ♖xc4 ♕xa2+ (20 ... ♗b5 doesn't help: 21 ♔e3 ♕xa2 22 ♖cc1 ♕xg2 23 ♕d2 ♕g3 24 ♕h2, etc.) 21 ♔e3 ♕xg2 22 ♖hc1 f5 23 e5! g5 24 hg ♕h2 25 e6 b5 26 ♖c7 1–0.

Polugayevsky won in confident style. The main game we are examining will also end quickly in his favour. Does this mean that the outlook as a whole is grim for Black? No – it turns out that **13 ... ♖fc8!** is a good deal more accurate. After the end of the main game, we shall consider what a difference it makes to occupy the c-file with the other rook.

14 h5   e5

Without this central advance Black can hardly hope for counter-play. Let us look at the alternatives:

(a) **14 ... e6** 15 hg hg 16 e5! (but not immediately 16 ♕d3 b5 17 ♗b3 ♘b4 18 ♕d2 ♖xc1+ 19 ♘xc1 ♘c6 20 ♕d3 b4 21 ♘e2 ♖d8, and Black has very strong counterplay in the centre. Lputian–Dvoiris, Simferopol 1988, continued 22 ♗h6? ♗xd4! 23 ♕h3 ♗f6 24 ♗e3 ♗c8 25 ♘f4 ♘e7, and White got nowhere. 22 ♔g1 was better) 16 ... ♘e7 17 ♕d3 ♖fe8 18 ♗d2 ♕a4 19 ♗b3 ♖xc1+ 20 ♗xc1 ♕b4 21 ♕h3 ♔f8 22 ♗h6 ♘g8 23 ♗xg7+ ♔xg7 24 ♕h8+ ♔f8 25 ♖h7 ♔e7 26 ♕g7 ♔d8 27 ♕xf7, and it is all over; Grünberg–Gauglitz, E. Germany 1989.

(b) **14 ... b5** 15 ♗b3 e5 (in the present circumstances, this counter-stroke in the centre is not good) 16 hg hg 17 de! (Black was vainly hoping for 17 d5? ♘d4 18 ♖xc8 ♖xc8 19 ♘xd4 ed 20 ♗xd4 ♗xd4 21 ♕xd4 ♖c1+ 22 ♗d1 f6 23 g3 ♕a4! 24 ♕xa4 ba 25 ♔g2 ♖a1 26 ♗f3 ♖xa2 27 ♖c1 a6, when the black bishop settles on b5 and the pawn on a4 acquires formidable strength) 17 ... ♘xe5 18 ♖xc8 ♗xc8 (18 ... ♖xc8 19 f4 ♘g4 20 ♗xf7+!) 19 ♘f4 ♗b7? (loses at once, but then Black also has a hard time in other

variations: 19 ... ♖e8 20 ♘xg6 ♘xg6 21 ♕h5 ♗e6 22 ♕h7+
♔f8 23 ♗c5+ ♘e7 24 ♗xe6 fe 25 ♖h3, and wins; or 19 ... b4
20 ♘d5 ♖e8 21 ♗g5 ♗b7 22 ♔g1 ♗xd5 23 ♖xd5, etc.) 20
♘xg6! ♘xg6 21 ♕h5 1–0; Dautov–Huzman, Kecskemet 1989.
Black resigned because he cannot simultaneously defend the knight
on g6 and the h7-square.

	15	hg	hg
	16	d5!	

More energetic than 16 ♗d2 ♕b6 17 ♖b1 ♕c7 18 d5 ♘a5! 19
♗d3 ♘c4, with a good game for Black; Guseinov–Huzman, Baku
1988.

| | 16 | ... | ♘d4 |

After 17 ... ♘e7 18 ♗g5, White has a solid advantage.

| | 17 | ♘xd4 | ♖xc4 |

17 ... ed 18 ♗xd4 ♖xc4 19 ♖xc4 ♕a6 (19 ... ♗b5 20 ♗xg7,
and wins) **20 ♕d3** transposes into the game continuation. At move
18, it might seem that Black can improve with **18 ... ♗b5 19
♗xg7 ♖xc4** (19 ... ♗xc4+ 20 ♖xc4!) **20 ♖xc4 ♗xc4+ 21 ♔g1
♔xg7 22 ♕d4+**, and after 22 ... f6 23 ♕xc4 ♕e1+ 24 ♕f1 ♕xe4
the endgame is more pleasant for Black (Huzman and Vaikerman).
However, in place of the check on d4, Polugayevsky unearthed
the quiet move **22 ♕c1!!** *(24)*.

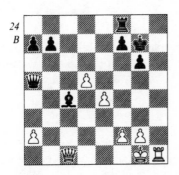

In spite of his extra piece, Black is helpless:
(a) **22 ... ♖c8** 23 ♕h6+ ♔f6 24 ♕f4+ ♔e7 25 ♕e5+ ♔d7 26
♖h7 ♖f8 27 ♕e6+ ♔d8 28 ♕d6+ ♔e8 29 ♕b8+ ♔e7 30 d6+!
(b) **22 ... ♕c5** (22 ... ♕b4 23 a3!) 23 ♕b2+! f6 24 ♕xb7+ ♖f7 25
♖h7+ ♔xh7 26 ♕xf7+ ♔h6 27 ♕xf6, and Black has no defence.

(c) **22 ... f6 23 ♖h3!** (another quiet move, looking for all the world like a study; instead, the straightforward 23 ♕h6+ ♔f7 24 ♕h7+ ♔e8 25 ♕xg6+ ♔d8 26 ♖h7 ♕e1+ 27 ♔h2 ♕xf2 28 ♕g7 ♕f4+ leads only to a draw). Now Polugayevsky gives two variations:

(c1) **23 ... ♕xa2** 24 ♕h6+ ♔f7 25 ♕h7+ ♔e8 26 ♕xb7 ♕a1+ 27 ♔h2 ♕e5+ 28 g3 ♕d4 29 ♕c8+ ♔f7 30 ♕d7+ ♔g8 31 ♕h7 mate.

(c2) **23 ... ♗a6** 24 ♕h6+ ♔f7 25 ♕h7+ ♔e8 26 d6! ♕e5 27 ♕c7 ♗b5 28 ♖h7, and it is all over.

	18	**♖xc4**	**♕a6**

As we already know, 18 ... ed 19 ♗xd4 ♗b5 loses to 20 ♗xg7.

	19	**♕d3!**	**ed**
	20	**♗xd4**	**♗b5** *(25)*

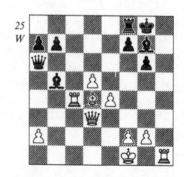

One's first impression is that Black has defended himself while keeping the extra piece. But the unexpected continuation was:

	21	**♕h3!**	**♗xc4+**
	22	**♔g1**	**f6**
	23	**♕h7+**	**♔f7**
	24	**♖h6!**	

1–0

A fine game. But let us go back to move 13, where Black could have played a little differently with **13 ... ♖fc8!**. This innovation was used in Nogueiras–Ljubojević, Barcelona 1989. Now, after **14 h5 e5** 15 hg hg 16 d5 ♘d4 17 ♘xd4 ed 18 ♗xd4 ♖xc4! 19 ♖xc4 (19 ♗xg7 ♕a6!) 19 ... ♕a6 20 ♕d3 ♗b5, we reach the same position as in diagram 25, with the difference that Black's rook is on a8, not f8. This little nuance reverses the verdict on the position. Black has an escape square on f8 for his king, and already holds victory in his hands, seeing that 21 ♕h3 (which settled matters in Polugayevsky–Kudrin) is unplayable; there is no threat of ♕h7 mate, and Black simply captures the bishop on d4.

I should add that in answer to 14 h5, Ljubojević refrained from 14 ... e5, preferring to retreat to the back rank with his knight: **14 ... ♘d8**. Incidentally, this retreat too was made possible by ... ♖f8–c8 – the rooks are not now disconnected. There followed: 15 hg hg 16 ♗d2? (a most unfortunate move) 16 ... ♕a4! (Black seizes the initiative. Mere equality results from 16 ... ♕b6 17 ♖b1 ♗a4 18 ♕e1 ♕f6 19 ♖c1 ♘e6, while in this line 18 ... ♕c7? actually loses to 19 ♖c1 ♕d7 20 f3 ♗xd4 21 ♕h4 ♕d6 22 ♗b4!; Dragomaretsky–Krasenkov, Moscow 1989) 17 ♗b3 ♕a6 18 ♔g1 ♕d3 19 ♖xc8? (it isn't so clear after 19 ♗h6) 19 ... ♖xc8 20 e5 ♗e6! 21 ♔f1 ♗xb3 22 ab ♖c2! and Black won.

One month later, the position after 13 ... ♖fc8 arose in a game Polugayevsky–Ftačnik, Haninge 1989. Polugayevsky now innovated with **14 e5!**, and only after 14 ... ♘d8 continued with 15 h5. Alas, a third beautiful win was not to be: 15 ... ♗b5 16 ♗xb5 ♕xb5 17 hg hg 18 ♔g1 ♖xc1 19 ♘xc1 ♘e6 20 ♕g4 ♖c8 21 ♕h4? (in Polugayevsky's view, 21 ♕e4 would have kept some initiative for White) 21 ... ♕b1 22 ♕h7+ ♔f8 23 ♔h2 ♕f5 24 ♘e2 ♖c2 25 ♖c1? (this allows Black to pick up a pawn and go into a won ending; it was essential to play 25 ♖e1, with drawing chances) 25 ... ♖xc1 26 ♘xc1 ♘xd4! 27 f4 ♕e4 28 ♕h3, and now instead of 28 ... ♘f5 (after which Black took 35 moves to win), Ftačnik demonstrated a quicker method: 28 ... ♘e6 29 ♗d2 g5 30 ♕c3 ♔g8 31 g3 gf 32 gf ♘xf4 33 ♕c8+ ♔h7 34 ♕g4 ♗xe5 etc.

So the keen debate about the fascinating variation 10 ♖c1 is far from being resolved.

3 Modern Exchange Variation

Game No. 8
Shirov–Akopian
Tbilisi 1989

1	d4	♘f6
2	c4	g6
3	♘c3	d5
4	♘f3	♗g7
5	cd	♘xd5
6	e4	♘xc3
7	bc	c5
8	♖b1	0–0
9	♗e2	

It is interesting that the 1976 edition of *ECO* gave this set-up no more than a cursory mention. Yet in the last few years, the system with 8 ♖b1 has virtually become the most popular choice against the Grünfeld Defence, perhaps even surpassing the old variation in which the bishop is brought out to c4.

Another method of developing the white pieces, behind that strong pawn centre which characterises the Exchange Variation, involves an early ♗c1–e3. In this case, the light-squared bishop is brought to e2 (later than usual), and the queen's rook may occupy either c1 or d1 (after ♕d1–d2). This variation was an object of dispute in my last match with Kasparov – see Games No. 14 and 15.

I would add that the popularity of the variation with ♖b1 and ♗e2 is above all associated with the names of the young grandmasters Boris Gelfand and Alexander Halifman.

9	...	♕a5

The main line for Black is 9 ... cd 10 cd, and only then 10 ... ♕a5+. We shall deal with it in Games 11–13. The fairly popular moves 9 ... b6 and 9 ... ♘c6 are examined in Games 9 and 10.

As for 9 ... ♗g4, it has gone out of use. White gains the advantage, either with the immediate 10 ♖xb7, or after sacrificing the d-pawn: 10 0–0 cd 11 cd ♗xf3 12 ♗xf3 ♗xd4 (12 ... ♕xd4 13 ♕xd4 ♗xd4 14 ♖xb7) 13 ♖xb7.

10   0–0

Of course, sacrificing the pawn on a2 is part of White's plan. Whether he will be able to work up a dangerous initiative in return is another question. Incidentally, at the beginning of the 1980s White used to prefer 10 ♖b5 ♕xc3+ (10 ... ♕xa2 11 ♖xc5 is worse for Black) 11 ♗d2 ♕a3 12 ♖a5 ♕b2 13 ♖xc5, and at last Black would take the pawn with 13 ... ♕xa2. White would then continue 14 ♖a5, 14 ♕c1, or 14 0–0, leading in all cases to a complex game with chances for both sides.

10   ...   ♕xa2 *(26)*

At this point, capturing the c-pawn is extremely risky. White's best reply to 10 ... ♕xc3 is 11 d5. Let us see how play might develop: 11 ... ♕a5 (if 11 ... ♘d7, then 12 ♗g5 ♖e8 13 ♕a4 is unpleasant, while 12 ... ♗f6 loses virtually by force: 13 ♗d2 ♕a3 14 ♕c2 ♘e5 15 ♖b3 ♘xf3+ 16 gf ♕a4 17 ♗b5 ♕d4 18 ♗c3) 12 ♗g5 ♕c7 13 ♕c1 (another good line is 13 ♕d2 ♗g4 14 ♖fc1 b6 15 h3 ♗xf3 16 ♗xf3 e5 17 d6 ♕c6 18 ♗e7 ♖e8 19 ♗e2 ♘d7 20 ♗b5 ♕b7 21 ♕c2; Legky–Veingold, Lvov 1984) 13 ... ♗g4 14 ♗f4 ♕c8 15 e5 ♘d7 16 ♖e1 (or 16 ♕e3, connecting the rooks and increasing the pressure in the centre) 16 ... ♘b6 17 d6 ed 18 ed, and in return for the pawn White has a highly promising position; Chiburdanidze–Malaniuk, Odessa 1982.

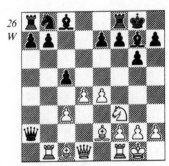

26
W

11   ♗g5   ♕e6

An interesting alternative is 11 ... ♘d7 12 ♗xe7 ♖e8 13 ♗d6 cd 14 ♘xd4 ♘f6 15 f3 ♘d5!? 16 ♖a1 ♕b2 17 ♕a4 ♗f5 18 ed

♗xd4+ 19 ♕xd4 ♖xe2 20 g4 ♖d2 21 ♕b4 ♗d3 22 ♕xb2 ♖xb2 23 ♖fd1, with equality; Vaiser–Dvoiris, Barnaul 1984. Vaiser suggests **15 ♖a1 ♕b2 16 ♘b5!? ♘xe4 17 ♗a3 ♕d2 18 ♘c7.**

12 ♕d3!?

A valuable idea, first employed in Epishin–Henkin, Barnaul 1988. Formerly, White used to advance one of his central pawns here. For example: 12 e5 ♖d8 13 ♕a4 ♕c6 (13 ... ♗d7 14 d5 ♗xa4 15 de f6 16 ef ef 17 ♗c4! ♖e8 18 ♗f4 b6 19 ♗d5 ♗c6 20 c4! gave White a clear advantage in Yusupov–Tukmakov, Moscow 1983) 14 ♕b3 ♗e6 (14 ... ♕c7 15 ♗c4 ♖f8 16 e6 f6 17 ♗h4 ♘c6 18 ♗g3 ♕d8 19 ♕a2 cd 20 cd b6 21 d5 ♘e5 22 ♖fd1 ♔h8 23 ♘xe5 fe 24 d6! gave White a large plus in another game Yusupov–Tukmakov, Erevan 1982) 15 c4 cd 16 ♗xe7 ♖c8 17 ♘xd4 ♗xc4! 18 ♘xc6 ♗xb3 19 ♘xb8 ♗e6 20 ♗d6 ♗f8 21 ♗f3 ♗xd6 22 ♗xb7 ♗xb8 23 ♗xa8 ♗xe5 24 ♗b7 ♖c2 25 ♖fc1 ♖a2 26 ♖d1 ♗c7 27 ♖a1 ♖b2 28 ♖db1 ♖d2 29 ♖d1 ♖b2 ½–½; Damjanović–Schmidt, Athens 1984. This one game serves to illustrate the harmlessness of 12 e5.

12 ... b6

After **12 ... ♕d6** 13 ♕e3, or **12 ... ♘d7** 13 ♕e3 ♘f6 14 ♘e5!, the initiative is with White. On the other hand, **12 ... ♖d8!?** deserves to be tried.

13 d5

In this case, 13 ♕e3 is no good: 13 ... ♗a6! 14 d5 ♕d6 15 c4 e5!, and White has nothing for the pawn.

13 ... ♕d6 (27)

14 e5!

The point of White's play. He now obtains the two bishops and a big advantage in space and development. Still, Black does have two extra pawns.

Again 14 ♕e3 would be well answered by 14 ... e5!.

	14	...	♗xe5
	15	♘xe5	♕xe5
	16	♕d2	

But not 16 f4? ♕d6 17 ♕e3 ♖e8, or 16 ♕e3? ♕xe3 17 fe ♖e8! 18 d6 e5! 19 ♗e7 ♗e6 20 ♗f3 ♘d7 21 ♗xa8 ♖xa8.

| | 16 | ... | ♕d6 |

Perhaps 16 ... ♘d7 does more to limit White's options. The virtually forced continuation is 17 ♗f3 ♕d6 18 ♖fe1 f6 (worse alternatives are 18 ... ♘e5? 19 ♖xe5! ♕xe5 20 ♖e1 ♕f5 21 d6 ♗d7 22 de ♖fe8 23 ♗xa8 ♖xa8 24 h3, and 19 ... f6 20 ♖e6! ♗xe6 21 ♗f4 ♕d7 22 de ♕xd2 23 ♗xd2) 19 ♖e6 fg 20 ♖xd6 ed 21 ♖e1 a5, and the position is unclear.

| | 17 | ♕e3! | |

Here this move is entirely in place, and better than 17 ♗f3 ♘d7 (see the previous note), or 17 ♗f4 e5 18 de ♕xd2 19 ♗xd2 fe 20 ♗f3 ♖xf3! 21 gf ♗b7.

| | 17 | ... | ♖e8 |

But not 17 ... f6 18 ♗f4.

| | 18 | ♗f3 | ♘d7 |

The play hinges on some subtle points. In many lines the counter-stroke ... e7–e5 is good, but not here: 18 ... e5? 19 de ♖xe6 20 ♖bd1! and wins.

| | 19 | ♗f4 | |

It is only now that White deviates from the game Epishin–Henkin already referred to. That game went **19 ♖fe1 ♘f6** (19 ... f6 20 ♕e6+!) **20 c4 ♗f5 21 ♖a1**, and after **21 ... a6?!** 22 ♗f4 ♕d7 23 h3 h5? 24 ♗e5 ♔h7 25 ♕f4 ♖g8 26 ♕g5, White quickly won. But instead of 21 ... a6 Black has **21 ... e5!**, after which White doesn't have adequate compensation for the two pawns, for example: 22 de ♖xe6 23 ♗xa8 (23 ♕c3 ♘e4!) 23 ... ♖xe3 24 fe. In Epishin's view, White can improve with **21 ♖bd1 ♗g4!** (otherwise 22 h3) 22 ♗xf6 ♗xf3 23 ♗e5 ♗xd1 24 ♗xd6 ed 25 ♕c3, but Henkin has indicated a line in which Black again has nothing to fear: 25 ... ♗e2 26 f3 b5! 27 cb ♗xb5 28 ♖xe8+ ♖xe8, 29 ♕f6 ♖e1+ 30 ♔f2 ♖e2+ 31 ♔g3 c4 32 ♕xd6 a6. But then, the text move should not have brought White any concrete gains either.

19	...	♛f6
20	d6	♜b8
21	♜bd1 *(28)*	

21 de is bad: 21 ... ♜xe7 22 ♛d2 ♘e5 23 ♗g5 ♘xf3+ 24 gf ♜d7! 25 ♛xd7 ♛xg5+, and Black wins.

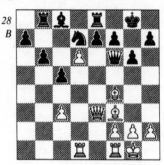

21	...	e5?

A serious mistake. He could not have solved his problems with **21 ... ♗b7** 22 de ♜xe7 (22 ... ♗xf3 23 ♜xd7 ♗g4 24 ♜xa7 ♜bc8 25 ♜e1) 23 ♜xd7! ♜xe3 24 fe ♗xf3 25 ♗xb8 ♛xc3 26 ♜xf3 ♛e1+ 27 ♜f1 ♛xe3+ 28 ♔h1 ♛e8 29 ♜fd1! and wins. But the essential move was **21 ... e6!**, and already after 22 ♗c6 ♛d8 23 ♜fe1 b5 it is White who has to think about equalising.

22	♗g5	♛g7

If 22 ... ♛f5, then 23 ♗e4 ♛e6 25 ♗d5 ♛f5 25 f4!, while 22 ... ♛h8 is well answered by 23 ♗c6.

23	♗h6	♛f6
24	♗c6!	♜e6?

24 ... ♛d8 25 f4 ♗b7 26 ♗xd7 ♛xd7 27 fe f5! was more tenacious, although after 28 ♗g5 ♗e4 29 ♗f6, White has an advantage due to the subsequent h4–h5.

25	♗g5	♛g7
26	f4	h6

If 26 ... f6, then 27 f5! gf 28 ♗h6 ♛g6 29 ♜f3 f4 30 ♜xf4!

27	♗e7	ef
28	♛xf4	g5
29	♛a4	♘e5
30	♗d5	♗b7
31	♛xa7	♘d7
32	♗xb7	

1–0

Game No. 9
Halifman–Pribyl
Leningrad 1989

1 d4 ♘f6 2 c4 g6 3 ♘c3 d5 4 ♘f3 ♗g7 5 cd ♘xd5 6 e4 ♘xc3 7 bc c5 8 ♖b1 0-0

	9	**♗e2**	**b6**
	10	**0-0**	

Another familiar plan is **10 ♗e3 ♗b7 11 e5 ♘c6 12 h4**, with a kingside attack. However, in a game Nemet–Korchnoi, Switzerland 1985, Black seized the initiative with **11 ... cd! 12 cd ♘a6 13 ♕d2 ♘c7 14 h4 ♘d5 15 h5 ♘xe3 16 fe e6 17 ♗d3 ♖c8.** There is also another possibility (after 11 ... cd 12 cd): **12 ... ♗e4! 13 ♖c1 ♘c6 14 h4 ♖c8 15 ♘g5 ♗xg2 16 ♖h2 ♗d5 17 h5 ♘b4 18 hg hg 19 a3 ♘a2,** and Black is clearly better; Vaiser–I. Sokolov, San Bernadino 1989.

In Cebalo–I. Sokolov from the same tournament, White launched his attack at once with **10 h4!?**. His opponent's ineffective response unexpectedly led to a quick and crushing defeat: 10 ... ♗g4 (10 ... ♗b7 is more logical) **11 ♔f1!?** cd **12 cd ♘d7** (and here, the right continuation is 12 ... ♘c6 13 d5 ♗xf3 14 gf ♘d4) **13 e5! ♖c8 14 ♗e3 ♘b8 15 h5! ♕d5 16 hg hg 17 ♕d2 ♖fd8 18 ♖h4! ♗xf3 19 gf ♗xe5? 20 ♖b5! ♕e6 21 ♖xe5,** and it is all over.

	10	**...**	**♗b7**
	11	**♕d3** *(29)*	

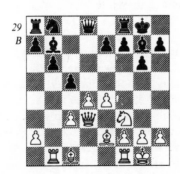

	11	**...**	**♗a6**

In earlier games, Black played 11 ... cd 12 cd e6 13 ♗g5 ♕d6, but as a rule failed to equalise. Here is one example: 14 ♕e3 ♖c8 15 ♖fd1 ♘d7 16 h4 ♖c2 17 e5 ♕c7 18 ♗d3 ♖c3 (18 ... ♖xa2 19

♖bc1) 19 ♕e2 ♗d5 20 ♖bc1 h6 21 ♗e3 ♖d8 22 h5! with a big advantage; Lputian–Lalić, Sarajevo 1985.

12 ♕e3

12 ♕c2 promises White less. Chernin–Dorfman, Moscow 1984, continued 12 ... cd 13 cd ♕c8 14 ♕d1 ♗xe2 15 ♕xe2 ♕a6 16 ♕xa6 ♘xa6 17 ♗a3 ♖fd8 18 d5 f5 19 ♗xe7 ♖d7 20 d6, and the players agreed a draw.

12 ... cd

12 ... e6 is too timid; after 13 dc ♗xe2 14 ♕xe2 bc 15 ♗f4 ♕c8 16 ♗d6 ♖d8 17 e5 ♕c6 18 h4 ♘d7 19 c4! a6 20 ♖fe1 ♘b6 21 ♕e4, Black has no prospects whatsoever; Lerner–Gorelov, Ivano–Frankovsk 1982.

In the last few years, Black has tried moving his queen to c8 or d7 without exchanging pawns in the centre. These experiments have been unsuccessful, for example: **12 ... ♕c8** 13 d5 ♗xe2 14 ♕xe2 ♗xc3 15 e5 ♕f5 16 ♖b3 ♗a5 17 ♘h4 ♕d7 18 ♗h6, with advantage; Halifman–Lau, Rotterdam 1988. Or **12 ... ♕d7** 13 dc bc (13 ... ♗xe2 14 ♕xe2 bc is safer) 14 ♖xb8!? ♖axb8 15 ♗xa6 ♕a4 16 ♕e2, with a won position; Gelfand–I. Sokolov, Yugoslavia 1988.

13 cd ♕d7

A recommendation of Grandmaster Gavrikov. A much earlier game Browne–Martz, USA 1982, went 13 ... ♗xe2 14 ♕xe2 ♘c6 15 d5 ♘d4 16 ♘xd4 ♗xd4 17 ♖d1 ♗g7 18 ♗a3 ♕d7 19 e5, with a clear advantage to White.

14 ♗a3

14 ♗xa6 ♘xa6 15 ♕a3 ♘c7! gives White nothing; Halifman–Epishin, Leningrad 1988, continued 16 ♖d1 ♖fc8 17 ♗b2 ♘b5 18 ♕d3, and now Halifman recommends 18 ... e6!

Black also obtains a good game after **14 ♖d1?!** ♕a4 15 ♗d2 ♗xe2 16 ♕xe2 ♖c8 17 e5 ♘a6 18 e6 f6 (18 ... f5!) 19 d5 ♕c4 20 ♕xc4 ♖xc4; Lputian–Zilberstein, Blagoveshchensk 1988. However, Salov's innovation **14 d5!?** deserves attention. After 14 ... ♗xe2 15 ♕xe2 ♕a4 16 ♗g5 ♖e8 17 ♖fc1, White obtained a slight edge in Salov–I. Sokolov, Haifa 1989.

14 ... ♗xe2

Another possibility is **14 ... ♖e8 15 d5** ♗xe2 16 ♕xe2 ♕a4 17 ♕e3 ♘d7 18 ♖fc1 ♖ac8 19 h3 ♖xc1+ 20 ♖xc1 ♘f6 21 ♘d2 ♗h6!, as in Gelfand–Malishauskas, Vilnius 1988. However, Pribyl gives **15 ♖fc1!** as more accurate.

15 ♕xe2 ♖e8

Black is not in a hurry to bring his knight out. In Gelfand–Groszpeter, Palma de Mallorca 1989, Black played 15 ... ♘c6, and after 16 d5 ♘e5 17 ♘xe5 ♗xe5 18 f4 ♗d6 19 ♗b2 e6 20 ♖bd1 White gained the initiative and soon won.

16 ♖fc1 e6
17 ♖c3 ♖c8

17 ... ♘c6? loses to 18 ♕b5 ♖ac8 19 ♖bc1 a6 20 ♕xb6.

18 ♖xc8+

18 ♖bc1 ♖xc3 19 ♖xc3 ♘c6 20 ♕b5 ♖c8 21 ♖c4 ♕b7 leads to equality.

18 ... ♕xc8
19 ♖c1 ♕b7

An alternative is **19 ... ♕a6 20 ♕e3 ♘d7 21 ♖c7 ♘f6** (21 ... ♕a4 22 h3) **22 ♘e5 ♖c8!** 23 ♖xf7 ♕b5 24 g3 ♕b1+ 25 ♔g2 ♕xe4+ 26 ♕xe4 ♘xe4 27 ♖xa7 ♗xe5 28 de ♖c2, with full equality; Dzhandzhgava–Malishauskas, Uzhgorod 1988. A better line for White, according to Halifman, is **20 ♕xa6 ♘xa6 21 ♔f1**, with some advantage.

20 ♕c4 ♘a6 *(30)*

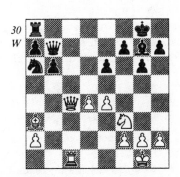

This position had first occurred only a few days earlier, in the game S. Ivanov–Pribyl from the same international tournament (Leningrad 1989). After 21 d5 ed 22 ed ♖d8 23 d6 ♘c5! 24 ♗xc5 bc 25 ♕xc5 ♕a6 26 h4 ♖xd6 27 ♘g5 h6, the players agreed a draw. The main game we are examining was to end in victory for Black, but that was hardly the rightful outcome. For the moment Halifman doesn't want to settle for a draw, and adds fuel to the flames.

21	h4	♖d8
22	e5!?	h6
23	h5	gh
24	♖c3	b5!
25	♕c6	♕xc6
26	♖xc6	♘b8
27	♖c7	♗f8
28	♗xf8	♔xf8 *(31)*

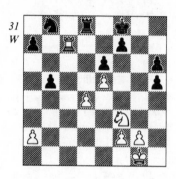

31
W

29 d5!

White's last chance – he hopes for success by sacrificing another pawn. As Pribyl has pointed out, a forced draw results from 29 ♖xa7 ♘c6 30 ♖b7 ♘xd4 31 ♘xd4 ♖xd4 32 ♖xb5 ♖d1+ 33 ♔h2 ♖d2.

29	...	ed
30	♘d4	♖e8!
31	f4	♖e7
32	♖c5	♘a6
33	♖xd5	

In the event of 33 ♖c6 ♘c7 34 ♖xh6, Black can save himself with 34 ... ♔g7! (but not 34 ... ♘e6? 35 ♘f5 ♖c7 36 ♖h8 mate) 35 ♖xh5 ♘e6 36 ♘f5+ ♔g6 37 ♘xe7+ ♔xh5 38 ♘xd5 ♔g4.

33	...	♘c7
34	♖d6	♘e6
35	♘c6	♖c7
36	f5	♘g5
37	f6?	

Now all White's previous work comes to nothing. After 37 e6! Black would still have to struggle for the draw.

37 ... ♔g8 38 ♔f1 ♔h7 39 ♘b4 a5 40 ♘d5 ♖c1+ 41 ♔e2
♖c2+ 42 ♔e3 ♖xg2 43 ♖d7 ♖g3+ 44 ♔e2 ♖g4 45 ♔d3 h4 46
♔e3 ♖a4 0–1

Game No. 10
Halifman–Henkin
Leningrad 1989

1 d4 ♘f6 2 c4 g6 3 ♘f3 ♗g7 4 ♘c3 d5 5 cd ♘xd5 6 e4 ♘xc3
7 bc c5 8 ♖b1 0–0

    9   ♗e2   ♘c6
    10   d5

White is unsuccessful with 10 ♗e3 cd 11 cd ♕a5+ 12 ♗d2
♕xa2; Paunović–Ristić, Vrnjacka Banja 1983. In comparison with
the variation 9 ... cd 10 cd ♕a5+, which we examine in Games
11–13, Black has the useful extra move ... ♘c6.

    10   ...   ♘e5

Safer than taking the pawn. Let us look at that possibility: 10
... ♗xc3+ 11 ♗d2 ♗xd2+ 12 ♕xd2 ♘a5 (moving that knight
to b8 or d4 is worse. An example of the latter is 12 ... ♘d4 13
♘xd4 cd 14 ♕xd4 ♕a5+ 15 ♕d2 ♕xd2+ 16 ♔xd2 ♖d8 17 ♔e3
b6 18 ♖bc1 e6 19 ♗c4 e5 20 ♗b3 ♗d7 21 ♖c7 a5 22 d6, and
Black has numerous problems; Kasparov–Natsis, Malta Ol 1980)
13 h4 (White may also castle, with e4–e5 to follow) 13 ... ♗g4
14 h5 ♗xf3 15 gf! (not allowing the knight onto c4). Despite the
simplification, White's attacking potential is very noticeable, for
example: 15 ... e6 16 ♕h4 ♕f6 17 hg ♕xg6 18 ♕h2 ♔h8 19 ♔d2!
f6 20 ♖bg1 ♕f7 21 de ♕e7 22 ♖g6, and the attack continues;
Bjarnason–Grünberg, Biel 1985.

    11   ♘xe5   ♗xe5
    12   ♕d2 *(32)*

White can also play 12 c4 at once, for example: 12 ... ♕d6!?
(12 ... ♕a5+ occurs more often) 12 ♕d2 ♗d4 14 ♗b2 ♗xb2 15
♖xb2 e5 16 0–0 b6 17 ♖b3, with a complicated position; Gelfand–
Ghinda, Halle 1987. Alternatively Black has an interesting counter-
sacrifice of a pawn: 12 ... f5 13 ef ♗xf5 14 ♖xb7 ♕d6 15 ♖b3.
Perhaps he should now go in for immediate exchanges with 15 ...
♗e4 16 ♗f3 ♗xf3 17 ♖xf3 ♖xf3 18 ♕xf3 ♖f8, trying to exploit
his advantage in development. Danner–Shvidler, Biel 1982, saw
instead 15 ... ♗d7 16 ♕d3 ♗f5 17 ♕d2 ♗e4 18 ♗g4 ♗xg2 19
♗e6+ ♕xe6 (19 ... ♔h8 20 ♖g1 ♗e4 21 ♖h3 with an attack!) 20 de

♗xh1 21 ♕e2 ♖f5 22 f3 ♖af8 23 ♗h6 ♖8f6 24 ♕e4, and Black has worries. A move that looks fairly logical is **12 ... ♕c7**, covering the pawn on b7 and preventing White from castling. A correspondence game Danner–Nesis (1983–5) continued 13 h3 f5 14 ef ♗xf5 15 ♖b3 ♗d4 16 0–0 e5, and Black achieved a sound position.

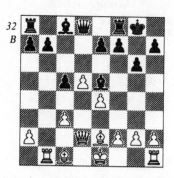

In the first half of the 1980s, Black almost invariably played 12 ... e6 here, and after 13 f4 he retreated his bishop to g7 or h8. I do not plan to give a thorough study of the positions which then arise, but it is worth reminding the reader of the difference that the choice of retreat square makes – or more exactly, of why it is essential to withdraw the bishop into the corner.

Consider the variation **12 ... e6 13 f4 ♗g7** 14 c4 ♖e8 15 e5 f6 14 d6 fe 17 ♗b2 ef 18 ♗xg7 ♔xg7 19 0–0 *(33)*.

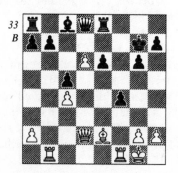

Practice has abundantly shown that 19 ... ♖f8 20 ♖xf4 ♖xf4 21 ♕xf4 secures White a distinct plus. But at move 19 Black cannot play 19 ... e5, on account of 20 d7!, and the pin on the 7th rank will be lethal.

However, if earlier Black plays **13 ... ♗h8**, and accordingly 18 ♗xh8 ♔xh8 occurs, then 19 0-0 *can* be answered effectively by 19 ... e5!, giving Black a solid position after 20 ♖fd1 ♕d7 21 ♕d5 ♖b8 22 ♕xc5 b6; Bikhovsky–Polovodin, Irkutsk 1983.

All the same, I should point out that after *13 ... ♗h8 14 c4 ♖e8 15 e5 f6*, White doesn't have to play 16 d6; he has the stronger *16 f5! (34)*.

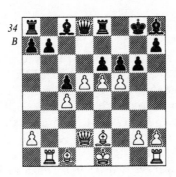

34
B

16 ... ed

Other pawn captures are no better: 16 ... ef 17 e6! followed by 18 0-0 and 19 g4; 16 ... fe 17 fg (17 fe ♕h4+ 18 ♔d1 doesn't look bad either) 17 ... hg 18 0-0 ed 19 cd ♕d6 20 ♖b3 ♗g7 21 ♖g3 etc.; 16 ... gf 17 ♖b3 ♖e7, and now 18 ♗b2, 18 d6 and 18 ♕h6 are all highly unpleasant for Black.

17 fg

Practice has also seen 17 e6 d4 18 g4 b6 19 ♗f3 ♖b8 (19 ... ♗a6!?) 20 ♕g2 ♕c7 21 0-0 g5 22 ♗d5 ♕e7 23 h4, with the initiative; Vaiser–Pribyl, Sochi 1984.

17 ... hg, and now White has two lines:

(a) *18 0-0* ♖xe5 19 ♗f3 d4 20 ♖e1 ♕e8 21 ♗a3 ♗f5 22 ♖xe5 ♕xe5 23 ♗d5+ ♕xd5 24 cd ♗xb1 25 ♗xc5, and Black is in a bad way; Cebalo–Raicević, Cáorle 1984.

(b) *18 cd* ♖xe5 19 0-0 b6 20 d6 ♗e6 21 ♗f3 ♖c8 22 ♗b2 f5 23 ♕h6! and White has a won position; Agzamov–Pribyl, Sochi 1984.

12 ...   b6

A comparatively new idea. Black limits the effect of his

opponent's rook on the b-file, and makes b7 available to his own
bishop.

13	f4	♗g7
14	c4	e6

14 ... e5 looks logical, but the following two examples from
recent practice show that it is not so simple for Black to achieve
equality.

Epishin–Ftačnik, Belgrade 1988, went **15 0–0 ef** 16 ♕xf4 ♗d4+
17 ♗e3 ♗xe3+ 18 ♕xe3 ♕e7 19 ♕f4 (Epishin gives 19 e5! ♖e8
20 e6 fe 21 ♗f3 as even stronger) 19 ... f6 20 a4! with the better
game for White.

Gelfand–Ftačnik, Debrecen 1989, deviated with **15 ... f5!?** 16
♗b2 ♕d6 17 ♕c3 ♖e8 18 ♗d3 ♖e7? (in Ftačnik's view, 18 ...
fe 19 ♗xe4 ♖e7 20 f5 gf 21 ♗xf5 e4 leads to unclear play) 19 ef
gf (19 ... e4 20 f6 ed 21 fe! and wins) 20 fe! ♗xe5 21 ♕d2 ♗xh2+
22 ♔h1 ♗e5 23 ♕g5+ ♔g6 24 ♕xe7 ♕h6+ 25 ♔g1 ♕e3+ 26
♔h1 ♕h6+ 27 ♔g1 ♕e3+ 28 ♖f2! ♗h2+ 29 ♔xh2 ♕xe7 30
♖f3! ♕d6+ 31 ♖g3+ ♔f7 32 ♖f1 h5 33 ♗xf5 h4 34 ♗g6++
♔g8 35 ♗h7++! ♔xh7 36 ♖f7+ ♔h6 37 ♗c1+ 1–0.

15 ♗b2

Considerably stronger than **15 0–0**, which Black used to meet
with **15 ... ♖e8**. But **15 ... ♗d4+!** is better; after 16 ♔h1 ♖e8
17 ♗d3 ed 18 ed ♗f5! 19 ♗xf5 gf, Black obtained good play in
Novikov–Krasenkov, Odessa 1989. The game continued very
sharply and ended in a draw; here is how: 20 ♗b2 ♕f6 21 ♗xd4
cd 22 ♖be1 ♖e4 23 g4 ♖ae8 24 gf ♕xf5 25 ♖g1+ ♔f8 26 ♕d3!
♕xf4 27 ♕a3+ ♖8e7 28 ♖ef1 ♕h4! 29 ♕d6 ♖g4 30 ♕d8+ ♖e8
13 ♕d6+ ♖e7 32 ♕d8+ ♖e8 33 ♖xf7+ ♔xf7 34 ♖f1+ ♖f4! 35
♕c7+ ♔g8 36 ♕xf4 ♕xf4 37 ♖xf4 d3! 38 ♖d4 ♔f8 39
♖xd3 ♖e1+ ½–½.

15	...	♗xb2
16	♖xb2	♖e8
17	e5	

On 17 0–0, Black would equalise with 17 ... ed.

17	...	♗b7
18	0–0	ed
19	♗f3	f6
20	♖e1	fe *(35)*

This position arose for the first time in Kudzhma–Henkin,
Kramatorsk 1989. In that game Black obtained a fine position

after 21 ♖xe5 ♛f6!. There followed 22 ♛e1 (22 ♗xd5+ was more to the point, giving equality after 22 ... ♗xd5 23 ♛xd5+ ♚h8) 22 ... ♖xe5! 23 ♛xe5 (23 fe ♛f4) 23 ... ♛f7 24 ♖e2 (better is 24 cd ♖e8, when Black has a minimal edge) 24 ... dc 25 ♗g4 ♛g7! and White's position is not easy.

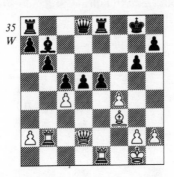

35
W

	21	fe!

A significant refinement.

	21	...	♛c7
	22	♗xd5+	♗xd5
	23	♛xd5+	♚g7
	24	e6	♖ad8
	25	♛f3	♖e7

He should have blockaded the pawn with his queen, although after 25 ... ♛e7 26 ♖be2 White still has the more pleasant position.

	26	♖f2	♛d6
	27	♛f6+	♚g8
	28	♛g5!	

This accurate move casts doubt on Black's set-up. After the immediate 28 h4 ♖de8, White would have to acquiesce in a draw with 29 ♛f7+ ♚h8 30 ♛f6+. But now 28 ... ♖de8 is answered by 29 ♛d5! ♖d8 30 ♖d2! with a won position.

	28	...	♚g7
	29	♛f6+	♚g8
	30	♛g5	♚g7
	31	h4!	♖de8
	32	♛d5	♖d8
	33	♛g5	

Of course not now 33 ♖d2? ♛g3!, and it is Black who wins.

33	...	♖de8
34	♖d2	♕c6?

As Henkin has shown, the only defence was **34 ... ♕c7**. Then
35 h5?! ♖xe6 36 h6+ ♔f8 37 ♖xe6 ♖xe6 38 ♖d8+ ♔f7 39 ♖h8
♕d6 40 ♖xh7+ ♔g8 41 ♖g7+ ♔h8 42 ♖xa7 ♖e1+! 43 ♔f2
♖e5 44 ♖a8+ would lead to a draw. Still, after the quiet **35 ♖de2**
White would retain some positional advantage.

35	♕e5+	♔g8 *(36)*

36	♖d7!

Black's pieces are stalemated.

36	...	b5

36 ... h5 doesn't help: 37 ♖e3, followed by 38 ♖g3. If **36 ...
♕a4**, White's simplest course would be 37 h5 ♕xc4 38 ♖xe7 ♖xe7
39 ♕b8+ ♔g7 40 h6+! ♔xh6 42 ♕f8+ ♖g7 43 e7.

37	cb	♕xb5
38	h5	♕b6
39	♖xe7	♖xe7
40	h6	c4+
41	♔h1	♕d8
42	♖b1!	♖c7
43	♕f4!	

After 43 ♕d5 ♖c8!, or 43 ♕d4 ♕f8!, Black could still hold on.

43	...	g5

The threat was 44 e7!

44	♕xg5+!	

1–0

Game No. 11
Vaiser–Pein
Budapest 1989

1 d4 ♘f6 2 c4 g6 3 ♘c3 d5 4 ♘f3 ♗g7 5 cd ♘xd5 6 e4 ♘xc3
7 bc c5 8 ♖b1 0–0

9	♗e2	cd
10	cd	♕a5+

At the present time, the exchange on d4 followed by the check with the queen is Black's most popular choice in this variation.

11	♗d2

Formerly, 11 ♕d2 was seen more often, but in the resulting endgame White can hardly count on a plus. For that reason, the search for the initiative now proceeds on different lines, and involves a pawn sacrifice. This variation of the Grünfeld occurred only once in my encounters with Kasparov – in the 13th game in Seville, where 11 ♕d2 ♕xd2+ 12 ♗xd2 was played *(37)*. Let us briefly examine that game.

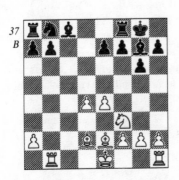

37
B

12 ... e6 (in answer to 12 ... b6 at once, White has various choices: 13 ♗d3, 13 d5 or 13 ♖c1, but best of all is 13 0–0. Then after 13 ... ♗b7 14 d5 ♗a6 15 ♖fe1 ♗xe2 16 ♖xe2 ♘a6 17 ♗e3, White has the better chances. If 17 ... f5, Gutman recommends 18 ♗d4! fe 19 ♖xe4 ♗f6 20 ♘e5!. If 17 ... ♖fe8, he recommends 18 ♖c2!, instead of 18 ♘d4 ♗xd4 19 ♗xd4 e6 20 de, which led to a draw in Halifman–Tseshkovsky, Minsk 1985) 13 0–0 (13 ♗c4, 13 ♖c1 and even 13 h4 have been seen, but there is no point in starting active operations with incomplete development) 13 ... b6 14 ♖fd1 (it is hard to decide how to arrange the rooks on the first rank; 14 ♖fe1, 14 ♖bc1 and 14 ♖fc1 have also been played.

As the d-pawn is due to advance, I place a rook behind it) 14 ...
♗b7 15 d5 ed 16 ed ♘d7 (16 ... ♗xd5 loses to 17 ♗b4 ♖d8 18
♗c4) 17 ♗b4 ♖fc8 18 ♗e7 (neither 18 ♘d4 nor 18 ♗b5 gives
White anything. But now his initiative looks fairly substantial –
for example 18 ... ♗f8 19 d6 ♗xe7 20 de ♘f6 21 ♖e1!. However,
Black manages to find a powerful retort which solves all his
opening problems) 18 ... ♗f6! 19 d6 ♔g7! 20 ♖e1 (20 ♗xf6+
is answered by 20 ... ♔xf6, but not 20 ... ♘xf6 211 d7 ♖d8 21
♘e5!) 20 ... ♖c5 21 ♗b5 ♗c6 22 ♗xc6 ♖xc6 23 ♖bd1 ♗c3 24
♖e3 f6 25 g4 g5 26 h4 h6 27 hg hg 28 ♘d4 (now Black seizes the
initiative; the correct line was 28 ♖c1 ♖ac8 29 ♗d8! with equality)
28 ... ♗xd4 29 ♖xd4 ♖h8 30 ♖e1 ♖c2 (Black could have
continued quite actively with 30 ... ♖c3 31 ♔g2 ♔f7; but now
peace ensues quickly) 31 a4 a5 32 f4! ♔g6 33 fg ♔xg5 34 ♖f1
♔g6 35 ♖f2 ♖hc8 36 ♖df4 ♖xf2 ½–½.

| 11 | ... | ♕xa2 |
| 12 | 0–0 | b6 *(38)* |

The main variations are 12 ... ♘d7 and 12 ... ♕e6; these will
feature in Games 12 and 13. There is no point in exposing the
knight to a pawn attack: after 12 ... ♘c6 13 d5 ♘e5 14 ♘d4,
White has clearly the better chances. But then, in the last few
years, practice has shown that 12 ... b6 is also dangerous for
Black. The present game will convince us of this.

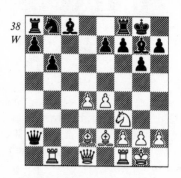

38
W

| 13 | ♕c1! | ♕e6 |

The alternative is 13 ... ♗b7 14 ♗c4 ♕a4 15 ♗b5 ♕a2 (now
of course White can force a draw by repetition, as occurred for
instance in Chernin–Dvoiris, Lvov 1990; but that is not much of
an achievement) 16 ♖e1! (but not 16 ♕e1? ♕c2! 17 d5 ♗a6! 18

♕e3 ♗xb5 19 ♖xb5 ♘a6 20 ♖bb1 ♘c5 21 ♗b4 a5!, and Black seizes the initiative; Yusupov–Korchnoi, Reykjavik 1988) 16 ... ♖c8 17 ♕d1 e6 18 ♕e2 ♘c6 19 ♕e3 ♖d8 (19 ... e5 is no better: 20 d5 ♘d4 21 ♘xd4 ed 22 ♕f4 ♗f8 23 ♖a1 ♕c2 26 ♗d7! with more than enough for the pawn; Halifman–Epishin, Vilnius 1988) 20 ♖a1 ♕b2 21 ♗xc6 ♗xc6 22 ♗c3 ♕b3 23 ♖eb1 ♕c2 24 ♘d2 ♗h6 25 ♕xh6 ♕xc3 26 ♘f3 f6 27 ♖c1 ♕b2 28 ♕f4! ♚g7 29 ♕c7+ ♗d7, and now instead of 30 ♕d6, as played in Epishin – Mark Tseitlin, Leningrad 1988, Epishin gives 30 ♖cb1! ♕e2 31 ♖e1 ♕b5 32 ♖xa7 ♖xa7 33 ♕xd8 ♗e8 34 e5 ♖f7 35 h3, with the advantage.

14	♗c4!	♕xe4
15	♖e1	♕b7
16	♗b4	♗e6
17	♖xe6!	

A typical exchange sacrifice giving White a dangerous initiative.

17	...	fe
18	♘g5 *(39)*	

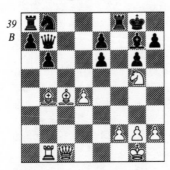

39
B

18	...	♘c6

A novelty which, however, does not solve all Black's problems.

In Gelfand–Dorfman, Minsk 1986, Black played **18 ... ♚h8**, which gave him a won position after **19 ♘xe6 ♘d7 20 ♗xe7?** ♖fc8. In Vaiser–Andrianov, Naberezhnie Chelny 1988, White's play was strengthened: **19 ♖b3! ♘d7 20 ♖h3 ♘f6?** (loses at once. A few days later, in a game Konyashkin–Titlyanov, Black replied 20 ... h5!, and after 21 ♕b1 ♖f5 22 ♘f7+ ♚h7 23 ♗xe6 ♘f6 24 ♗xf5 gf 25 ♕xf5+ ♚g8 26 ♕g6 ♕e4 27 ♘h6+ ♚h8 28 ♘f7+, the game had to end in perpetual check. However, the right line was 21 ♕d1! ♘f6 22 ♕b1 ♕c6 23 ♗xe6, with numerous threats)

21 ♕b1! ♘h5 22 ♖xh5 ♖f6 23 ♖xh7+ ♚g8 24 ♕b3 ♕c6 25 ♕h3 1–0.

19	♘xe6	♚h8
20	♗c3	

But not 20 ♗d5? ♖fc8 21 ♘g5 h6, and Black has everything in order.

20	...	♗f6

After 20 ... ♖f6 21 ♘xg7 ♚xg7 22 d5 ♘d8 23 d6! ♖c8 24 ♕e3 e6 (24 ... ed? 25 ♗xf6+ ♚xf6 26 ♕d4+ ♚g5 27 ♖b3 and wins) 25 ♗xf6+ ♚xf6 26 ♕d4+ ♚f7 27 ♖d1, White's advantage is indisputable.

21	♕h6!	♖g8

The decisive mistake. In Vaiser's opinion, 21 ... ♖f7! 22 ♘c5 ♕c8 23 ♗xf7 bc 24 ♗xg6 ♕g8 25 ♗e4 leads to unclear play.

22	♖e1	♖g7

In his analysis Vaiser has shown that on 22 ... ♘d8, White attains his goal with 23 ♘f8!

23	g4!	♘a5

23 ... g5 is no better: 24 ♗d3! ♖f7 25 ♗g6 ♚g8 26 ♗xf7+ ♚xf7 27 d5!

24	♗d3	♕c6
25	♗a1	♖f7

Things also go badly for Black in the endgame that results from 25 ... ♕f3 26 g5 ♕h5 27 ♕xh5 gh 28 f4 ♖gg8 29 ♚f2 ♗g7 30 ♘xg7 ♚xg7 31 ♖xe7+ ♚f8 32 ♖xh7.

26	g5	♗g7
27	d5!	♕xd5
28	♗xg7+	♚g8
29	♗xg6	

1–0

Game No. 12
Polovodin–Maslov
Leningrad 1990

1 d4 ♘f6 2 c4 g6 3 ♘c3 d5 4 ♘f3 ♗g7 5 cd ♘xd5 6 e4 ♘xc3 7 bc c5 8 ♖b1 0–0 9 ♗e2 cd 10 cd ♕a5+ 11 ♗d2 ♕xa2

12	0–0	♘d7

Over the last three years, a good many games and analyses relevant to this move have accumulated. I shall here quote the most important of them.

13 &b4

The natural move, which is usually played almost automatically. However, in Nemet–Kozul, Liechtenstein 1989, White decided to postpone this active bishop sortie and drive the queen away: 13 &a1 &e6 (13 ... &b2 is also playable) 14 &b1 &b6 15 &d3 &d8 16 &fc1 b6 17 &b4 &f6! (but not 17 ... &b7 18 e5!) 18 &e5 &b7 19 &c6 &xc6 20 &xc6 a5 21 &d2 (other bishop moves are answered by 21 ... b5, when White has inadequate compensation for the pawn) 21 ... &c8 22 &ac1 &xc6 23 &xc6 &a8 24 d5 &d7. Black's chances are better; here is how the game ended: 25 &a3 &d4 26 &h6 &e8 27 &b5? &c5! 28 &c7 &d8 29 &a7 &b8 30 &xe8 &xa7 31 &h3 &b8 32 &c6 &xe4 33 d6 &xd6 34 &d7 &f5 35 &d2 &e5 0–1.

13 ...   &b6 (40)

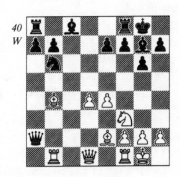

40
W

Before proceeding to the game continuation (14 &e5), let us look at some alternatives.

The exchange of the pawns on e4 and e7 took place in Vaiser–Kozul, Ptuj 1989: **14 &xe7 &e8 15 &a1** (or 15 &c5 &xe4 16 &d3 &e8 17 &a1 &b2 with a draw, but Black also has the interesting reply 15 ... &d7!) 15 ... &e6 16 &c5 &xe4 17 &e5 &xe5 18 &f3 &xh2+ 19 &xh2 &f4+ 20 &g1 &d7 21 &xa7 &f6 22 &c1 &f5 23 &e1 &xe1+ 24 &xe1 &f4. White has the advantage of the bishop pair, which compensates for the pawn minus.

An equal game results from **14 &b5 &d7 15 &xd7 &xd7 16 &xe7 &fe8**; Riemersma – Conquest, Dordrecht 1988. It is worth considering **14 d5**, with the threat of 15 &xe7.

The game Halifman–Gavrikov, Moscow 1988, took the following interesting course:

14 ♕d3!? ♖e8 15 ♘g5!

Exploiting the unfavourable placing of the enemy queen, White sets up the threat of 16 ♖a1. The tactical justification, given by Halifman, is: 15 ... ♗xd4 16 ♗d1! ♖d8 (16 ... ♗e6 17 ♕xd4 ♕xb1 18 ♘xe6 fe 19 ♗c3, or 16 ... ♕c4 17 ♕f3 and 18 ♗b3) 17 ♗b3 ♗xf2+ (17 ... ♕xf2+ 18 ♔h1) 18 ♔h1 ♖xd3 19 ♗xa2 and wins.

15 ... ♗e6 16 d5 ♗d7

The attempt to take advantage of the queen on the d-file with 16 ... ♖ad8 is no good in view of 17 de f6 18 ♕h3 fg 19 ♗b5.

17 ♕f3 f5!

The only move. 17 ... ♗f6 loses at once to 18 ♗xe7!, while 17 ... f6 18 ♖a1 ♕c2 19 ♖fc1 ♕b2 20 ♗c3 ♕b3 21 ♖cb1 ♕c2 22 ♖b2 is also bad for Black.

18 ♗d3 ♗f6 19 ef

Rather recklessly played. 19 ♘e6 or 19 h4 was stronger, and may have given a sharper attack.

19 ... ♗xg5 20 fg ♕xd5 21 ♗e4 ♕e6 22 ♗d2!

Not 22 ♕h5 h6 23 f4 ♕xe4 24 fg, which fails to the intermediate check 24 ... ♕e3+.

22 ... hg!

Other moves quickly lose.

23 ♗xg5 ♗c6 24 ♗xc6 ♕xc6 25 ♕h3 ♕d5 26 ♗e3

Here White had the much stronger 26 ♕h6! ♕f7 27 ♗e3, winning the pawn back and retaining a positional advantage.

26 ... ♘c4 27 ♕g4 ♔g7 28 ♗d4+ ½-½.

So 14 ♕d3 gave White a dangerous attack. However, the vulnerability of the queen on d3 was emphasised in a game Tukmakov–Gavrikov, Moscow 1989, which went **14 ... ♗e6!** *(41).*

Black threatens 15 ... ♗c4, which Makarichev suggested parrying with **15 ♘d2 ♖fd8 16 d5**. But then Black would carry out much the same decisive tactical operation as in the actual game: 16 ... ♗xd5! 17 ed ♘xd5! and there is no defence against 18 ... ♘xb4 or 18 ... ♘f4. The correct line for White is **15 ♖a1 ♕c4 16 ♗xe7 ♕xd3 17 ♗xd3 ♖fe8 18 ♗c5 ♗c4 19 ♗xc4 ♘xc4**, with a roughly equal ending; or 15 ... ♕b3 16 ♗xe7 ♖fe8 17 ♗c5 ♘a4 18 ♕xb3 ♗xb3 19 ♗b5 ♘xc5 20 ♗xe8 ♖xe8 21

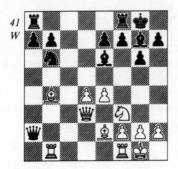

♖a3, as in S. Ivanov–Novik, USSR 1989, and now 21 ... ♗c4! 22 dc ♗xf1 23 ♔xf1, again with an equal position.

Tukmakov played **15 d5??**, not even suspecting the danger awaiting him: 15 ... ♘xd5!, an attractive stroke which decides the issue at once. After 16 ed ♗f5, not only the rook on b1 but also the bishop on e2 is left under attack, and White could very well cease resistance. This actually happened 12 moves later.

14   ♘e5 *(42)*

14 ♖a1 ♕e6 15 ♕c2 is interesting, but has yet to be tried out in practice. It was Neverov who suggested jumping to e5 with the knight, and the move was first played in a game Alterman–Rogozhenko, USSR 1989.

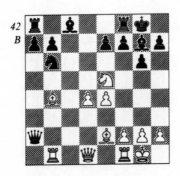

14 ...   f6

In the original game with this line, Black decided to eliminate the knight at once, and was quickly crushed: **14 ... ♗xe5** 15 de ♕e6 16 ♕d4 ♗d7 17 f4 f6 (17 ... ♗c6!? was more tenacious; after 18 f5 ♕d7, the play isn't so clear) 18 ef ♕xf6 19 ♕e3! ♖ac8

20 ♗c5 ♗c6 21 f5 ♕e5 22 ♖xb6! ab 23 ♗c4+ ♖f7 24 ♗xf7+! and White won.

The retreat of the queen to e6 in these circumstances led to disaster in Ivanov–Maslov, Leningrad 1990: **14 ...** ♕**e6** 16 fe f5 16 ♗c5 fe 17 ♗xb6 18 de ab 19 ♕d4 ♕c6 20 ♖fc1 (or 20 ♗c4+ ♗e6 21 ♗xe6+ 22 ♖xb6 ♕f5 23 ♖xb7, with the better chances) 20 ... ♖a4 (he should have played 20 ... ♕d7 21 ♕xb6 ♕d8, with a complex struggle) 21 ♕d1! ♕d7 22 ♖xc8! and wins.

14 ... ♗**e6** is also dangerous for Black: 15 ♗xe7 ♖fe8 16 ♗h4! (stronger than 16 ♗c5 ♗xe5 17 de ♗c4 18 ♗xc4 ♕xc4, with equal chances; Halifman–Kindermann, West Berlin 1989) 16 ... g5 (16 ... ♖ec8 may be better) 17 ♗xg5 (or 17 ♗g3 ♖ad8 18 ♗b5 ♖f8, as in Sakayev–Novik, USSR 1990, and now 19 ♕h5! f6 20 d5 fe 21 de ♕xe6 22 ♕xg5 with a clear plus) 17 ... f6 18 ♖a1 ♕b3 (18 ... ♕b2 19 ♘d3 ♕xd4 20 ♗e3 ♕xe4 was better) 19 ♕d2 ♖ac8 20 ♗d1 ♕c3 21 ♕xc3 ♖xc3 22 ♗d2, and White wins.

15 ♘c4!

In the game Shevelev–Lagunov, USSR 1989, in which 14 ... f6 was played for the first time, White withdrew his knight to f3, giving Black a good place for his queen: 15 ♘f3 ♕f7! 16 ♕c1 ♗d7 17 ♕a3 ♖fc8! 18 ♗xe7 (otherwise 18 ... ♗f8) 18 ... ♖e8 19 ♗c5 ♖xe4 20 ♖xb6 (20 ♗xb6 ♖xe2 is worse) 20 ... ♖xe2 21 ♖xb7 a5 22 ♕d3 ♖ee8 23 d5 *(43)*.

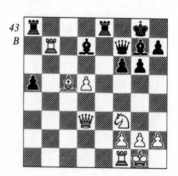

Now after 23 ... ♖ab8 24 ♖a7 a4, the game was eventually drawn. Lagunov points out an interesting trap that Black could have set: 23 ... ♖ec8! 24 ♗a3 (also after 24 ♖a7 ♖xa7 25 ♗xa7 a4, the advantage is with Black) 24 ... ♗f5! 25 ♕b5 ♗d3! and wins.

Apart from the retreat of the knight at move 15, practice has seen **15 ♖a1 ♕e6 16 ♗g4 f5 17 ef gf 18 ♗f3 ♖d8 19 ♖e1 ♗xe5 20 ♖xe5 ♕xe5 21 de ♖xd1+ 22 ♖xd1 ♔f7**, with a roughly equal game; Neverov–Malishauskas, Podolsk 1989. Or **16 ♘d3!? ♕xe4?** (16 ... ♕f7 is safer) **17 ♗f3 ♕f5 18 ♖e1 ♖e8 19 ♗c5 ♗d7 20 ♗xb7 ♖ab8 21 ♖xa7** with the advantage; Agrest–Maslov, USSR 1990.

| | 15 | ... | ♘xc4 |
| | 16 | ♖a1 | ♘b2! |

16 ... ♕b2 loses the queen to 17 ♗xc4+ ♔h8 18 ♖b1!. On the other hand, **16 ... ♘e3** transposes into the game after 17 ♖xa2 ♘xd1.

	17	♖xa2	♘xd1
	18	♗c4+	♔h8
	19	♖xd1	*(44)*

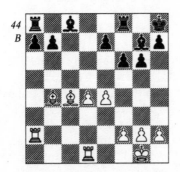

44
B

How should we assess this rook and bishop ending? Black is a pawn up, and has two connected passed pawns on the queenside. White has powerful pawns in the centre, and the more active bishops. Overall, White's position looks the more attractive, and indeed in the present game his conduct of the ending brings success. (From now on, I shall make use of the winner's notes.)

| | 19 | ... | ♗d7 |

After **19 ... a6 20 f3 ♖e8 21 ♗b5 ♗e6 22 d5 ab 23 ♖xa8 ♖xa8 24 de ♗f8 25 ♖d7 ♖a6 26 ♗xe7 ♗xe7 27 ♖xe7 ♖b6 28 ♖e8+ ♔g7 29 ♖b8 ♖xe6 30 ♖xb7+** (threatening ♖xb5), White would gain a clear advantage (Almeira). But a better move, undoubtedly, was **19 ... ♖d8**, clarifying the position in the centre at once: 20

♗xe7 ♖e8 21 ♗c5 ♖xe4 22 ♖xa7 ♖xa7 23 ♗xa7. Material equality is restored, and White has a minimal edge.

20 ♗xe7 ♖fe8
21 ♗d6

The game Petursson–Almeira, Lyon 1990, went 21 ♗c5 b6, and only then 22 ♗d6. After 22 ... ♗e6 23 d5 ♗d7 24 ♗d3 f5 25 ef gf, White utilised the weakening of a6 with 26 ♗a6!

21 ... ♖ec8

After **21 ... ♗f8** 22 ♗xf8 ♖xf8 23 ♗d5 ♗c6 24 ♗xc6 bc 25 ♖a6 ♖fc8 26 f3, the double rook endgame is difficult for Black. The ingenious tactical trick **21 ... ♖xe4** 22 ♗d5 ♗e6 doesn't turn out so well after 23 ♗xe4 ♗xa2 24 ♗xb7. A safer line for Black is **21 ... ♗e6** 22 d5 ♗d7 23 ♗d3 f5 24 ef gf.

22 ♗f7 a5

22 ... ♗f8 23 ♗xf8 ♖xf8 24 ♗d5 ♗c6 25 ♗xc6 bc 26 ♖a6 similarly leads to a bad ending for Black.

23 f4!

The advance of the centre pawns quickly decides the game.

23 ... ♖a6

Black could resist more stubbornly with 23 ... ♗f8 (23 ... ♗h6 24 g3) 24 ♗xf8 ♖xf8 25 ♗d5 ♗c6 26 ♗xc6 bc 27 ♖c1 ♖fd8 28 ♖a4, although even then it isn't simple to hold the ending.

24 e5 ♗f8
25 ♗d5!

A tactical resource which consolidates White's advantage. After 25 ♗xf8 ♖xf8 26 ♗d5 b5!, the black pawns would already be much the more dangerous.

25 ... ♖a7

If 25 ... ♗xd6, the intermediate move 26 ♗xb7 is decisive. Nor can Black save himself with 25 ... ♖xd6 26 ed b6 27 ♖b1 ♗xd6 (27 ... ♖b8 28 ♖xa5!) 28 ♖xb6 ♗xf4 29 ♔f2 ♗xh2 30 ♖xf6.

26 ♗xf8 ♖xf8
27 e6 ♗c8

Other moves likewise fail to rescue Black: 27 ... ♗c6 28 ♗b3 a4 29 d5 ♗b5 30 d6!, or 27 ... ♗b5 28 ♖b2 ♗a4 29 ♖a1 ♗c6 30 ♗c4.

28 ♖e2 b5

If 28 ... b6, then 29 ♗c6 ♖e7 30 d5, with a won position.

29 ♗c6 ♖e7

30	d5	b4

Or 30 ... ♖d8 31 ♗xb5 ♖xe6 32 ♖xe6 ♗xe6 33 de ♖xd1+ 34 ♔f2 ♖d2+ 35 ♔f3, and the pawn queens.

31	♖a1
	1–0

Game No. 13
Gelfand–Ivanchuk
Tilburg 1990

1 d4 ♘f6 2 c4 g6 3 ♘c3 d5 4 cd ♘xd5 5 e4 ♘xc3 6 bc ♗g7 7 ♘f3 c5 8 ♖b1 0–0 9 ♗e2 cd 10 cd ♕a5+ 11 ♗d2 ♕xa2

12	0–0

The present game will feature **12 ... ♗g4** – we shall come to it shortly.

In Games 11 and 12, we looked in detail at **12 ... ♘d7** and **12 ... b6**. Since the black queen must return to its own camp sooner or later, the immediate **12 ... ♕e6** is also sometimes played. Let us digress a little from our principal game and consider this manoeuvre. White protects his pawn with **13 ♕c2**, giving this position *(45)*:

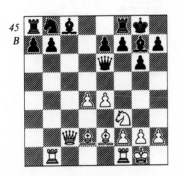

45
B

The queen doesn't feel very comfortable on e6, and it is now best to move it to d6 or c6.

Gelfand–Kindermann, Debrecen 1989, went **13 ... ♕d6 14 d5** b6 (14 ... ♘a6 is safer) 15 ♗b4 ♕d8 16 ♖fd1 ♘a6 17 ♗a3 ♘c5 18 ♘d4 ♗xd4 19 ♖xd4 ♕d6 20 ♕c3 ♕f4 21 ♗b5 ♗d7 22 ♗xd7 ♘xd7 23 ♗xe7 ♖fe8. At this point, as Gelfand has shown, White could have won beautifully with 24 d6 ♖ac8 25 ♖c4! ♕xe4 (25 ... ♖c5 26 ♖xc5 ♘xc5 27 ♕d4) 26 ♖xc8 ♕xb1+ 27 ♕c1 ♕xc1+

28 ♖xc1 f5 29 ♖c7 ♘f8 (29 ... ♘c5 30 ♖xc5!) 30 h4, etc. Instead he played 24 g3?, and after 24 ... ♕e5 25 ♗a3 ♖ac8 26 ♕d2 ♖c2 27 ♕xc2 ♕xd4 28 ♖e1 ♘c5 29 ♗xc5 bc 30 ♖d1 ♕xe4 31 ♕xc5 ♕f3!, a level ending arose and a draw soon resulted: 32 ♖c1 (32 ♕d4? ♖e4!) 32 ... ♖d8 33 ♖e1 ♖xd5 (33 ... ♕xd5? 34 ♖e8+) 34 ♖e8+ ♔g7 35 ♕f8+ ♔f6 36 ♕e7+, ½-½.

Interestingly enough, the position in diagram 45 occurred in another game between the same players a year later (Dortmund, 1990). This time, after 13 ... ♕d6 Gelfand innovated with the immediate **14 ♗b4!**. There followed 14 ... ♕d8 15 d5 ♗g4 (14 ... b6 transposes into the previous game, which should not have turned out well for Kindermann) 16 ♖fc1 ♘a6 17 ♗a3 ♗xf3 18 gf! (White has obtained a definite plus) 18 ... ♕d7 19 ♗xa6 ba 20 ♕c7 ♕h3 21 ♕g3! ♕xg3 22 hg, and Black has a miserable position.

Gelfand–Kamsky, Tilburg 1990, went **13 ... ♕c6** 14 ♕d3 ♕d6 15 ♗b4 ♕d8 16 ♕a3 (of course White had no reason to exchange queens, but then his queen didn't feel too comfortable on d3 either) 16 ... ♘c6 17 ♗c5 *(46)*.

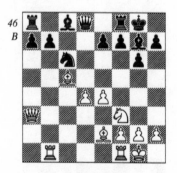

After lengthy manoeuvres (... ♕d8–a5–a2–e6–c6–d6–d8), the black queen has returned to its 'rightful' place. Several tempi have been lost, and in addition White is threatening d4–d5. However, Black found an interesting tactical resource: 17 ... ♗xd4!? 18 ♘xd4 ♘xd4 19 ♗xe7 ♘xe2+ 20 ♔h1 ♕e8 21 ♗xf8 ♕xf8 22 ♕e3 a5 (while White surrounds the knight, the black a-pawn speeds forward) 23 ♕xe2 a4 24 ♖b5 ♕e7 25 ♖a1 ♗e6 26 e5 a3 27 ♕f3 a2 28 ♕xb7 ♕d8 (Black is the exchange down, but his far advanced a-pawn enables him to save himself) 29 h3 ♖c8 30 ♖b2

♕g5 31 ♖bxa2 (forcing the issue) 31 ... ♖c1+ 32 ♖xc1 ♕xc1+
33 ♔h2 ♗xa2 34 ♕a8+ ♔g7 35 ♕xa2 ♕f4+ 36 g3 ½–½.

And now, one more digression: the new move **12 ... a5!?** was
played in Hébert–Kozul, Toronto 1990. No other examples are
available, but in this case the advance of the rook's pawn brought
Black success: 13 ♗g5 a4 14 ♗b5 (better is 14 ♕d3) 14 ... ♗d7
15 ♗xd7 ♘xd7 16 ♖xb7 ♕e6 17 d5 ♕xe4 18 ♖xd7 a3 19 ♖xe7
♕b4 20 ♖ee1 a2 21 ♗e7 ♕b5 22 ♕d2? (the right course was 22
♗xf8 a1(♕) 23 ♕xa1 ♖xa1 24 ♗xg7 ♖xe1 25 ♖xe1 ♔xg7 26
h4! ♕xd5 27 ♖e3, with equality) 22 ... ♖fc8 23 d6 a1(♕) 24 ♖xa1
♖xa1 25 ♖xa1 ♗xa1 26 h3 ♕d7, and Black won.

<h2 style="text-align:center">12 ...   ♗g4</h2>

Black leaves his pawn on b7 undefended, but takes aim at the
white d-pawn. 13 ♖xb7 ♗xf3 14 ♗xf3 ♗xd4 15 e5 ♘a6 16
♖xe7 ♖ad8 leads to sharp play, with material equality.

<h2 style="text-align:center">13 ♗g5!   h6</h2>

In the game Sakayev–Bukhman, USSR 1989, Black retreated
with 13 ... ♕e6, and there followed: 14 d5 (at this point, taking
the b-pawn doesn't pay at all: 14 ♖xb7 ♕xe4 15 ♖xe7 ♕d5, with
advantage to Black) 14 ... ♕xe4 (or 14 ... ♕d7 15 ♕b3 b6 16
♕a3, and White has the initiative) 15 ♕d2! f6 (the preliminary 15
... a5 was better: 16 ♖xb7 f6 17 ♗e3, with compensation for the
pawn) 16 ♗e3 a5 17 ♖fc1! ♖c8 18 h3 ♗d7 19 ♖xc8+ ♗xc8
20 ♗d3 ♕a4 (20 ... ♕xd5 loses to 21 ♖c1 ♕d7 22 ♗c4+ ♔h8
23 ♗e6! ♕xe6 24 ♕d8+ ♕g8 25 ♖xc8) 21 ♗c5 ♕d7 22 ♕e2
♗f8 23 ♗c4 ♔h8 24 ♖b6 ♘a6 25 ♗d4 ♘c7 26 ♘e5! fe. White
could now have won immediately with 27 ♕xe5+ ♔g8 28 d6+
e6 29 dc.

<h2 style="text-align:center">14 ♗e3   ♘c6</h2>

Ivanchuk twice reached this position in the Manila Interzonal,
1990. Gurevich–Ivanchuk continued: 14 ... b6 15 h3 ♗xf3 16
♗xf3 e5 17 d5 ♘d7 18 ♖e1 ♖fd8 19 ♕d3 ♘c5 20 ♕b5 ♗f8 21
♖ed1 ♘b7 22 ♖a1 ½–½.

<h2 style="text-align:center">15 d5   ♘a5</h2>

In the game between the same opponents in Manila, Black
preferred 15 ... ♘e5, and after 16 ♖xb7 e6 17 ♖e1 ♗xf3 18 gf
♖fd8 19 d6 ♕a3 20 d7 ♕e7 21 ♗b5 ♕h4 22 ♗f1 a draw was
agreed. White has a strong passed d-pawn, but his king's residence
is weakened, which gives Black sufficient counterchances. In the
present case Ivanchuk is attempting to improve on his play, but

Gelfand succeeds in exploiting the position of the knight on the edge of the board.

16	♗c5	♗f6
17	e5!	

The positional sacrifice of a second pawn.

17	...	♗xe5
18	h3	♗xf3
19	♗xf3	♖fe8

In a detailed examination of the game, Gelfand and his trainer Kapengut indicate the stronger 19 ... ♖ae8 20 d6 (20 ♖e1 ♘c4 21 ♖xb7 ♗d6 22 ♖xa7 ♕d2 leads to equality) 20 ... ed 21 ♗d5 ♘c4 22 ♕g4 (the tempting 22 ♖xb7 dc 23 ♕f3 ♘d2 24 ♕d3 comes up against 24 ... ♗h2+! 25 ♔xh2 ♘xf1+ 26 ♔g1 ♕a1! – Ivanchuk; but 22 ♗b4! is worth considering) 22 ... dc 23 ♕xg6+ (if 23 ♗xc4, Black can defend his g-pawn with 23 ... ♕c2) 23 ... ♗g7 24 ♖xb7 ♘e5! 25 ♕xg7+ ♔xg7 26 ♗xa2 ♖b8 27 ♖xa7 ♖a8, with equality.

20 d6!

Now it turns out that Black cannot take the d-pawn, so he has to part with the exchange.

20 ... ♕c4

The endgame which now arises is difficult for Black, but the alternatives are thoroughly bad: 20 ... ed 21 ♗d5 ♘c4 22 ♖xb7, or 20 ... ♕e6 21 d7 ♖ed8 22 ♕a4 ♘c4 23 ♗xb7 ♖ab8 24 ♗xa7.

21	d7	♕xc5
22	de(♕)+	♖xe8

For the moment Black is quite well off from the material point of view, with three pawns – more than the equivalent – for the exchange. His pieces, however, are badly co-ordinated, and this leads to more losses.

23 ♕a4

23 ♕d7 looks tempting, with the aim of exploiting the exposure of the black king after 23 ... ♕c8 24 ♕b5 ♗c7 25 ♖fc1 ♖d8 26 ♕c5 ♘c6 27 ♗xc6 ♗d6 28 ♕e3!. But the raid with the queen would be refuted by 23 ... ♔f8! 24 ♖b5 ♕c7.

23 ... ♘c6

24 ♖xb7

After 24 ♖fc1 ♕d4 25 ♖c4 ♕d7 26 ♖xc6 bc 27 ♗xc6 ♕f5! 28 ♗e4 ♕c8, it is Black who has the better game.

24 ... ♖c8

25   ♗xc6

25 ♖b5 ♕c3! 26 ♗xc6 ♕xc6 is insufficient to win.

25   ...   ♖xc6

26   ♖xe7

Already the advantage in material is with White.

**26 ... ♕xe7 27 ♕xc6 ♗d4 28 ♕d5 ♗b6 29 g3 h5 30 ♔g2
♔g7 31 ♖b1 ♕e2 32 ♕f3 ♕e6**

White's advantage is indisputable, but to convert it to a win he
needs to exchange queens.

**33 ♕c3+ ♔h7 34 ♖e1 ♕d5+ 35 ♕f3 ♕d7 36 ♖d1 ♕e7 37
♖d3 ♔g7 38 ♕c6 ♕e2 39 ♖f3 ♕a2? 40 ♕c3+ ♔g8 41 ♕b3**

White's main task is accomplished; the rest is simpler.

**41 ... ♕xb3 42 ♖xb3 ♔f8 43 ♔f3 ♔e7 44 ♖b2 ♔e6 45 ♔e4
♔d6 46 ♖d2+ ♔e6 47 ♔f4 ♔f6 48 ♖c2**

The rook cannot be prevented from penetrating the Black
position.

**48 ... ♗d4 49 ♔e4 ♗b6 50 ♖c6+ ♔e7 51 f4 ♗d7 52 ♖f6
♔e7 53 ♖c6 ♔d7 54 ♔d5 ♗c7 55 ♖c4 a5 56 ♖c6 ♗d8 57 ♖a6
♔e7 58 ♔e4 ♗c7 59 ♔d5 ♗d8 60 ♖a7+ ♔f6** *(47)*

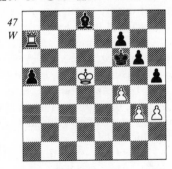

61   ♖a8!

Now if 61 ... ♗c7, White wins with 62 ♔c6, as the bishop is
trapped. If 61 ... ♔e7, then 62 ♔c6, and an original zugzwang
decides the game; once the possible kingside pawn moves are
exhausted, Black must move his a-pawn for lack of anything else.

61   ...   ♗e7

62   ♖xa5

1–0

White cannot be stopped from approaching the f-pawn with his
king and then winning it with the aid of the rook, after which
further resistance is senseless.

Game No. 14
Karpov–Kasparov
World Championship (15th game)
Lyon 1990

Before proceeding with this game, I should explain that nearly all the material for the present book was assembled before my last match – the fifth – with Kasparov; and that when I began putting the manuscript in order immediately the match was over, I allotted two places to the four Grünfeld games played in New York and Lyon. The point is that the ninth game of the match was spoilt by my blunder in the ending, while in the thirteenth I never managed to extract much from the opening; so I decided not to include either of them among the principal (numbered) games. The fifteenth and seventeenth match games were a different matter – they were assigned to places 14 and 15. But once I set about annotating the first of these games – with my impressions of it still fresh – I unexpectedly realised that it contained a far greater number of interesting subtleties and unusual situations than might at first have been supposed. Immersing myself in the analysis, I detected – strangely enough – more and more new ideas and problems which had to be looked into. The result was that whereas in other cases I had merely told the story of a game, here I produced something more like a novel.

To be sure, by the exhaustive analysis, by the sheer abundance of the variations given, this game stands clearly apart from all others in the book. What is offered here for the reader's attention is virtually the definitive theory of an important Grünfeld system that was tested out in this match.

1	d4	♘f6
2	c4	g6
3	♘c3	d5

Ever since the World Championship Match of 1986, the Grünfeld Defence has been firmly incorporated into Kasparov's repertoire, and together with the King's Indian it today constitutes his main weapon against the closed openings. Obviously his choice of the Grünfeld in the present match was no surprise to me.

4   cd

Essentially, this seems to me to be more logical than 4 ♗f4 (to which I turned during the 1986 match), or 4 ♘f3 ♗g7 5 ♕b3 dc 6 ♕xc4 (another popular line which was thoroughly tested both in 1986 and in the Seville encounter of 1987). The merit of the plan initiated by 4 cd is that White creates a strong pawn centre within the shortest number of moves!

4	...	♘xd5
5	e4	♘xc3
6	bc	♗g7

There was a time when it was thought essential to start undermining the pawn centre at once with 6 ... c5. The argument was that otherwise (after 6 ... ♗g7), White could play 7 ♗a3, as recommended by Simagin, and hold up Black's flank counter-thrust for a long time. But now the bishop move to a3 is considered fairly innocuous on account of 7 ... ♘d7 (or 7 ... 0–0 8 ♘f3 ♘d7) 8 ♘f3 c5.

7   ♗e3

The development of forces which commences with this move is less thoroughly explored than 7 ♗c4 c5 8 ♘e2, or 7 ♘f3 c5 8 ♖b1 (7 ♕a4+ and 7 ♗b5+, which are coming into fashion, do not appeal to me). Together with my team of seconds I had prepared this variation specially for the match. It must be said that, in the main, my hopes of gaining an opening advantage with it were not unrealised.

7	...	c5
8	♕d2 *(48)*	

White still has quite a wide choice of continuations here. Thus, 8 ♗b5+ is playable, as are 8 ♘f3 and 8 ♖c1, two lines which tend to transpose.

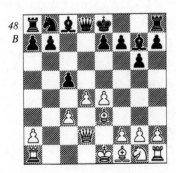

This is the position that formed the starting point for the theoretical contest in the games (and analysis!) of the 1990 match.

Kasparov endeavoured four times to equalise for the Black side, in opposition to my efforts to develop an opening initiative. The overall score (+1 =3 to White) may be considered acceptable to both sides, and testifies rather to the problematic character of the variation than to the attainment of a definite verdict.

8 ... 0–0

In the ninth game, where I tried this system for the first time, Kasparov chose a more straightforward plan, exchanging pawns in the centre. That game is also a very important one, so we will now embark on a long digression to look at it in detail:

   8 ... cd 9 cd ♘c6 10 ♖d1

   ECO only considers 10 ♘f3 ♗g4 11 ♖d1 (nor can White count on anything after 11 ♗b5 0–0 12 ♗xc6 bc 13 ♖c1 ♗xf3 14 gf ♕d7) 11 ... 0–0 12 ♗e2 ♖c8 13 0–0 b6 (13 ... ♗xf3 14 ♗xf3 e5 15 d5 ♘d4 doesn't look bad either) 14 d5 ♗xf3 15 gf ♘e5 16 ♖c1 ♕d7 17 f4 ♘c4!. After 18 ♗xc4 ♕g4+, Black is guaranteed a draw; Haïk–Granda, Dubai Ol 1986.

   10 ... ♕a5 (49)

   The game Kozul–Dorfman, Marseille 1989, in which the innovation **10 ♖d1** was tried out, went **10 ... e6** 11 ♘f3 0–0 12 ♗b5!? (the tempting 13 ♗h6 is parried by 13 ... ♕a5 14 ♕xa5 ♘xa5 15 ♗xg7 ♔xg7 16 ♗d3 ♗d7 17 ♔d2 ♖fc8, or by the quite good alternative 13 ... f5!? 14 ♗xg7 ♔xg7 15 e5 ♕d5 16 ♗e2 b6 17 0–0 ♗b7, retaining counter-attacking possibilities in the middlegame) 12 ... ♗d7 13 0–0 (after 13 ♗h6 ♗xh6 14 ♕xh6, the reply 14 ... ♕a5+ is rather risky on account of 15 ♖d2. Similarly, 13 ... ♘e5 14 ♘xe5 ♗xb5 15 ♗xg7 ♔xg7 is inadequate in view of 16 h4. But 13 ... f5 14 ♗xg7 ♔xg7, as in the previous note, is fully viable, since 15 e5 is met by 15 ... ♘xe5 16 de ♗xb5 17 ♕b4 ♕b6 – the simple 17 ... ♕e8 is also possible – 18 ♘g5 ♖fe8 19 ♖d6 ♗c6 20 ♘xe6+ ♔g8, with complications; or 18 ♘d4 ♖ad8, with the idea of answering 19 ♕xb5 with 19 ... ♖xd4!, or 19 ♕e7+ with 19 ... ♔g8! 19 a4 ♗d7, or 19 ♘xb5 with 19 ... ♖xd1+ 20 ♔xd1 a6 21 ♕e7+ ♖f7) 13 ... a6 (13 ... ♘e5 is unconvincing; although 14 de ♗xb5 15 ♕b4 ♕e8 16 ♖fe1 b6 is satisfactory for Black, the unassuming 14 ♗e2 gives White the better prospects) 14 ♗e2 ♕a5 15 d5 ♕xd2 (of course not 15 ... ♗c3? 16 dc! ♗xd2 17 ♗xd2, with a won position) 16 ♖xd2 ed 17 ed ♘e7, and the ending clearly favours White. For example, he can play to restrict the knight's mobility with 18 d6 ♘f5 (18

... ♘c6 19 ♗b6) 19 ♗b6 and then g2–g4; or else 18 ♗c5 ♖fe8 19 d6 ♘f5 20 g4 ♘h6 21 h3, with the advantage.

In Seirawan–Sokolov, Novi Sad Ol 1990, Black played the modest **10 ... 0–0**, but after 11 ♘f3 ♗g4 12 ♗e2 ♖c8 13 0–0 ♕d7 14 h3, he sacrificed his bishop: 14 ... ♗h5 15 g4 ♗xg4 16 hg ♕xg4+ 17 ♔h2 ♕xe4 18 ♘g5 ♕f5 19 f4 e6 20 ♗d3 ♕f6 21 ♗e4. Black's compensation for the piece is insufficient, and White eventually prevailed.

Whatever the reason, Kasparov preferred to exchange queens ...

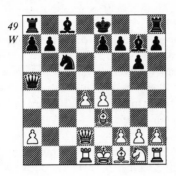

49
W

11 ♕xa5 ♘xa5 12 ♘f3

This endgame had arisen once before, in Yusupov–Gulko, Linares 1989. On that occasion White preferred 12 ♗d3 0–0 13 ♘e2 ♗d7 14 ♖c1 ♖fc8 15 ♔d2 e6 16 ♖xc8+ ♖xc8 17 ♖c1 ♖xc1 18 ♘xc1 ♔f8, and the minor piece ending was quickly drawn after 19 ♘e2 a6 20 ♗f4 ♘c6 21 ♗d6+ ♔e8 22 ♔c3 ♗f6 23 ♗c7 ♗e7 24 f3.

12 ... 0–0

Here 12 ... ♗g4 is premature on account of 13 ♗b5+.

13 ♗e2 ♗d7 (50)

14 ♗d2!

Typical of Grünfeld endings. If the knight retreats, then after 14 ... ♘c6 15 d5 ♘e5 (in the event of 15 ... ♘d4 16 ♘xd4 ♗xd4 17 ♗b4 ♗f6 18 f4 a5 19 ♗a3 ♗c3+ 20 ♔f2 ♖fe8 21 ♖b1, or 20 ... ♗b4 21 ♗xb4 ab 22 ♖d2, Black has many problems) 16 ♘xe5 ♗xe5 17 f4 ♗c7 18 ♖c1 ♖fc8 (18 ... ♗b6 19 ♗b4 ♖fc8 20 ♔d2) 19 ♗e3 e6 20 ♗c4, White goes ahead with his policy of constriction. 19 ♔f2 is also playable.

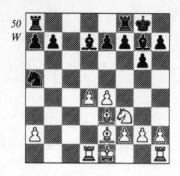

14 ... b6 15 0–0

After pondering it for a long time, I refrained from doubling Black's pawns with 15 ♗xa5 ba, for he would then acquire an adequate initiative. However, as Zaitsev has shown, 15 ♗a6!? was more promising. The analysis of this endgame points to the conclusion that the entire variation, beginning with 8 ... cd, fails to secure equality for Black.

15 ... ♖fd8?!

This appears to be the root cause of his subsequent troubles. A more natural choice seems to be 15 ... ♖fc8 16 ♖c1 (if 16 ♗a6, then 16 ... ♖c2 17 ♗xa5 ♖xa2 18 ♗b7 ♖b8. Therefore White should first play 16 ♗xa5 ba, and then 17 ♗a6 ♖c2 18 ♖c1 ♖xa2 19 ♖c7 ♖d8, but even so, Black is risking nothing after 20 h3 ♖a3! 21 ♖xa7 ♖xf3 22 gf ♗xd4 and 23 ... ♗xh3) 16 ... ♗g4 (16 ... ♘c6 is problematic; Black aims to answer 17 ♗a6 with 17 ... ♘xd4 18 ♗xc8 ♘xf3+ 19 gf ♗xc8 20 ♔g2 ♗e6, or if 20 ♖c7, then 20 ... ♗h3. In either case Black has definite compensation for the exchange, but is it sufficient for equality? Thus, in the last variation, after 21 ♖fc1 e5 22 ♖b7!, the rook cannot be dislodged from the seventh rank: 22 ... ♗c8 23 ♖xa7!) 17 ♗a6 (on 17 d5, Black has 17 ... ♗b2, when neither 18 ♖b1 ♗xf3 19 gf ♖c2 20 ♖fd1 ♗c3 nor 18 ♖xc8 ♖xc8 19 ♖b1 ♗xf3 20 gf ♖c2 21 ♖d1 ♗c1 presents him with any danger) 17 ... ♖xc1 18 ♖xc1 ♗xf3 19 gf ♗xd4 20 ♖c7. White regains the sacrificed pawn, but cannot achieve more than that.

16 ♖c1 ♗g4 (51)

Again a straightforward decision. Perhaps it was worth preparing an exchanging operation with 16 ... a6!? 17 ♖b1 (17 ♖c7 ♗b5 18 ♗xb5 ab 19 d5 ♘c4 20 ♗b4 ♗f6 21 ♗xe7 ♗xe7 22

♖xe7 ♖xa2 leads to complications, since 23 ♘d4 b4 24 ♘c6? b3 25 ♘xd8 b2 looks too hazardous for White, while 23 ♖b1 f5!? 24 ♘g5 fe 25 ♘xe4 ♘d2 should lead to a draw) 17 ... ♗b5 18 ♗xb5 ab 19 ♖xb5 ♘c4 20 ♗b4 ♖xa2 21 ♖c1?! ♗xd4! 22 ♖xc4 ♗xf2+ 23 ♔f1 ♖d1+ 24 ♘e1 ♗xe1 25 ♗xe1 ♖aa1. Nor does 17 ♗f4 produce the expected effect: 17 ... ♗b5 18 ♗xb5 ab 19 ♗c7 ♖d7 20 ♗xb6 ♘c4. Or if 17 ♗g5, then 17 ... h6! 18 ♗xe7 ♖e8, and Black restores the balance. However, it is worth considering 17 d5!? ♗b5 18 ♖fe1 ♖ac8, with possibilities for both sides.

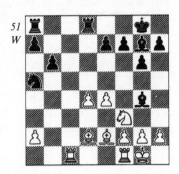

51
W

17 d5 ♘b7

Devices such as 17 ... e6 18 h3 ♗xf3 (18 ... ed 19 hg de 20 ♗xa5 ef 21 ♗xf3 ba 22 ♗xa8, and Black has a lost position) 19 ♗xf3 ed 20 ed fail to help Black – he is still faced with the same inferior ending.

18 h3

White would be wasting time with 18 ♗b4 e6, while 18 ♖c7?! is a mistake owing to 18 ... ♘c5! (18 ... ♖d7 19 ♖fc1, with the initiative) 19 ♖xe7?! ♗f6 20 ♖c7 ♘xe4.

18 ... ♗xf3

Nor is 18 ... ♗d7 19 ♗b4 e6 20 ♗a6 any better for Black.

19 ♗xf3 ♘c5 20 ♗e3 ♖ac8 21 ♗g4! ♖b8

Or 21 ... ♖c7 22 ♗f4 ♖b7 23 ♖fd1, and White has a large plus, since 23 ... ♘xe4? loses at once to 24 ♖c8 ♖xc8 25 ♗xc8. White also retains a substantial advantage with 22 f4 (with a view to 22 ... h5 23 ♗f3, and the pawns creep forward) 22 ... f5!? 23 ef gf (23 ... ♖xd5 24 fg hg 25 ♖fd1 ♖xd1+ is also a grim outlook for Black) 24 ♗xf5 ♖xd5 25 ♖xc5! ♖dxc5 (if 25 ... ♖cxc5, then 26 ♗e6+ ♔f8 27 ♗xc5 ♖xc5 28 ♖d1!, and Black is in a difficult position after either 28 ... ♗b2 29 ♖d8+ ♔g7 30 g4 ♘f6 31 ♗b3, or 28 ... ♗h6 29 ♖d8+ ♔g7 30 g3! ♘f6 31 ♗b3) 26 ♗e6+ ♔f8 27 ♖d1 ♔e8 (27 ... ♖c8?? fails to 28 ♗xc5, and 27 ... ♗b2 28 ♗xc5 bc 29 ♖d8+ ♔g7 30 g4 ♘f6 31 ♗c4 brings Black no relief either) 28 ♗xc5 bc 29 ♖b1! (astonishing domination with full material equality) 29 ... ♗d4+ 30 ♔h2 ♔f8 31 ♖b8+ ♔g7 32 g4 ♘f6 (he can't save himself with 32 ... ♖c6 33 ♖g8+ ♔f6 34 ♗d5 ♖d6 35 g5+ ♔f5 36 ♖f8+ ♔g6 37 ♗e4+ ♔g7 38 ♖e8 ♖e6 39 ♗d5 ♖e2+ 40 ♔g3 h5 41 ♔h4, or 40 ... h6? 41 ♖g8+ ♔h7 42 g6 mate) 33 ♗c4 e6 34 ♖e8 ♖e7 35 g5+ ♔f7 36 ♖c8 ♔g6 (36 ... ♔g7? 37 f5!, or 36 ... ♗e3 37 ♔g3) 37 ♔g3 h6 38 h4 hg 39 hg e5 40 ♖c6+ ♔g7 41 f5, with a simple win.

The reader will agree that these variations are pretty, although rather long. But now to return to the game, i.e. the 9th match game:

22 ♖c4

A mistake would be 22 ♗xc5 bc 23 ♖xc5 ♖b2 24 ♖a5 ♗d4, when White's material advantage is neutralised by Black's pressure against f2.

22 ... h5

A difficult ending results from 22 ... ♘xe4 23 ♖xe4 f5 24 ♗xf5! gf 25 ♖xe7, or 22 ... f5 23 ♗xc5 bc 24 ef gf (not 24 ... ♖xd5? 25 f6!) 25 ♗xf5 ♗d4 26 ♗e6+ ♔g7 27 ♔h2 (27 ♖a4 ♖b7 28 ♖d1?! is less convincing in view of 28 ... ♖b2 29 ♖xa7 ♗xf2+ 30 ♔h2 ♗h4, when neither of the alternatives bring a clear result: 31 d6 ♗f6! 32 d7 – not 32 de?? ♗e5+ 33 ♔g1 ♖xd1 mate – 32 ... ♗e5+ 33 ♔g1 ♔f6 34 ♗g4 e6 35 ♖a6 ♗d4+, or 31 ♖f1 ♗f6 32 ♖xe7+ ♗xe7 33 ♖f7+ ♔g6 34 ♖xe7 ♖xa2 35 d6 ♖a6! 36 d7 ♖xe6 37 ♖xe6+ ♔f7 38 ♖h6 ♔g7 39 ♖d6 c4) 27 ... ♖b2 28 ♖a4 ♖b7 29 f4, with a technically won position for White.

23 ♗f3 e6 24 ♖d1 ed 25 ed

Stronger than 25 ♖xd5 ♖e8!, when Black is defending actively.

25 ... ♗e5 (52)

At first sight it seems that on blocking the d6-square, Black will have constructed an almost impregnable fortress.

26 g4!

This breaking-up of the pawn chain dispels any illusions of equality. The endgame was and still is unattractive for Black.

26 ... hg 27 hg ♘b7?!

Perhaps 27 ... ♖bc8 or 27 ... ♖b7 was more logical, but even

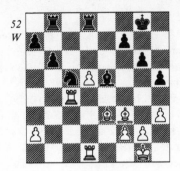

so, by deploying his forces in the same way as in the game –
g4–g5, ♔g1–g2, and the transfer of the rooks to the h-file – White
would clearly have the better chances.

28 ♖a4

For good measure, Black's knight is now driven onto a bad
square, since 28 ... ♖a8 fails to 29 d6.

28 ... ♘a5 29 g5!?

It is also worth considering 29 ♖e4!?

29 ... ♖bc8 30 ♗e2 ♗d6

If 30 ... ♖c2, a good reply is 31 ♗d3 ♖c3 (31 ... ♖b2? 32 ♗c1,
and the rook is trapped) 32 ♗a6, after which White again carries
out the plan beginning with ♔g1–g2.

31 ♔g2!?

More accurate than 31 ♗a6 ♖c2 32 ♔g2, which could be met
by 32 ... ♗c5 33 ♗d3 ♖c3; whereas now, 31 ... ♖c2 32 ♗d3
would immediately put Black in a critical position.

31 ... ♗c5 (53)

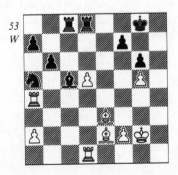

32 &d2??

An absurdity! I make the *second* move of the variation 32 &f4 &d6 33 &d2, which would give White somewhat the better chances. If instead 33 &c1 &f8 34 &b2 ♖c5! (but not 34 … &g7 35 &f6!, when 35 … &xf6 36 gf ♖d6 37 ♖h4 ♖xf6 38 ♖dh1, or 37 … g5 38 ♖h6, leads to catastrophe) 35 ♖h4 &g7 36 &f6 ♖dxd5! 37 ♖dh1 ♖xg5+! 38 &xg5 ♖xg5+, the play is quite sharp. White's best line is 32 &f4 &d6 33 &xd6 (33 &a6 ♖c7 brings White to a dead end) 33 … ♖xd6 34 ♖h4 ♖c5 (34 … ♖c2 loses to 35 ♖dh1 ♔f8 36 ♖h8+ ♔e7 37 ♖e1 ♔d7 38 &g4+ ♔c7 39 ♖c8+) 35 ♖dh1 ♔f8 36 ♖h8+ ♔e7 37 &f3, with a considerable endgame advantage.

32 … ♖xd5 33 &f3 ♖dd8 34 &xa5 ½–½.

It is not without good reason that we have so thoroughly examined the first duel with this variation. It is useful for the reader to understand that the assessment of the endgame plays a key role in this particular Grünfeld line.

Instead of 8 … 0–0 or 8 … cd, Black frequently chooses **8 … ♕a5 9 ♖b1 cd** (the prophylactic 9 … a6, defending against ♖b5, can be met by 10 ♖c1!?. White sets up the positional threat of d4–d5 – since the c3 point is defended! – and compels his opponent to go into an ending with 10 … cd 11 cd ♕xd2+ 12 ♔xd2. This ending is even more favourable to White, since the point b6 in Black's camp has been weakened. Epishin–Gutman, Frankfurt 1990, saw instead 10 … ♘d7 11 ♘f3 0–0 12 &d3 ♘b6 13 &h6! cd 14 &xg7 ♔xg7 15 cd ♕xd2+ 16 ♔xd2, and White had the advantage). The game Kozul–Polajžer, Ptuj 1989, continued: **10 cd ♕xd2+ 11 ♔xd2 0–0 12 ♘f3 e6** (more precise than the immediate 12 … ♖d8 13 &d3 ♘c6 14 d5 ♘a5 15 ♔e2 b6 16 ♖hc1 e6 17 &g5 f6 18 &d2, when White's characteristic bishop manoeuvre to shake up the black position brings tangible results) **13 &d3 ♘c6 14 ♖hc1 ♖d8 15 e5 f6!?** (15 … f5 16 h4 h6 17 ♔e2 &f8 18 g3 ♘b4 19 &c4 b6 20 ♘e1! is less effective for Black; Damjanović–Kozul, Belgrade 1989. Also 18 ♖c4!?, recommended by Zaitsev, deserves serious attention. Black cannot develop his queenside freely: 18 … ♘e7 19 ♖g1! ♘d5 20 g4 b5 21 ♖xc8 ♖axc8 22 gf ef 23 &xf5, and White has more than enough for the exchange) **16 ♔e2 fe 17 de ♘xe5 18 ♘xe5 &xe5 19 &e4 ♖b8 20 ♖c5 &d6?!** (according to *Informator 47*, 20 … &d4 21 ♖a5 e5 22 &xd4 ♖xd4 23 f3 gives White a big advantage, but this verdict is obviously exaggerated. After the simple 23 ... ♗e6 24 ♖xa7 ♗c4+ 25 ♔e3 b5 26 f4 ♖bd8, threatening 27 ... ♖xe4+ 27 ♔xe4 ♗d3+, Black is out of danger. If instead 24 ... ♖bd8 25 ♖bxb7! ♖d2 26 ♔e3, the position remains unclear; neither 26 ... ♗c4 27 f4!, nor 26 ... ♖xa2 27 ♖g7+ ♔f8 28 ♖xh7, nor 26 ... ♖xg2 27 ♖g7+ ♔f8 28 ♖xh7 gives Black a cast iron draw) 21 ♖a5 a6 22 ♗b6 ♖d7 23 h4!? ♗c7 24 ♔e3 ♗xb6+ ♖xb6, and White succeeded in realising his positional advantage.

We can see that this result was due to the somewhat unfortunate 20 ... ♗d6?!. However, at move 16, White had an opportunity to strengthen his play: **16 ef** (the difference between 15 ... f6 and 15 ... f5 now disappears) 16 ... ♗xf6 17 ♔e2 ♘xd4+ (the attempt to develop with 17 ... e5 leads to a worse position: 18 de ♘xe5 – not 18 ... ♗xe5? 19 ♖xc6 and wins – 19 ♘xe5 ♗xe5 20 ♗e4 ♖b8 21 ♗xa7! ♖a8 22 ♗b6 ♖xa2+ 23 ♔e1 ♖e8 24 ♗d5+ ♗e6 25 ♖c8!) 18 ♘xd4 ♗xd4 19 ♗xd4 ♖xd4, and now White has the better chances after either 20 ♔e3 e5 21 ♖b5, or 20 ♖c7 b6 (20 ... e5 21 ♖bc1 ♖d8 22 ♖e7) 21 ♖bc1 ♗d7 22 ♔e3 e5 23 f4! ♖d8 24 ♗c4+ ♔h8 25 fe.

Evidently it is due to considerations of this kind that Black has recently been giving preference to the move-order starting with 8 ... 0–0.

9 ♘f3

Earlier, one of the main lines here was **9 d5**, but then it was discovered that Black obtains a fine game with 9 ... e6!, for example: 10 ♗xc5?! ♕c7! 11 ♗d4 ♗xd4 12 cd ed 13 e5 ♘c6 14 ♗e2 f6 15 ef ♖xf6 16 ♘f3 ♗g4 17 0–0 ♖e8, and already Black has the initiative. Perhaps an even more accurate method is 11 ... ed!? 12 ♗xg7 ♔xg7 13 ed ♖e8+ 14 ♗e2 ♗g4 15 ♕d4+ ♔g8 16 f3 (16 d6 ♕c6) 16 ... ♗f5, and it is obvious that Black's initiative compensates for the sacrificed pawn.

9 ♖c1 leads to the same kind of position as in the game, if Black replies **9 ... ♕a5**. It acquires original overtones only in the case of **9 ... ♘d7** *(54)*.

There can follow:
10 ♗d3!?
Better than 10 d5 ♘f6 11 f3 (11 ♗d3 b6 12 c4 ♘g4 13 ♗f4 e5!) 11 ... e6 (after 11 ... b6 12 ♗b5 ♘e8 13 ♗c6 ♖b8 14 ♗f4?! ♘d6 15 e5 ♘c4 16 ♕e2 ♘a5 17 e6 ♘xc6 18 dc ♖a8 19 ef+ ♖xf7 Black obtains a good position, but the correct line for White is

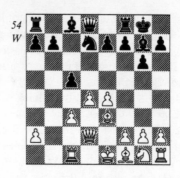

13 ♗xe8!? ♖xe8 14 ♘e2 e6 15 c4 ed 16 ♗a6 17 ♔f2 ♕h4+ 18 g3 ♕h3 19 ♘f4 ♕d7 20 ♖he1. Now, as Vaiser demonstrates, Black should play 20 ... ♖xe3! 21 ♔xe3! ♗d4+ 22 ♔e2 g5 23 ♘d3, with complications. In Vaiser–Romanishin, Sochi 1983, Black neglected this opportunity and ended up in a difficult position after 20 ... ♖e7 21 ♔g2 ♖ae8 22 d6! ♖e5 23 ♘d5) 12 c4 ♖e8 13 ♘e2 b6 14 ♘c3 (14 e5 ♘xd5!) 14 ... ♗a6 15 ♗e2 (or 15 e5 ♘d7 16 f4 f6, and White can't maintain his centre) 15 ... ♘d7 16 0–0 ♘e5 17 ♘d1 ed 18 cd ♗xe2 19 ♕xe2 f5! and Black firmly seizes the initiative; Spassov–Tseshkovsky, Moscow 1985.

10 ... e5!

This pawn-break is the point of Black's whole set-up. If now 11 d5, Black plays 11 ... f5! and obtains strong counterplay.

11 ♘f3 ed 12 cd cd 13 ♘xd4

An interesting alternative is 13 ♗xd4!? ♗xd4 (13 ... ♘f6 14 h3 ♖e8 15 0–0 ♘xe4 16 ♗xe4 ♗xd4 17 ♗xg6 ♗xf2+ 18 ♕xf2 hg 19 ♘e5 leads to a double-edged position) 14 ♘xd4 ♘f6 15 ♗b1 ♕b6 16 0–0 ♖d8 17 ♖fd1 ♗g4 f3 ♖d7 19 fg ♖ad8 20 ♖c4 ♘xg4, with unclear play (Yusupov).

13 ... ♘e5 14 ♗e2 ♕h4!?

Or 14 ... ♘g4 15 ♗xg4 ♗xg4 16 0–0, which is also good for Black.

15 0–0 ♕xe4 16 ♘b5 ♗e6 17 ♖fd1! ♗f6 18 ♘d6 ♕h4 19 ♗f4 ♖fd8 20 ♘e3 ♘g4 21 ♕f3 ♗e5!? 22 ♗xe5 ♘xe5 23 ♕xb7 ♘g4 24 ♗xg4 ♕xg4

The chances are equal; Yusupov–Timman, Belgrade 1989.

These fairly authoritative examples show that in the current state of theory, 8 ♕d2 0–0 9 ♖c1 is inadequate to give White an advantage.

9 ... ♕a5

In the seventeenth match game, Kasparov refrained from the queen excursion to a5, preferring **9 ... ♗g4** (see Game No. 15).

I should also mention the variation **9 ... cd 10 cd ♗g4 11 ♖c1** ♗xf3 12 gf e6 13 ♗b5 ♘c6 (the pawn sacrifice is justified, since after 13 ... a6 14 ♗a4 it is not simple for Black to complete his development) 14 ♗xc6 bc 15 ♖xc6 ♕d7! 16 ♖c4 (or 16 ♖a6 ♕b5 17 ♕e2 ♕b1+, and White achieves nothing) 16 ... f5! (precisely calculated – 17 0–0 fe 18 fe e5!, and to avoid coming under attack White has to permit a draw with 19 d5! ♕g4+ 20 ♔h1 ♕f3+ etc.) 17 d5 fe 18 fe ed 19 ♕xd5+ ♕xd5+ 20 ed ♖fd8, and Black has a satisfactory endgame, as 21 ♖c5 can be answered by 21 ... ♗f8! 22 ♖b5 a6; Vilela–Armas, Bayamo 1988. White might consider the prospects offered by **11 ♖b1!?** or **11 ♘g5!**, on the lines of Game No. 15.

10 ♖c1 e6 *(55)*

Another popular line here is the transition to an ending with 10 ... cd 11 cd ♕xd2+. Compared with the variation 7 ♘f3 c5 8 ♖b1, the rook on c1 is more mobile, which increases White's possibilities. Play might continue:

12 ♔xd2

More precise than capturing with the knight. Let us take a close look at the latter: 12 ♘xd2 e6 13 ♘b3 (after 13 ♗b5 ♗d7! 14 ♗xd7 ♘xd7 15 ♔e2 ♖fc8 16 ♘c4 ♗f8 17 ♗f4 ♖c6 18 ♘a5?! ♖a6 19 ♘xb7 ♖xa2+ 20 ♔f3 e5! 21 de ♖e8 22 ♖a1! ♖b2! White had some difficulties to overcome in Hübner–Adorjan, Bad Lauterberg 1989) 13 ... ♖d8 14 ♗g5 f6 15 ♗e3 ♗f8 (or 15 ... f5 16 ef gf 17 ♗b5 ♘d7 18 0–0 ♘f6 19 ♗g5 ♗d7 20 ♗c4 b6 21 ♘d2 ♖e8 22 ♘f3 ♗c6 23 ♘e5 ♗d5 24 ♗b5 ♖ec8 25 a4 ♘e4 26 ♗f4 ♗f8 27 f3, with advantage to White; Karpov–Hübner, Tilburg 1980) 16 ♗c4 ♘c6 17 ♔e2 ♗d7 18 ♖hd1 ♔g7 19 f3 ♖ac8 20 d5 ed 21 ♗xd5 ♗e8 22 ♘c5 ♗xc5 23 ♗xc5 ♗f7, and the game heads towards a draw; Johansen–Hort, Martigny 1986.

12 ... ♖d8

Another well-known continuation is 12 ... ♘c6.

13 ♗b5 ♗g4 14 ♖c7 ♘c6 15 d5 ♖ab8!

Black does badly with 15 ... e6? 16 ♘g5! ed 17 ♘xf7 ♖dc8 18 ♖xc8+ ♖xc8 19 ♘d6 ♖c7 20 ♖c1! de 21 ♘xb7 ♖d7+ 22 ♔e1 ♖xb7 23 ♗xc6 ♖e7 24 ♗d5+ ♗e6 25 ♗g5! ♗xd5 (25 ... ♖e8 26 ♖c8!) 26 ♗xe7 ♗xa2 27 ♖c8+, and White's win is not in doubt; Ftačnik–Smejkal, Trenčianske Teplice 1979.

16 ♗f4!

In Mikh. Tseitlin–Schmidt, Lodz 1980, White played the inadequate 16 ♗xc6 bc 17 ♖xc6 e6 18 d6 ♖b2+ 19 ♔d3 ♖xa2 20 ♖hc1 (or 20 h3 ♗xf3 21 gf ♗e5, and Black has no problems) 20 ... e5! 21 ♖1c2 ♗d7! 22 ♖6c5 ♖xc2 23 ♔xc2 f6, with the more pleasant position for Black.

16 ... e6 17 ♘g5 ed 18 ♘xf7 ♖dc8!? 19 ed ♖xc7 20 ♗xc7 ♖c8 21 dc ♖xc7 22 ♗c4!? ♔f8 23 ♘d8 bc 24 ♘e6+ ♗xe6

Again, the draw cannot be avoided.

In practice, as a rule, Black nonetheless steers clear of this ending, since White does after all dictate the play.

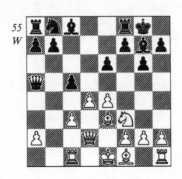

55
W

11   ♗h6!

A new, and quite effective, idea of Zaitsev's. By exchanging bishops, White attempts to exploit the weakening of the dark squares in his opponent's camp. I proceeded less convincingly in the 13th game of the match, in which the diagrammed position arose by a different move-order (9 ♖c1 ♕a5 10 ♘f3 e6). Now is the best time to pause and examine that game.

11 d5

Practice has also seen **11 ♗e2** cd 12 cd ♕xd2+ 13 ♘xd2 ♘c6 14 d5?! ed 15 ed ♘d4, with equality; or **11 ♗d3!?** ♖d8 12 ♗g5 f6 13 ♗e3 cd 14 cd ♕xd2+ 15 ♔xd2 ♘c6 16 ♖c4 ♗d7 17 ♖b1 ♗f8 18 ♔e2 b6 19 ♗d2 ♖ac8, with unclear play; Blees–Mikhalchishin, Budapest 1990.

11 ... ed 12 ed ♖e8!?

A game Lputian–Tukmakov, USSR 1989, went 12 ... ♗f5 (12 ... ♘d7 13 ♗d3 b5! 14 c4 ♕xd2+ 15 ♘xd2 bc 16 ♗xc4 should have led to equality in Ftačnik–Hartston, Skara 1980: 16 ... ♗b7

17 0–0 ♘e5. But after 13 c4!? ♕xd2+ 14 ♘xd2 b6 15 ♗e2, White has a minimal edge) 13 ♗e2 ♘a6!? 14 0–0 ♖ad8 15 ♗xa6 ♕xa6 16 ♗xc5 ♖fe8 17 c4 ♖c8 18 ♗d4 ♖xc4, with equality.

13 ♗e2 ♗f5 14 0–0 ♘d7 15 h3

A useful prophylactic move. Instead, Piket–Korchnoi, Wijk aan Zee 1990, went 15 ♕b2 ♘f6 (15 ... ♘b6 is also sufficient for equality; Seirawan–Olafsson, Novi Sad Ol 1990, continued 16 ♕b3 c4 17 ♗xc4 ♖xe3 18 fe ♕c5 19 ♗b5 a6 20 ♗e2 ♘xd5 21 ♕xb7 ♖e8 22 ♗xa6 ♗xc3 ½-½) 16 ♗c4?! (16 ♕xb7 is more logical: 16 ... ♕xa2 17 ♗b5 ♖ab8 18 ♕a6 ♕xa6 19 ♗xa6 ♘xd5 20 ♗xc5 ♘xc3 21 ♘d4, maintaining the balance) 16 ... ♕b6! 17 ♕a3 ♗f8 18 ♖cd1 ♗d6 19 h3 a6 20 ♗h6 ♕c7 21 ♕c1 ♕d7 22 ♗f4 ♗e4 23 ♘g5 b5 24 ♗xd6 ♕xd6 25 ♘xe4 ♘xe4 26 ♗d3 c4 27 ♗xe4 ♖xe4, with advantage to Black in the queen and rook ending.

15 ... ♘b6

The prophylactic reply **15 ... h5!?** is also worth considering. In reply, 16 c4?! is dubious: 16 ... ♕xd2 17 ♘xd2 ♗d4! 18 ♗xd4 ♖xe2 19 ♗e3 ♖e8, with the highly unpleasant threat of 20 ... ♖8xe3. Therefore White would have to content himself with exchanging bishops: 16 ♗d3 ♗xd3 17 ♕xd3, which allows 17 ... ♕xa2 18 ♕b5 ♘f6 19 c4 b6 20 ♖fd1 with complex play.

After **15 ... ♘f6** 16 c4 ♕xd2 17 ♘xd2 ♘e4 18 ♘xe4 ♖xe4, White would still retain a microscopic plus.

16 g4 ♗d7 17 c4 ♕xd2 18 ♘xd2 ♘a4

If 18 ... ♗d4, then 19 ♗xd4 ♖xe2 20 ♗e3 f5 21 ♖fe1 ♖xe1+ 22 ♖xe1 fg 23 hg ♗xg4 24 ♗xc5, and White's game is somewhat preferable.

19 ♗f3 ♘c3 (56)

The more restrained 19 ... b6 is also playable.

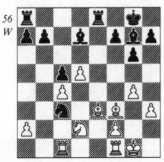

20 ♖xc3!? ♗xc3 21 ♘e4 ♖xe4!

An opportune counter-stroke. After 21 ... ♗g7 (21 ... ♗d4? 22 ♗xd4 cd 23 ♘f6+ and wins) 22 ♘xc5, with a pawn for the exchange, White would retain a powerful initiative.

22 ♗xe4 ♖e8 23 ♗d3 b6 24 ♔g2 f5!? 25 gf ♗xf5 26 ♗xf5 gf 27 ♖d1

Holmov recommends 27 ♖c1 ♗f6 (27 ... ♗d4? 28 ♗xd4 cd 29 ♖d1 ♖e4 30 f3, and endgame difficulties arise for Black) 28 ♔f3 ♖e4 29 ♗f4, and the bishop threatens to penetrate to Black's rear. Hence a more accurate reply is 27 ... ♗g7 28 ♔f3 ♖e4, preventing 29 ♗f4? because of 29 ... ♖xf4+!. If 29 d6 (29 ♖c2 ♗e5) 29 ... ♔f7 30 ♖d1, then 30 ... ♗d4 *is* playable.

27 ... ♔f7

Not 27 ... ♖e4? 28 ♗g5!

28 ♖d3 ♗f16 29 ♖a3 a5 30 ♖b3 ♗d8 31 ♖c3 ♗c7 32 a4 ♔f6 33 ♔f1 f4 34 ♗c1 ♔f5 35 ♖c2 ♖g8 36 ♖e2 ♗e5 37 ♗b2! ♗d4! 38 ♗xd4 cd 39 ♖e7! d3!

The immediate 39 ... ♖c8 is weaker: 40 ♔e2 ♖xc4 41 ♔d3, and Black is faced with problems (41 ... ♖xa4? 42 d6).

The amusing 39 ... f3 40 ♖xh7 ♖g1+ 41 ♔xg1 d3 fails to 42 ♖f7+.

40 ♔e1! ♖c8!

One more precise move that is indispensable to Black.

41 ♔d2 ♖xc4 42 ♔xd3 ½–½.

After the forced 42 ... ♖xa4 43 d6 ♖a1 44 ♔c2 (44 ♔c4 ♖d1) 44 ... ♖a2+ 45 ♔c3 ♖a1, the draw is unavoidable. We now return once again to the 15th match game.

	11	...	♘c6
	12	h4!	*(57)*

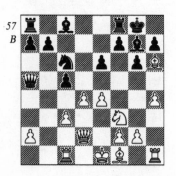

This is the whole point; White forces his opponent to go into an ending, as the threat of h4–h5 is quite unpleasant. A factor of considerable importance is that with the dark-squared bishops exchanged, the white king will find a comfortable central post on e3.

12	...	cd
13	♗xg7	♔xg7
14	cd	

14 h5 is hazardous: 14 ... dc 15 ♖xc3 ♖d8 16 ♗d3 ♔g8!, but not 16 ... ♘b4 17 hg ♘xd3+ 18 ♖xd3 (18 ♔e2! is interesting) 18 ... ♕xd2+ 19 ♖xd2 ♖xd2 20 ♔xd2 hg 21 e5, with approximate equality.

14	...	♕xd2+
15	♔xd2	♖d8
16	♔e3	♗d7 *(58)*

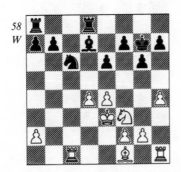

58
W

The only way. Postponing development with 16 ... h6 (aiming to meet 17 h5 with 17 ... g5) could be costly to Black after 17 ♗b5 ♗d7 18 ♗xc6 ♗xc6 19 ♘e5.

17 ♖b1

As the answer ... b7–b6 would be bad for Black on account of ♗a6, which gains control of the c-file, this transfer of the rook is very useful. Incidentally, 17 ♗b5 would fail to the unexpected 17 ... ♘xd4! 18 ♘xd4 e5! with complete equality.

17	...	♖ab8
18	♗d3	

It was worth considering an immediate 18 h5!?, since in the game Black could now have played 18 ... h6 to frustrate this plan.

	18 ...	♘e7

Kasparov probably rejected 18 ... h6 because of 19 g4 ♗e8 (nor can he rid himself of his troubles with 19 ... f6 20 g5 hg 21 hg 22 ♖h6 ♖h8 23 ♖xh8 ♔xh8 24 d5, when White has the better prospects) 20 g5 h5 21 ♖hc1, and relying on his powerful centre White can proceed with a long-term plan for pressure on both flanks.

	19	h5

19 ♖hc1, recommended by Krasenkov, is answered by 19 ... ♖bc8! and Black has already solved most of his problems.

	19	...	f6
	20	hg	hg
	21	♖h2 *(59)*	

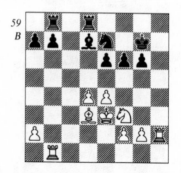

Rather slow. White could have set his opponent more problems with **21 g4!?**. The threat to break up Black's kingside structure is highly unpleasant. Replies which fail to help are 21 ... g5 (21 ... ♗c6 22 ♗c4!) 22 e5! ♘d5+ 23 ♔d2 ♖h8 24 ♖xh8! ♔xh8 25 ♖h1+ ♔g8 26 ♖h6, and 21 ... ♖h8 22 ♖xh8 ♔xh8 23 g5 f5 24 ♘e5 ♗e8 25 ♗a6 b6 26 ♖c1 or 26 f3.

It seems Black would have to play **21 ... e5 22 de ♗xg4 23 ef+ ♔xf6**. White would then carry out a similar idea to one which will arise in the actual game (with the difference that the black pawn is on b6 and the white rook on h1): **24 ♘d4 ♖d7 25 ♖h4 ♖bd8 26 e5+** (26 ♖xg4 ♖xd4 27 e5+ ♔xe5 28 ♖xd4 ♖xd4 29 f4+ ♖xf4 30 ♖b5+ ♘d5+ 31 ♖xd5+ ♔xd5 32 ♔xf4 draws) **26 ... ♔xe5 27 ♖b5+ ♘d5+ 28 ♖xd5+ ♖xd5**, but this plan loses its force because the c6 square has not been weakened. There is likewise no danger to Black in **24 e5+!? ♔g7** (24 ... ♔e6 25

♘g5+!) 25 ♘g5 ♘d5+ (stronger than 25 ... ♖xd3+ 26 ♔xd3 ♗f5+ 27 ♔d2! ♗xb1 28 ♖xb1) 26 ♔e4 (26 ♔d2? ♘f4 27 ♖b3 ♗f5, and it is Black who wins) 26 ... ♘c3+! (after 26 ... ♗f5+ 27 ♔f3! ♗xd3 28 ♖h7+ ♔g8 29 ♖bh1, there is no defence against the mate threats) 27 ♔e3, and everything ends happily as in a good vaudeville: 27 ... ♘d5+ 28 ♔e4 ♘c3+ etc.

21 ... b6

One can understand Black's wish to avoid the unattractive endgame that results from 21 ... ♖h8 22 ♖xh8 ♔xh8 23 ♗a6! b6 (23 ... ♗c8 24 ♗b5! or 24 ♗c4) 24 ♖c1, or 23 ... ♗c6 24 ♗c4 ♗d7 (24 ... f5 25 ♖h1+ ♔g7 26 ♘g5 ♔f6 27 ♔f4 fe 28 ♖h7 ♖f8 29 g4, threatening 30 ♘xe4+ ♗xe4 31 g5 mate; the only defence is 29 ... ♘d5+, but then Black loses his rook after 30 ♗xd5 ed 31 ♖c7!) 25 g4.

22 g4

Kasparov now plays very ingeniously:

22 ... e5!?
23 de ♗xg4 (60)

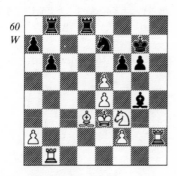

60
W

24 ef+

24 ♖bh1 has been recommended as stronger. But let us see whether it is. 24 ... ♖xd3+! (inadequate alternatives are 24 ... ♗xf3 25 ♖h7+ ♔f8 26 ♖h8+ ♘g8 27 ♗c4! ♗xh1 28 ef ♔e8 29 ♗e6, and 24 ... fe 25 ♘xe5 ♗e6 26 ♖h7+ ♔f6 27 f4 ♖bc8 28 ♘f3! ♗g8 29 ♘g5! ♗xh7 30 ♖xh7 ♖xd3+ 31 ♔xd3 ♖f8 32 ♔e3 ♘c6 33 ♖c7 ♘e7 34 ♘h7+) 25 ♔xd3 ♗xf3 26 ♖h7+ ♔f8 *(61)*.

27 ♖1h3 (forced, since 27 ef ♘g8! 28 ♖1h3 ♗xe4+! draws; nor does 28 ♖1h4 help, in view of 28 ... g5!, and when the rook moves,

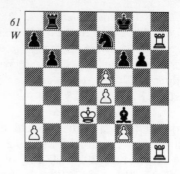

Black again has 29 ... $\triangle$xe4+!) 27 ... $\triangle$g4 (the attempt to weave a mating net for the white king, with 27 ... $\triangle$g2 28 Ξg3 $\triangle$f1+ 29 $\triangle$e3 fe 30 Ξf3+ $\triangle$g8 31 Ξxe7 Ξd8, fails to the simple 32 Ξxe5) 28 Ξg3 f5 29 $\triangle$e3 Ξe8! 30 Ξh8+ $\triangle$g8, and Black is out of danger. It remains for us to consider 28 ef Ξd8+! 29 $\triangle$e3 (29 $\triangle$c3 Ξc8+! 30 $\triangle$b2 $\triangle$xh3 31 fe+ $\triangle$e8 32 Ξxh3 $\triangle$xe7 33 Ξh7+ $\triangle$e6 34 Ξxa7 Ξf8, and Black has everything in order) 29 ... $\triangle$g8 30 Ξg3 $\triangle$xf6 31 Ξh8+ $\triangle$e7 32 Ξxd8 $\triangle$xd8 35 e5 $\triangle$d5+ 34 $\triangle$d4 $\triangle$e6 35 Ξxg6 $\triangle$d7, and Black's defence cannot be breached.

So the move suggested by the annotators, 24 Ξbh1, fails to justify their hopes.

> **24** ... **$\triangle$xf6**
> **25** **$\triangle$d4**

25 e5+ $\triangle$g7 (25 ... $\triangle$e6?! 26 $\triangle$g5+) is not dangerous for Black.

> **25** ... **Ξb7?!** *(62)*

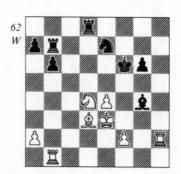

This move was probably based on miscalculation in the main variation. But even after the more precise **25 ... ♖h8** (25 ... ♔g7 leads to an unattractive minor piece ending after 26 ♖bh1 ♖h8 27 ♖xh8 ♖xh8 28 ♖xh8 ♔xh8 29 ♔f4) 26 ♖bh1 ♖xh2 27 ♖xh2 ♔g7, White can play, for example, 28 f3 (28 ♔f4 is premature in view of 28 ... ♖d8 29 ♔e5 g5! 30 ♘e6+ ♗xe6 31 ♔xe6 ♖xd3 32 ♔xe7 ♖d2!), and it is not easy for Black to save himself.

Has Black no other suitable defence, then? Zaitsev suggests **25 ... ♖e8!?**, with the idea of answering 26 ♗b5 (26 ♔f4 ♖bd8) with 26 ... ♘f5+! 27 ♘xf5 (risky alternatives are 27 ♔f4 g5+! 28 ♔xg4 ♖xe4+, and 27 ♔d3 ♖ed8! 28 ♖b4 ♖xd4+! 29 ♖xd4 ♗e2+!) 27 ... ♖xe4+ 28 ♔xe4 ♗xf5+. A complete demonstration of the geometric co-ordination of the black pieces.

26 f3

At this point, White could have put his opponent in a critical position by playing **26 ♖h4!**. How is Black to defend?

The obvious-looking **26 ... ♖bd7** (26 ... ♗e6 loses to 27 e5+) suffers a fiasco after 27 e5+! ♗xe5 (27 ... ♔g5 28 ♖xg4+! ♔xg4 29 ♖g1+ is crushing) 28 ♖b5+ ♘d5+ 29 ♖xd5+ ♔xd5 (Black comes out a piece down after 29 ... ♖xd5 30 ♘c6+ ♔f6 31 ♘xd8 ♔g5 32 ♖h8) 30 ♖xg4. It is notable that this line was indicated by Mephisto, the World Microcomputer Champion. True, Black can still struggle on: 30 ... ♖e8+!? 31 ♔f3 (after 31 ♗e4+ ♔c4!, the black king slips across to the queenside, creating counterchances; while after 31 ♔d2 ♖f7 32 f3, Black is not devoid of hope although he clearly stands worse), and now 31 ... ♔c5 32 ♘b3+! or 31 ... ♔e5 32 ♘c6+ allows White to re-group effectively, so Black must play 31 ... ♖f7+ or 31 ... ♖f8+; though in either case, after 32 ♔g3, the two pieces are much stronger than the rook and pawn.

Another try is **26 ... ♘f5+**. If now 27 ♘xf5 gf 28 f4 (if 28 ef, then 28 ... ♖xd3+, while after 28 ♖g1 ♖bd7 29 ♗b5 ♖e7 30 f3 ♔g5 31 ♖hh1 Black is guaranteed a draw with 31 ... ♖xe4+! 32 fe f4+ 33 ♔f2 ♖d2+ etc.) 28 ... fe 29 ♗xe4 ♗f5!, there follows a lengthy combination with a happy end: 30 ♖h6+! ♔g7 31 ♗xf5 ♔xh6 32 ♖h1+ ♔g7 33 ♖h7+ ♔f6 34 ♖xb7 ♔xf5 35 ♖xa7 ♖e8+! 36 ♔f3 ♖e1 37 ♖f7+ ♔e6 38 ♖b7 ♔f5 39 ♖xb6 ♖f1+ 40 ♔e3 ♖f3+! 41 ♔d4 (capturing the rook leads to a classic stalemate) 41 ... ♖a3 42 ♖b2 ♔xf4 43 ♔c5 ♖a8 44 ♖b4+ ♔e5 45 a4 ♖c8+, and the draw is elementary.

Nonetheless there is a way for White to win. He should answer 26 ... ♘f5+ with **27 ef ♖e7+ 28 ♗e4!** gf 29 ♖xg4 etc.

26	**...**	**♖bd7**

If 26 ... ♗d7 or 26 ... ♗c8, then 27 f4 is strong.

27	**♖b4**	**♗e6**

The best defence. **27 ... ♗xf3?** is refuted by 28 ♖f2, and **27 ... ♘c6** by 28 ♘xc6 ♖xd3+ 29 ♔f4 ♗h5 30 e5+!. If **27 ... ♖e8**, then 28 ♖a4. The matter is more complicated after **27 ... ♗h5** 28 f4! ♘c6 29 e5+ ♔g7 (29 ... ♔f7 30 ♗c4+ is bad for Black) 30 ♘e6+ ♔g8 31 ♘xd8 ♘xb4 32 ♗c4+ ♘d5+ 33 ♔e4 ♖xd8 34 ♗xd5+ ♔g7 35 ♖c2 ♖d7 36 e6 and 37 ♔e5. At move 30, if 30 ... ♔h8, then 31 ♗xg6, or if 30 ... ♔h7, then 31 ♖xh5+. One final possibility is 30 ... ♔h6 31 ♖b3 ♖e8 32 ♗xg6! ♔xg6 33 ♔e4 ♘xe5 34 ♖g3+ ♘g4 (34 ... ♗g4 35 f5+ ♔f6 36 ♖h6+ ♔e7 37 ♔xe5) 35 f5+ ♔h6 36 ♖xh5+ ♔xh5 37 ♖h3 mate.

28	**♖c2**

White could try playing for the win with **28 f4**, but Black has one satisfactory reply: 28 ... ♗g8! (if 28 ... a5?, then 29 ♖h7? is a mistake on account of 29 ... ♘f5+ 30 ef ab, but 29 e5+! ♔f7 30 ♖h7+ ♔g8 31 ♖xe7! ♖xe7 32 ♖xb6, or 31 ... ab 32 ♖xe6 ♖xd4 33 ♖xg6+, gives White a clear plus) 29 e5+ ♔g7 30 ♗e4, and the chances are about level.

28 ♗b5! looks a much stronger try. There follows 28 ... ♖c7 *(63)*

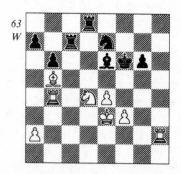

63
W

29 ♘xc6 ♖c3+ 30 ♔f4 ♗xe6 31 ♗c4+ ♔d6 (31 ... ♔f6 is dangerous: 32 ♖h7 g5+ 33 ♔g4! and the black king comes under a strong attack) 32 ♖d2+ ♔c7 (more precise than 32 ... ♔c5 33 ♖xd8 ♔xb4 34 ♗e6! g5+ 35 ♔xg5 ♖xf3 36 ♖d7 ♘c6 37 ♖c7,

and Black's troubles continue) 33 ♖xd8 ♔xd8 34 ♗e6 g5+ (34 ... ♘c6 can be met by 35 ♖c4! ♖xc4 36 ♗xc4 ♔e7 37 ♔g5, when White's chances are better) 35 ♔xg5 ♖xf3 36 ♖d4+ ♔e8 37 ♖d7 (also 37 ♗g4 ♖g3 38 ♔f4 ♖a3 39 ♗h5+ ♔f8 only leads to equality) 37 ... ♖g3+ (37 ... ♘c6 is unconvincing in view of 38 ♖c7 ♘d4 39 ♗d7+) 38 ♔f6 (an equal position results from 38 ♔f4 ♖g6 39 ♗f5 ♘xf5 40 ef ♔xd7 41 fg ♔e7 42 ♔e5 ♔f8! 43 ♔d5 ♔g7 44 ♔c6 ♔xg6 45 a4 ♔f6 46 ♔b7 a5) 38 ... ♖g6+ 39 ♔e5 ♖g5+ (Black loses after 39 ... ♘c6+ 40 ♔d5 ♘b4+ 41 ♔d6 ♘d3 42 ♖xa7, and has a difficult ending after 40 ... ♘e7+ 41 ♔d6 ♘c8+ 42 ♔e5) 40 ♔d6 ♘c8+ 41 ♔c7 ♖c5+ 42 ♔b7 ♖e5 43 ♗h3 ♘e7 44 ♔xa7 ♖xe4 45 ♔xb6 ♖e3, with a clear draw.

28	...	a5
29	♖a4	g5!
30	♗b5	♖d6
31	♗e2	♗d7
32	♖ac4	♖e8
33	♖b2	♘d5+

½-½

Black now has a tiny pull, but neither side can seriously count on winning.

Game No. 15
Karpov–Kasparov
World Championshp (17th game)
Lyon 1990

I have said that in my last match with Kasparov the Grünfeld Defence was played in four games. The first three of them, though containing fascinating struggles, ended in draws. We have covered all three together in the context of Game 14. In the seventeenth match game, which concluded our dispute in this opening, I finally succeeded in winning. That is why this example merits a separate number in the book.

1 d4 ♘f6 2 c4 g6 3 ♘c3 d5 4 cd ♘xd5 5 e4 ♘xc3 6 bc ♗g7 7 ♗e3 c5 8 ♕d2 0-0

| 9 | ♘f3 | ♗g4 |

Up to here, everything coincides with the fifteenth match game. From the notes to that game, the reader will derive a large amount of information about this opening line. In that game Kasparov played 9 ... ♕a5, and encountered distinct problems – as we saw. Consequently, this time he prefers a different method.

10   ♘g5!? *(64)*

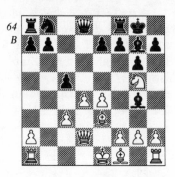

Perhaps White can hardly to without this thrust if he is to count on an advantage. But then I dare say the debate about this opening line will be continued further, and the assessment will undergo many alterations.

10   ...   cd
11   cd   ♘c6

If 11 ... h6, then 12 h3 is obligatory.

12   h3   ♗d7

An inferior choice is 12 ... ♗xd4 13 ♗xd4 ♕xd4 14 ♕xd4 ♘xd4 15 hg ♘c3+ 16 ♔d2 ♘xa1 17 ♗d3.

13   ♖b1   ♖c8!

The subtle tactical point lies in the highly attractive, though not complicated, line 14 ♖xb7 ♘xd4! 15 ♗xd4 ♗xd4 16 ♕xd4 ♖c1+ 17 ♔d2 (or 17 ♔e2 ♗b5+ 18 ♔e3 ♖e1+) 17 ... ♖d1+! 18 ♔xd1 ♗a4+, and White loses his queen. Hence he has to spend some time bolstering his centre.

14   ♘f3   ♘a5
15   ♗d3   ♗e6

The black pieces have securely fastened onto the c4-point. It is a rule in many Grünfeld variations that the domination of c4, in the absence of organic pawn weaknesses, guarantees Black counterplay.

16   0–0   ♗c4
17   ♖fd1   b5?! *(65)*

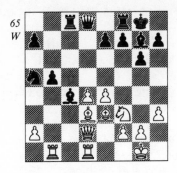

65
W

This might seem to be quite in order; Black strengthens his hold on c4. But in so doing, he commits a major positional error. From now on, his queenside pawn chain becomes vulnerable and causes him a great deal of worry. The modest 17 ... b6! would have been more appropriate.

> **18 ♗g5**

The first encouraging sign. The threat is not only 19 ♗xc4 ♘xc4 20 ♕b4 ♘d6 21 e5, but also, in some variations ♗xe7, deflecting the black queen.

> **18 ... a6**
> **19 ♖bc1**

I believe 19 ♖dc1!? was also worth considering. Then, for example, after 19 ... ♗xd3 20 ♖xc8 ♕xc8 21 ♕xd3 ♕b7, White would immediately have the highly effective break 22 a4, and if 22 ... b4, then 23 ♗d2, winning material.

> **19 ... ♗xd3**
> **20 ♖xc8 ♕xc8**
> **21 ♕xd3 ♖e8?!**

A passive move. **21 ... ♕b7 22 ♕a3 ♘c4 23 ♕xe7 ♕xe7 24 ♗xe7 ♖e8** was more flexible. It is possible that I would then have had to revert to the plan of ♖d1–b1 and a2–a4. After **22 ♖b1**, the reply 22 ... h6 is bad on account of 23 ♗d2!. The alternative **22 ♖c1** is less convincing, as after 22 ... h6 23 ♗f4 ♘c4, neither of White's options promises him anything to speak of: 24 ♘d2 ♖c8! 25 d5 ♘b2, or 24 d5 ♖c8 25 ♘d4 ♘b2 26 ♖xc8+ ♕xc8 27 ♕d2 ♘c4 28 ♘c6 ♘xd2 29 ♗xe7+ ♔f8 30 ♘xc8 ♘xe4.

Another interesting variation is **21 ... ♘c4 22 ♗xe7 ♖e8** (22 ... ♘b2 23 ♕b3 ♘xd1 24 ♗xf8 ♕c1 25 ♗a3 ♕a1 26 ♕c2!) 23

♟a3 ♘xa3 24 ♕xa3 ♜xe4 25 d5 ♟f8 26 d6 ♕d7 27 ♘g5, with complications.

22	**♜c1**	**♕b7**
23	**d5**	**♘c4**
24	**♘d2**	

A key factor in White's overall strategy. Evicting the last piece from c4, he seizes the vital file.

24	**...**	**♘xd2**

It was worth considering 24 ... h6 25 ♟f4 e5 (25 ... g5 26 ♟g3 ♘xd2 27 ♜c7 ♕b6 28 ♕xd2 favours White, as does 27 ... ♜c8 28 ♜xb7 ♜c1+ 29 ♚h2 ♘f1+ 20 ♕xf1 ♜xf1 31 ♜a7; another unsatisfactory line is 25 ... ♘xd2 26 ♕xd2 g5 27 ♜c7 ♕b6 28 ♜c6 ♕d4 29 ♕xd4 ♟xd4 30 ♟d2 ♜a8 31 ♟b4 ♚f8 32 d6! ed 33 ♜xd6) 26 ♟e3 (avoiding the sly trap 26 de?! ♜xe6 27 ♘xc4 ♕xe4! with instant equalisation) 26 ... ♘xe3 27 ♕xe3 ♜c8 28 ♘b3 ♟f8 29 ♘a5 ♜xc1+ 30 ♕xc1 ♕b6 31 ♘c6 f6, and Black can resist stubbornly.

25	**♟xd2**	**♜c8** *(66)*

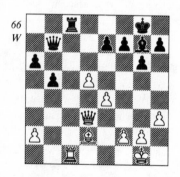

66
W

26	**♜c6!**	

In view of the variation **26 ... ♜xc6 27 dc ♕xc6 28 ♕d8+ ♟f8 29 ♟h6**, Black's position at once becomes critical. Of course, 27 ... ♕c7 28 ♕d7 ♟e5 29 ♟h6! would also lead to a simple win for White: 29 ... ♕xd7 30 cd ♟c7 31 e5! a5 32 ♚f1 b4 33 ♚e2 a4 34 ♚d3 ♟d8 35 ♚c4, etc.

26	**...**	**♟e5**
27	**♟c3**	**♟b8**

In the event of 27 ... ♝xc3 28 ♕xc3 ♖xc6 29 dc ♕c7 30 g3 a5
31 ♕c5 b4 32 ♕d5, or 30 ... f6 31 ♕b3+ ♔f8 32 ♕e6, the white
queen penetrates decisively to d7.

28	♕d4	f6
29	♝a5	

Even now White has to play carefully; not 29 ♖b6?? ♖xc3! 30
♖xb7 ♖c1+ and mates.

29	...	♝d6
30	♕c3	♖e8
31	a3	

Why hurry? The fruit will ripen of its own accord.

31	...	♔g7
32	g3	♝e5
33	♕c5	h5
34	♝c7	♝a1
35	♝f4	♕d7
36	♖c7	♕d8
37	d6!	

The death agony of the black pieces, suffocating on the edge of
the board, now commences.

37	...	g5
38	d7	♖f8
39	♝d2	♝e5
40	♖b7	

1–0

On 40 ... h4, Zaitsev gives 41 ♝a5! ♕xa5 42 ♕xe7+ ♔g6 (42
... ♖f7 43 ♕xf7+) 43 ♕h7+! ♔xh7 44 d8(♕)+. A paradox – to
win Black's queen, White must first sacrifice his own!

4 Russian System

Game No. 16
Ehlvest–Ernst
Tallinn 1989

1	d4	♘f6
2	♘f3	g6
3	c4	♗g7
4	♘c3	d5
5	♛b3	dc
6	♛xc4	0–0
7	e4	♗g4

The queen move to b3 (or the rarely played ♛a4+) constitutes what numerous theoretical manuals call the Russian System. But it incorporates various subsidiary systems which depend on Black's seventh move. At present, the Ragozin (or Prins) Variation, 7 ... ♘a6, enjoys the greatest popularity. This is evidently due to its appearances in the 1986 and 1987 World Championship matches, and the subsequent rapid development of its theory. The Smyslov Variation, 7 ... ♗g4, also occurred in two of the Karpov–Kasparov match games – I shall come to these presently. Among the rarer and somewhat passive continuations, I would menion 7 ... c6 (The Boleslavsky Variation), and 7 ... a6 with the idea of ... b7–b5 (the Hungarian Variation).

8 ♗e3

The most flexible move. The continuations 8 ♘g5 and 8 ♘e5 cause Black no harm.

8 ... ♘fd7 (67)

The critical position of the Smyslov Variation. White's most popular moves are 9 ♖d1, 9 ♗e2, 9 0–0–0, and the one he plays in this game.

9 ♛b3

The most active continuation. Instead of 9 ♔b3 White also has an interesting idea of placing his queen on c5: **9 ♖d1 ♘c6 10 ♗e2 ♘b6**, and now **11 ♕c5 ♕d6** *(68)*.

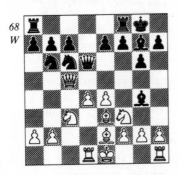

A large number of moves have been seen here: 12 ♕xd6, 12 ♘b5, 12 d5, 12 h3, 12 0–0. I would remind you of the famous game Botvinnik–Fischer, Varna 1962, which went **12 h3 ♗xf3 13 gf ♖fd8 14 d5 ♘e5 15 ♘b5 ♕f6 16 f4 ♘ed7 17 e5**, and now Fischer gave his opponent an unpleasant shock with 17 ... ♕xf4!. After some errors by both sides, however, this fascinating encounter was eventually drawn.

But White proves to have one other interesting move at his disposal. Without having been tried out before, it occurred twice in the return match for the World Championship in 1986, and for that reason I have decided to discuss it:

12 e5

A paradoxical decision at first sight. White not only leaves his pawn on e5 hopelessly weak, he allows a queen exchange too. But it is not as simple as all that.

12 ... ♕xc5 13 dc ♘c8

The more natural-looking 13 ... ♘d7 is met by 14 h3! ♗xf3 15 gf!, and the 'doomed' pawn on e5 is immune – since if either knight takes it, 16 f4! wins a piece. Otherwise White will protect the e-pawn with its neighbour, gaining a clear advantage.

14 h3!

This was played in the seventeenth match game (Karpov–Kasparov, Leningrad 1986). In the fifteenth game, where the novelty 12 e5 was used for the first time, I continued instead with 14 ♘b5, and after 14 ... ♖b8! 15 ♘xc7 e6! Black managed to obtain fully equal chances. The point is that the threat to surround the knight with 16 ... a6 compels White to lose a tempo with 16 ♘b5, whereupon the black knight on c8 quickly transfers itself to a convenient post. The game concluded: 16 ♘b5 ♘8e7 17 ♖d2 b6 18 cb ab 19 ♗g5 ♘f5 20 b3 h6 21 ♗f6 ♗xf3 22 ♗xf3 ♘xe5 (only now does Black recover the pawn) 23 ♗xe5 ♗xe5 24 0–0 ♖fd8 25 ♖fd1 ♖xd2 26 ♖xd2 ♖c8 27 g3 ♖c1+ 28 ♔g2 ♔f8 29 ♗e4 ♔e7 ½–½.

We now return to the seventeenth game:

14 ... ♗xf3

If 14 ... ♗e6, the sortie 15 ♘g5 is unpleasant: 15 ... ♘xe5 16 ♘xe6 fe 17 f4.

15 ♗xf3 ♗xe5

After 15 ... ♘xe5 16 ♗xb7 ♖b8 17 c6 ♘c4 18 ♖d7 ♘xb2, White can choose between two attractive possibilities: 19 ♘d5 and 19 ♘b5.

16 ♗xc6! bc 17 ♗d4 ♗f4 18 0–0

It is worth considering 18 ♘e2. A correspondence game Rümmele–Brummer (1988) continued 18 ... e5 19 ♗c3 f6 20 ♖d7 ♖f7 21 ♖d8+ ♔g7 (White also has a clear plus after 21 ... ♖f8 22 ♖xf8+ ♔xf8 23 ♘xf4 ef 24 ♗xf6) 22 ♘xf4 ef 23 ♔e2, with a won position. In Rümmel's view Black can play more precisely with 18 ... ♗h6 19 ♗c3 ♖b8 20 ♖d7 ♗g7 21 ♗xg7 (21 ♘d4! is interesting) 21 ... ♔xg7 22 b3 ♖b5 23 0–0 ♖xc5 24 ♖c1 ♖xc1+ 25 ♘xc1 ♘d6 26 ♖xc7, with a minimal edge for White.

18 ... a5?

The correct line is 18 ... e5 19 ♗e3 ♗xe3 20 fe ♘e7, as demonstrated in the game Karpov–Timman, Tilburg 1986, which continued:21 ♖d7 ♘f5 22 ♖xc7 ♖fc8! 23 ♖d7 ♖d8 24 ♖fd1 ♖xd7 25 ♖xd7 ♘xe3 26 ♖c7 ♖b8 27 b3 ♖d8! 28 ♘e4 ♖d4 29 ♘f6+

♔g7 30 ♖xc6 ♖d2 31 g4 ♘c2 32 ♔f1 ♘d4 33 ♖a6 ♘f3 ½–½.

*19 ♖fe1 a4 20 ♖e4 ♗h6 21 ♗e5 a3 22 b3 ♘a7 23 ♖d7 ♗c1
24 ♖xc7 ♗b2 25 ♘a4!*

The material balance is restored, but White's threats are mounting up.

25 ... ♘b5 26 ♖xc6 ♖fd8 27 ♖b6! ♖d5

Cunningly thought out; if 28 ♘xb2, then 28 ... ♖xe5! 29 ♖xe5 ab 30 ♖e1 ♘c3, and the b-pawn unexpectedly brings victory to Black. But avoiding the trap is quite simple.

28 ♗g3 ♘c3 29 ♘xc3 ♗xc3 30 c6 ♗d4 31 ♖b7 1–0

Black resigned in view of the inevitable c6–c7.

| | **9** | **...** | **♘b6** |

Alternatives are 9 ... c5 and 9 ... ♗xf3.

| | **10** | **♖d1** | **♘c6** |

Practice has also seen 10 ... e6, and 10 ... e5 11 de ♘8d7 with sharp play. With 10 ... ♘c6, Black provokes the advance d4–d5.

	11	**d5**	**♘e5**
	12	**♗e2**	**♘xf3+**
	13	**gf**	**♗h5**

As practice has shown, 13 ... ♗h3 is less convincing in view of 14 ♖g1!, and Black's bishop will soon have to retreat.

| | **14** | **a4** |

14 ♘b5 and 14 f4 are not dangerous for Black. We shall say a word about 14 ♖g1 presently.

| | **14** | **...** | **♕d7** *(69)* |

In such situations Black usually plays ... ♕c8 to defend his b-pawn, but here this is not necessary, since after 15 a5 ♘c8 16 ♕xb7 ♘d6 17 ♕c6 ♕h3! Black obtains good counterplay.

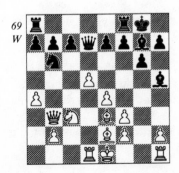

69
W

15   ♖g1!

An interesting idea. It used to be thought that White should not allow the queen onto h3. Hence the rook manoeuvre to g1 was carried out a move earlier; then after 14 ♖g1 ♕d7 (or 14 ... ♕c8), White could reply 15 ♖g3. In the present game, on the contrary, White 'tempts' the black queen to h3 and then even further – to h2. The result is mind-bending complications, which in fact were what attracted me to this game.

Formerly, the normal move from diagram 69 was 15 h4, for example: 15 ... a5 16 ♘b5 ♘c8 17 ♗d4 (Uhlmann–Kozma, Zinnowitz 1967, went 17 f4 ♗xe2 18 ♔xe2, and now 18 ... ♘d6! would have equalised) 17 ... ♗xd4! 18 ♘xd4 ♘b6 19 ♗b5 ♕d6, and the chances are level. I should mention that the exchange on d4 was suggested by Euwe. Long ago, in a game Smyslov–Botvinnik from the return World Championship Match of 1958, Black played instead 17 ... ♘d6, and White gained a distinct advantage.

15   ...   ♕h3

Black could also go after a different pawn – the one on a4 – but after 15 ... ♗xc3+ 16 bc ♕xa4 17 ♕xa4 ♘xa4 18 ♔d2, White has quite enough initiative for it.

16   f4   ♕xh2
17   ♔d2!

White's intention becomes clear: having lured the enemy queen into his camp, he aims to exploit its awkward position in order to work up a kingside attack.

17   ...   ♗xe2

The sharp variation 17 ... ♗xc3+ 18 bc ♗xe2 19 ♔xe2 ♕h5+ 20 ♔d3 ♖ab8 21 ♖b1 ♘d7 22 ♕d1 is also possible.

18   ♘xe2   c6

Black has to play energetically. If 18 ... ♕h3, then 19 f5 with unpleasant threats.

19   a5   ♘d7
20   ♘g3

White's plan of surrounding the black queen is quite consistent. After 20 ♕xb7 ♘f6! Black would have a promising position.

20   ...   cd

Black sacrifices a piece, but obtains a large number of pawns in return.

21   ♖h1   ♕g2

	22	⊈e2!	de

The only move, in view of the threatened 23 ⏘dg1.

	23	⏘xd7	e5!
	24	f5!	♛f3+

Ehlvest recommends 24 ... gf at once. Play could continue: 25 ⏘c5 (it must have been to prevent this move that Black gave check) 25 ... f4 26 ⏘xf8 ⏘xf8 27 ⏘f1 (27 ⏘hd1 e3) 27 ... ⏘h6! (of course not 27 ... fg 28 ♛xg3, with a won ending for White) 28 ⏘h1 ⏘g7, and White cannot improve the placing of his pieces.

	25	⊈e1	gf *(70)*

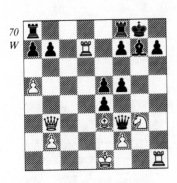

	26	⏘g1!

Once again the rook occupies the g-file, this time with even greater effect.

	26	...	f4

If 26 ... ⏘ad8 (26 ... ⏘ac8 27 ♛d1!), then 27 ♛d5 ⏘xd7 28 ♛xd7 f4 29 ♘f5 fe 30 fe is decisive.

	27	♘f5	fe
	28	♛xe3!	♛xf5
	29	♛h6	♛g6
	30	⏘xg6	hg
	31	♛h4!	

Now there is nominal material equality, but Black's pieces are very passively placed and he doesn't succeed in co-ordinating them.

	31	...	b6
	32	a6!	e3
	33	fe	e4
	34	b3	b5

34 ... ♝c3+ 35 ♔e2 ♝b4 doesn't help: 36 ♕xe4 ♝c5 37 ♕d5!

35 ♔e2 ♝c3 36 ♕e7 ♝a5 37 ♖xa7 ♖ae8 38 ♕a3 ♝c3 39 ♕c5 b4 40 ♖e7 ♖c8 41 ♕d5 1–0

Game No. 17
M. Gurevich–Kasparov
Moscow 1988

1	d4	♘f6
2	c4	g6
3	♘c3	d5
4	♘f3	♝g7
5	♕b3	dc
6	♕xc4	0–0
7	e4	♘a6 *(71)*

71
W

Introduced into practice by Ragozin as long ago as the 1930s, this variation has occurred three times in the encounters between Kasparov and myself. The nineteenth game of the return match in 1986 ended in a beautiful win for White, but in Seville (games 15 and 21) Kasparov succeeded in obtaining equality, and both games were drawn. I do not know if its occurrence in our matches was the reason, but since then the popularity of this variation has noticeably increased, and a good many games have been played enriching its theory. In the notes to the present game we shall examine the most interesting practical examples, including all three of the World Championship games to which I have referred.

In the diagram position, Gurevich developed his bishop on e2. Strange though it may seem, no fewer than ten other continuations have also been seen! The moves 8 ♕a4, 8 b4, 8 ♗e3, 8 h3, 8 e5, 8 ♖b1 and 8 ♗d3 have completely gone out of use. 8 ♕b3, 8 ♗g5 and 8 ♗f4 are also employed only rarely, and in any case they often amount merely to a transposition – the bishop is brought to e2 a little later. I shall now given one example of each of these three alternatives that I have said to be the most common.

G. Georgadze–Tukmakov, Odessa 1989, went **8 ♕b3** c5 9 d5 ♕b6! (9 … e6 is the usual continuation. The queen exchange gives Black a comfortable game) 10 ♕xb6 (perhaps White shouldn't be in a hurry to exchange; 10 ♗c4 or 10 e5 should be tested) 10 … ab 11 ♗c4 e6 12 de ♗xe6 13 ♗xe6 fe 14 0–0 ♘b4 15 h3 ♘d7 16 ♖d1 ♘c2 17 ♖b1 ♘d4 18 ♘e1 (better 18 ♘b5 e5 19 a3, with unclear play. Now Black seizes the initiative and quickly achieves a won position) 18 … ♘e5 19 a4 ♖ad8 20 ♗g5 ♖d7 21 ♗h4 h6 22 b3 g5 23 ♗g3 ♘ec6! 24 ♔f1 ♖fd8 25 ♘e2 ♘xe2 26 ♔xe2 ♘d4+ 27 ♔f1 b5! 28 ab ♘xb5 29 ♖xd7 ♖xd7 30 e5 ♘c3 31 ♖b2 b5! 32 ♖c2 b4 33 ♖c1 ♖d2 34 ♖a1 c4 35 ♘f3 ♖d8 0–1.

Flear–Ftačnik, Belgrade 1989, went **8 ♗g5** h6 9 ♗h4 c5 10 d5 b5! 11 ♘xb5 (*ECO* gives 11 ♕xb5 ♖b8 12 ♕e2 ♖xb2! 13 ♕xb2 ♘xe4 14 ♖c1 ♕a5, with advantage; if now 15 ♗xe7 ♖e8 16 d6 ♘xd6 17 ♕d2 ♖xe7+ 18 ♗e2, Black has the very strong 18 … ♗xc3 19 ♕xc3 ♕b5! 20 ♘g1 ♘b4 21 ♔f1 ♖xe2! 21 ♘xe2 ♗a6, and although White is two exchanges up, Black's attack is irresistible) 11 … ♕a5+ 12 ♘d2 ♖b8 (theory recommends 12 … ♘xe4, but the rook move is more precise) 13 0–0–0 (after the familiar 13 ♗g3 ♘xe4 14 ♕xe4 ♖xb5 15 ♗xb5 ♕xb5 16 ♕e2 ♕xb2 17 0–0 ♘b4, Black has excellent compensation for the minimal material deficit. But in castling queenside, the English grandmaster comes under a strong attack) 13 … ♘g4! 14 ♕b3 (14 ♗g3 ♗d7!) 14 … c4 15 ♗xc4 ♗d7 16 a4 ♖fc8 17 ♔b1 ♘c5 18 ♕a3 ♕xa4! 19 b3 ♗xb5! 0–1. After 20 ba ♗xc4+ 21 ♔c1 ♗b2+ 22 ♕xb2 ♘d3+, White suffers big material losses.

Eingorn–H. Olafsson, Reykjavik 1990, saw **8 ♗f4** c5 9 dc ♕a5 (9 … ♗e6 is also frequently played) 10 e5 ♘d7 11 a3 ♕xc5 *(72)*. This position was recently the object of a minor theoretical debate, associated with three games.

12 ♕e4 (in Eingorn–Gavrikov, Tallinn 1989, White played 12 ♘d5, and after the inferior reply 12 … ♖e8 he quickly reached a won position: 13 ♖d1 h6 14 h3 g5 15 ♕xc5! ♘dxc5 16 ♗e3 etc. Soon afterwards, in Piket–Ivanchuk, Tilburg 1989, Black

innovated with 12 ... ♘b6 and seized the initiative: 13 ♕xc5 ♘xc5 14 ♘xe7+ ♔h8 15 ♖c1 ♘e6! 16 ♗e3 ♗d7 17 ♗e2 ♖ae8! 18 ♗xb6 ab 19 ♘d5 ♗c6 20 ♖d1 f6! with clearly the better position. This time, it is Eingorn who himself changes the complexion of the game) 12 ... ♘b6 13 ♗e3 ♕c7 14 ♖c1 ♗f5 15 ♕h4 ♖ac8 16 ♗xa6 ba 17 0-0 ♕b7 18 ♘d4 ♘c4 19 ♗h6 ♗xh6 20 ♕xh6 ♘xe5 21 ♖fe1 f6 22 b4 ♖fd8 23 ♘xf5 gf 24 ♖xe5 ♖xc3 25 ♖c5 (but not 25 ♖xf5 ♕e4 26 ♖c5 ♕c2!) 25 ... ♖xa3 (the chances here are level) 26 ♖xf5 ♖ad3 27 ♖g5+ fg 28 ♕xg5+ ♔f8 29 ♕f5+ ♔e8 30 ♕h5+ ♔f8 31 ♕f5+ ½-½.

$$\textbf{8} \qquad \textbf{♗e2} \qquad\qquad \textbf{c5}$$
$$\textbf{9} \qquad \textbf{d5}$$

9 e5 is met by 9 ... ♘g4 10 h3 cd 11 hg dc 12 bc ♕a5, with a good game for Black.

White gains nothing from 9 dc ♗e6 10 ♕b5 ♖c8! 11 ♕xb7 ♘xc5 12 ♕xa7 ♖c7 13 ♕a3 (if 13 ♕a5 ♘cxe4, White can't play 14 ♘xe4 because of 14 ... ♖xc1+!) 13 ... ♘d3+ 14 ♗xd3 ♕xd3, with a very strong initiative for Black. This whole variation is given in the opening monographs. In M. Gurevich–Gavrikov, Moscow 1990, White varied with 11 c6 ♖xc6, and then 12 ♕xb7, but after 12 ... ♖xc3! 13 ♕xa6 ♘xe4 14 0-0 ♖c7 15 ♗f4 ♘d6! 16 ♗e5 ♕b8 17 ♗xg7 ♔xg7 18 b3 ♕b4 19 ♖ad1 ♘f5 20 ♖fe1 ♖b8 21 ♗f1 ♖b6, the game was level.

$$\textbf{9} \qquad \textbf{...} \qquad\qquad \textbf{e6}$$
$$\textbf{10} \qquad \textbf{0-0}$$

The bishop sortie 10 ♗g5 *(73)* should also be mentioned.

After **10 ... ed** (stronger than 10 ... h6 11 ♗xf6 ♕xf6 12 e5 ♕d8 13 d6!, or 10 ... ♕b6 11 ♗xf6 ♗xf6 12 e5 ♗g7 13 0-0,

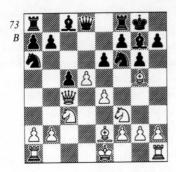

73
B

when practice has shown White's chances to be better) **11 ♘xd5**, Black has two options: 11 ... ♗e6 and 11 ... ♕a5+.

Belyavsky–Kasparov, Belfort 1988, went **11 ... ♗e6** 12 0–0–0 ♗xd5 13 ♖xd5 ♕b6 14 ♗xf6 ♕xf6 15 e5 ♕f5! (in Flear–Korchnoi, Lugano 1988, after 15 ... ♕e7 16 ♖hd1 ♖ad8 17 ♖xd8 ♖xd8 18 ♖xd8+ ♕xd8 19 e6 White obtained the better chances, although his initiative was gradually neutralised) 16 ♗d3 ♕c8! 17 ♖d1 (allowing his opponent to work up a dangerous attack. The right move was 17 ♖d6, with complex play) 17 ... b5! 18 ♕h4 ♘b4 19 ♗xg6 fg 20 ♖d7 ♕e8! 21 ♖e7 ♗h6+! 22 ♔b1 ♖d8 23 ♖d6 ♕c6! 24 a3 ♖xd6 25 ed ♕xd6 26 ab cb 27 ♕e4 b3 0–1.

Farago–Dorfman, Budapest 1988, continued instead **11 ... ♕a5+** 12 ♗d2 ♕d8 13 ♘xf6+ ♗xf6 14 e5 ♗g7 15 ♗c3 (Gutman recommends 15 0–0 ♗e6 16 ♕c1! ♕b6 17 ♗h6, with slightly the better game) 15 ... ♗e6 16 ♕b5 ♕e7 17 0–0 ♘c7 18 ♕a4 ♗d7 19 ♕c2 ♗c6, with equal chances.

| 10 | ... | ed |
| 11 | ed | ♖e8 *(74)* |

The move **11 ... ♗f5** might well transpose after 12 ♗f4 ♖e8; alternative ideas after 11 ... ♗f5 are discussed in Games No. 18 and 19.

After **11 ... b5** 12 ♕xb5! ♖b8 13 ♕a4 ♖b4 14 ♕d1! Black has no compensation for the pawn.

11 ... b6 is interesting – the knight on a6 is at once freed from its unwanted duty of defending the c-pawn. Tukmakov–Chiburdanidze, Biel 1988, went **12 ♖d1** (12 ♗g5 h6!) 12 ... ♘b4 13 a3 (13 ♕b3 ♗f5!) 13 ... ♗a6 14 ♕b3 ♗xe2 15 ♘xe2 ♘bxd5 16 ♘f4 c4 17 ♕xc4 ♕c7 18 ♕xc7 ♘xc7, and the position was completely equal. In Naumkin–Henkin, Moscow 1989, White instead played 12 ♘e5, but again achieved nothing: 12 ... ♘b4! 13 ♘c6 ♘xc6 14 dc ♗e6 15 ♕a4 ♕d4 16 ♕xd4 cd 17 ♘b5 ♘d5!, and after some sharp play the endgame concluded peacefully.

In Vladimirov–Fette, Groningen 1989, White answered 11 ... b6 with the valuable novelty **12 ♕h4!**. After just three moves, Black was in trouble: 12 ... ♘b4 13 ♗g5 ♗f5 (13 ... h6 14 ♗xh6 ♗xh6 15 ♕xh6 ♘bxd5 16 ♖ad1 ♕e7 17 ♖xd5! is also bad for Black) 14 ♖ad1. Vladimirov gives another variation which likewise favours White: 12 ... ♘xd5 13 ♘xd5 (or 13 ♗g5!) 13 ... ♕xd5 14 ♘g5 h6 15 ♗f3 hg 16 ♗xg5.

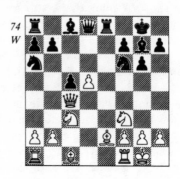

12 ♗f4

The fashionable development of the bishop on e3 (though with Black having played 11 ... ♗f5 instead of 11 ... ♖e8) is covered in Game No. 19.

After **12 ♖d1** (to prepare a quick advance of the d-pawn) **12 ... ♗f5**, we reach a position that occurred twice in the Seville match *(75)*. This is the appropriate moment to recall those games.

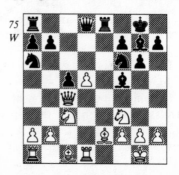

The 15th game of the 1987 match continued:

13 d6 h6

Not 13 ... ♘e4? 14 d7!

14 h3

In the 21st match game, I played 14 ♗f4 (see below). A suggestion of Gutman's is also interesting: 14 a3! ♘d7 (14 ... ♘e4 15 ♗e3!) 15 ♕a2! ♘b6 16 ♗e3! ♗e6 17 ♕b1. The queen has escaped from pursuit, and the d-pawn continues to fetter the opponent's pieces.

14 ... ♘b4 15 ♗f4 ♘d7 16 ♖d2 a6 17 ♕b3 b5 18 ♕d1 c4 19 a4! ♘c5 20 ab ♘bd3 21 ♗xd3 ♘xd3 22 ♖xd3! cd

The bishop on f5 has to be left where it is, to restrain the d-pawn; a weaker choice is 22 ... ♗xd3 23 ♖xa6 ♖xa6 24 ba ♕a5 25 ♕a4! ♕xa4 26 ♘xa4.

23 ♘d5! ab! 24 ♘e7+ ♔h7 25 ♖xa8 ♕xa8 26 ♘xf5 gf 27 ♕xd3 ♕e4 28 ♕xb5 ♖a8 29 ♗d2 ♖d8 30 ♕c5 ♕e6 31 ♗f4 ♗xb2 32 ♘h4 ♗f6 33 ♕xf5+ ♕xf5 34 ♘xf5 h5! 35 g4 hg 36 hg ♔g6 37 ♔g2 ♗b2 38 ♘e7+ ♔f6 39 ♘c6 ♖d7 40 ♘b8 ♖d8 41 d7 ♔e6 42 ♔f3 ♗a3 ½-½.

From diagram 75, the 21st game of the Seville match went:

13 d6 h6 14 ♗f4 ♘d7!

More accurate than 14 ... ♘h5 15 ♗e3, when the white bishop has enticed the enemy knight onto the edge of the board and itself settled in a good position.

15 ♖d2

Or 15 ♕b3 ♘b4 16 ♖d2, transposing; alternatively 16 ♗c4 ♕f6! 17 ♖d2.

15 ... ♘b4 16 ♕b3 ♗e6

Better than 16 ... a6 17 a3 ♘c6 18 ♘d5!.

17 ♗c4 ♘b6 18 ♗xe6 ♖xe6 (76)

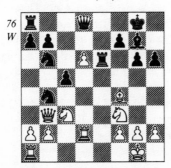

19 a3?

An unfortunate move. 19 ♘b5 is also bad: 19 ... ♖e4! 20 ♗e3 ♘c4 and Black has an excellent position. Instead, 19 ♗g3 ♘d3 20 ♘b5 (or 20 ♘d5 c4 21 ♕b5 ♘xd5 22 ♕xd5 ♘xb2 23 ♕xb7 c3 24 ♖c2) 20 ... c4 21 ♕a3 leads to double-edged play. In a simultaneous display with clocks, against six of the strongest American juniors (New York 1988), Kasparov reached the diagram position again in his game against Rao. But in answer to 19 ♗g3, he didn't jump to d3 with his knight; he chose the modest 19 ... ♕d7, and after 20 a3 ♘c6 21 ♕b5?! ♖c8! 22 ♖ad1? (22 ♘d5 is stronger) 22 ... ♗xc3 23 bc ♘e5! 24 ♕xd7 ♘xf3+ 25 gf ♘xd7, Black achieved a won endgame.

19 ... ♘d3!

The appearance of the knight at d3 causes a certain amount of confusion in the white camp. Capturing it, obviously, loses to the fork 20 ... c4!

20 ♗g3 c4 21 ♕c2 ♖c8 22 ♖ad1 ♕d7

Not 22 ... ♘xb2, which fails to 23 ♕xb2 ♘a4 24 ♘xa4! ♗xb2 25 ♖xb2 ♕a5 26 ♖b4.

23 h4 f5

Perhaps 23 ... ♖c6 or 23 ... ♖c5 was more accurate. The exchange sacrifice on d3 would then be ineffective; White would have to play 24 ♕b1 and then 25 ♘e1.

24 ♖xd3 cd 25 ♕xd3 ♘c4 26 ♕d5 ♘b6

Evidently, Kasparov's weakened king position is not to his liking, and he decides not to risk anything. And yet with 26 ... ♔h7! Black would have retained the better chances. You may ask what difference it makes whether the king goes to h8 or h7. In fact the difference is highly significant. After 26 ... ♔h8 (26 ... ♘xb2 27 ♖e1 ♖ce8 28 ♖xe6 ♖xe6 – 28 ... ♕xe6? 29 d7! – 29 ♘b5 ♔h7 30 ♘e5! ♗xe5 31 ♗xe5 ♘c4 32 f4! a6 33 ♘d4, with advantage) 27 ♘b5 ♘xb2 28 ♖b1 ♘a4 29 ♘c7 ♖xc7 30 dc ♕xd5 31 c8(♕)+ ♔h7 32 ♖xb7, it is White who has the winning chances. With the king on h7, the c-pawn would queen without check and the whole variation would fail.

27 ♕d3

More precise than 27 ♕b3 ♕f7! 28 ♘d5 (28 ♔h2 g4) 28 ... ♖d8, with the better chances for Black.

27 ... ♘c4 28 ♕d5 ♘b6 ½–½

12   ...   ♗f5

Again **12 ... b6** is possible. In Annageldiev–Arbakov, Uzhgorod 1988, there followed **13 d6** (13 a3 ♘c7 14 d6 ♘e6 gives White nothing, but 13 ♖fd1 ♘b4 14 ♕b3 ♗f5 15 ♖ac1 is worth trying) **13 ... ♘b4 14 ♘g5 ♕d7 15 ♕b3** *(77)*.

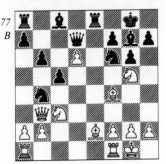

The position looks unpleasant for Black; after **15 ... ♗a6** 16 ♗xa6 ♘xa6, his knight has been thrown back again. But the Moscow master found a powerful resource: **15 ... ♖xe2!** (Black gives up the exchange but activates his bishops) 16 ♘xe2 ♗a6 17 ♘c3 (White takes the correct decision to return the exchange. 17 ♖fe1 is risky: 17 ... ♘d3 18 ♖ed1 h6! 19 ♘f3 ♘h5! with a fine game for Black, for instance 20 ♕d5 ♖e8! 21 ♖xd3 ♖xe2 22 ♘e5 ♗xe5 23 ♗xe5 ♖xe5! 24 ♕xe5 ♗xd3; but not 17 ... ♘h5 18 ♘g3! ♘xf4 19 ♖e7 c4 20 ♕f3, and Black comes to grief) 17 ... ♗xf1 18 ♖xf1 ♖e8 19 h3 h6 20 ♘f3 ♕f5. A complex position has arisen, with chances for both sides.

13   ♖ad1   ♘e4

13 ... ♕b6 has been played; White continues 14 ♕b5 or 14 ♘h4, with mutual chances.

13 ... ♘d7 appears to be weaker. Ivanchuk–Kotronias, Lvov 1988, continued 14 ♕b3 ♘b4 15 ♖d2 ♘b6 16 ♗b5 ♗d7 17 ♗g5 ♕c8 18 ♖c1 a5 19 ♘a4 c4 20 ♕d1 ♘xa4 21 ♕xa4 ♗xb5 22 ♕xb5 ♕f5 23 h4 c3 24 bc ♖ec8 25 c4, and Black came away empty-handed.

14   ♗d3

Before proceeding further with the main game, we must recall the 19th game of the return World Championship match (1986), in which I employed a prepared variation here.

14 ♘b5! (78)

The basic strategic conflict revolves round the d-pawn. If White succeeds in utilising its potential energy, the initiative will be his. If Black manages to blockade it securely, his position will be the more promising. In advancing my knight to b5 I was prepared to part with the b-pawn, aiming to develop an attack in the centre after 14 ... ♗xb2 15 d6 ♗f6 16 ♗d3! and 17 ♖fe1. Kasparov refuses the gift.

14 ... ♕f6!?

Taimanov recommended 14 ... g5, but after 15 ♗c1 g4 16 ♘e1 White has a clear positional advantage.

15 ♗d3

Considering what happened later in the game, many people gained the impression that Black's opening set-up had been refuted outright. But in chess such things rarely happen, and soon after the match Kasparov himself was to go back to this variation. In fact, in Belyavsky–Kasparov, Moscow 1987, it was White who first departed from precedent by advancing his d-pawn at once. The ensuing fierce struggle brought about a rapid depletion of forces: 15 d6 ♗d7 16 g3 g5 17 ♗e3 h6 18 ♘c7 ♘xc7 19 dc ♗c6 20 ♘d2 ♖ac8 21 ♘xe4 ♖xe4 22 ♕xc5 ♖xc7 23 ♖d6 b6 24 ♖xf6 bc 25 ♖xc6 ♖xc6 26 ♗f3 ♖xe3 ½–½.

15 ... ♘b4

Not wishing to be condemned to passive defence, Black plays *va banque*, but the exchange sacrifice fails to justify itself. It may have been worth taking the pawn with **15 ... ♕xb2**, even though this involves a definite risk. On the other hand, Black has a way of sacrificing a pawn himself. This improvement was worked out by Kasparov, who used it in a clock simultaneous display at a

Young Pioneers' tournament. His opponent in this game was the only master in the contest:

Dzhandzhgava–Kasparov, Baku (Simul) 1987: **15 ... ♖ad8!** (possibly it was because of this move that Belyavsky refrained from 15 ♗d3 and played 15 d6) 16 ♖de1 (16 ♖fe1 ♕xb2 17 ♗xe4 ♖xe4 18 ♖xe4 ♗xe4 19 ♕xe4 ♕xb5 20 d6 deserved consideration. Also worth noting is 16 ♘xa7 ♕xb2 17 ♘b5 ♘b4 18 ♗b1, when 18 ... ♘xd5 19 ♖xd5 ♖xd5 20 ♕xd5 ♕xb5 appears to fail after 21 ♘e5! However, 21 ... ♗xe5 22 ♗xe5 ♘d2! is better for Black – *ed.*) 16 ... ♕xb2 17 ♘c7 ♘xc7 18 ♗xc7 ♘d2! (a pretty resource, eliminating all inconveniences. In the sharp endgame, Kasparov easily outplays his young opponent) 19 ♖xe8+ ♖xe8 20 ♘xd2 ♕xd2 21 ♗xf5 gf 22 g3 ♗d4 23 d6 ♖e1 24 ♔g2 ♖xf1 25 ♕xf1 ♕xa2 26 ♕b5 ♔g7 27 ♔h3 ♕d5 28 ♕e8 ♕c4! 29 ♔g2 ♕c2 30 ♕e1 ♕a4! 31 ♕d2 ♕c6+ 32 f3 ♗f6 0–1.

At move 15, Black also has the interesting **15 ... ♗d7**. This occurred in Ivanchuk–Dorfman, Lvov 1988. The further course of the game was fascinating: 16 ♗e5 ♗xb5 17 ♕xb5 ♖xe5 18 ♘xe5 ♘d6! 19 ♘g4 ♕f4 20 ♕d7 c4 21 g3 ♘c5 22 ♕c7 ♕xg4 23 ♕xc5 ♕d7 24 ♗e2 ♗xb2 25 ♖b4 c3 26 ♗d3 a5 27 ♕f4 ♗a3 28 ♖fe1 ♗c5 29 ♔g2 b5 20 h4 h5 31 ♕f6 ♕d8 32 ♕xc3 ♗b4 33 ♕e5 ♗xe1 34 ♖xe1. The concentrated tactical crossfire has at last culminated peacefully; the players agreed a draw a few moves later.

16 ♘c7 ♘xd3 17 ♘xe8 ♖xe8 18 ♕xd3!

To Black's misfortune, 18 ... ♘xf2 or 18 ... ♘g3 would fail to the counter-stroke 19 ♕b5.

18 ... ♕xb2

For the exchange Black has a pawn and an active position, but the passed pawn on d5 has yet to reveal its full potential.

19 ♖de1

The straightforward 19 d6 ♖d8! 20 ♕e3 h5 21 ♖b1 ♕xa2 22 ♖xb7 ♕d5 23 ♖xa7 ♘xd6 24 ♗xd6 ♕xd6 25 ♘g5 is unpleasant for Black and was undoubtedly worth playing. But I decided to pin the knight, restricting the activity of the enemy pieces. White incidentally threatens 20 g4. Of course, 19 ♖fe1 doesn't work in view of 19 ... ♕xf2+ 20 ♔h1 ♕xe1+! 21 ♖xe1 ♘f2+ 22 ♔g1 ♖xe1+ and 23 ... ♗xd3.

19 ... ♕b4

The decisive mistake. After 19 ... ♘f6 20 ♖xe8+ ♘xe8 21 ♕e3,

White can realise his material advantage without trouble, but with 19 ... ♛xa2 20 ♛b5 (20 g4 c4!) 20 ... ♖d8 21 ♛xb7 ♛xd5, Black can hold out. In his notes to the game, Kasparov pointed out that after 22 ♛xd5 ♖xd5 23 g4, Black has the neat 23 ... ♘f6!.

   20 ♘d2!

Playing to exploit the pin is the chief factor in White's strategy.

   20 ... ♛a4 21 ♛c4

Forcing the queens off, whereas 21 ♘xe4 is not so clear: 21 ... ♖xe4 22 ♖xe4 ♗xe4 23 ♛d2 c4, with counterplay.

   21 ... ♛xc4 22 ♘xc4 ♗c3

Black would lose at once with 22 ... b5 23 ♘d2 ♘f6 24 ♖xe8+ ♘xe8 25 ♖e1 etc.

   23 ♘d2 ♗xd2 24 ♗xd2 ♗d7 (79)

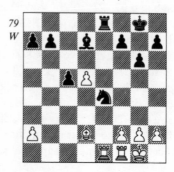

79
W

To many onlookers during the game, Black seemed to have 'wriggled out', and indeed done more than that. The bishop on d2 is attacked, and Black threatens ... ♗b5. But White is able to give the exchange back ... .

   25 ♗f4! ♗b5 26 f3! g5

After 26 ... ♗xf1 27 ♔xf1 ♘f6 28 ♖xe8+ ♘xe8 29 ♗e5!, the d-pawn finally shows its full capability: 29 ... f6 30 d6! and Black has to give up a piece.

   27 ♗xg5 ♗xf1

Nor is 27 ... ♘xg5 any better: 28 ♖xe8+ ♗xe8 29 h4!, winning the knight.

   28 ♔xf1 ♘d6 29 ♗e7 ♘c8 30 ♗xc5 ♖d8 31 ♖e5 f6 32 ♖f5 b6 33 ♗d4 ♘e7 34 ♗xf6 ♖xd5 35 ♖g5+ ♖xg5 36 ♗xg5 ♘c6 37 ♔e2 ♔f7 38 ♔d3 ♔e6

After 38 ... ♘b4+ 39 ♔c4 ♘xa2 40 ♔b3, the black knight is trapped.

39 ♔c4 ♘e5+ 40 ♔d4 ♘c6+ 41 ♔c4

Here the game was adjourned, and Black resigned without resuming. After 41 ... ♘e5+, White can achieve his ends with either 42 ♔b5 or 42 ♔d4 ♘c6+ 43 ♔e4, and the white pawns are not to be stopped.

We now return to the main game, which concluded very quickly:

14	...	♗xc3
15	bc	b5
16	♕xb5	♘xc3
17	♕xa6	

The correct plan, involving an exchange sacrifice, was demonstrated by Gurevich in another game: 17 ♕c4!? ♘xd1 18 ♖xd1 ♗xd3 19 ♖xd3 ♕b6 20 ♖b3 ♕f6 21 g3! ♖ad8 22 ♗g5 ♕d6 23 ♗f4 ♕f6 24 a3!; M. Gurevich–Kotronias, Reykjavik 1988. The black knight is badly placed, and the activity of White's pieces assures him of more than enough for the exchange.

17	...	♗xd3
18	♕xd3	

If 18 ♖xd3, then 18 ... ♘e2+ 19 ♔h1 ♘xf4 is good for Black.

18	...	♘e2+
19	♔h1	♘xf4
20	♕c4	♕d6 *(80)*

In an earlier game Ptin–Lau, played in a postal tournament (1975), Black continued with 20 ... ♕f6, leading to equality.

It is strange that thirteen years later (this game was played in the 55th USSR Championship), Grandmaster Gurevich – who is one of Kasparov's seconds, too – should bring about this position again. It is only now that Black plays a new move, and the resulting position can already be assessed as good for him.

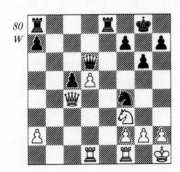

80
W

21   ♖fe1

After **21 g3** (21 ♘g5 ♕e5! 22 ♘f3 ♕f5) 21 ... ♘h5 22 ♖fe1 (22 ♘d2 ♘f6 23 ♘b3 ♖ac8) 22 ... ♘f6 23 ♖xe8+ ♖xe8 24 ♖c1 ♖c8 25 ♖d1 ♖d8, Black has a slight advantage.

Apparently, **21 ♘d2 ♘xd5 22 ♘e4** (but not 22 ♘b3 ♖ad8) 22 ... ♕f4 (22 ... ♕e5) 23 ♕xc5 ♖xe4 24 ♕xd5 ♖ae8 would have maintained equality (Kasparov). Incidentally, after 21 ♘d2 a bad line for Black is **21 ... ♖ad8** 22 ♘e4 ♕e5 23 f3 ♔g7 24 d6 ♕b2 25 ♖g1 ♕b4 26 ♕c1! ♘e2 27 ♕a1+ ♘d4 28 ♖b1! ♕a5 29 ♖bc1 ♕b6 30 ♖gd1 ♖e6 31 ♘xc5 ♖exd6 32 ♖c4, and White wins; Annageldiev–Chudinovskikh, Yalta 1989.

White's unfortunate rook move leads to a quick catastrophe.

21   ...   ♖xe1+

22   ♘xe1

White has also a difficult position after 22 ♖xe1 ♘xd5 23 ♖d1 ♘b6 24 ♕xf7+ ♔xf7 25 ♖xd6 ♔e7, but now Black succeeds in increasing his advantage decisively.

22   ...   ♖b8!

23   a3

23 ♘c2 loses to 23 ... ♕xd5!. If 23 g3, Black has 23 ... ♖b4!, while 23 ♘d3 is met by 23 ... ♘xd3 24 ♕xd3 ♖b2.

23 ... ♖b2 24 f3 ♕e5! 25 ♕e4 ♕g5 26 g3 ♕h5 27 h4 ♘e2 28 ♕e8+ ♔g7 29 d6 ♘xg3+ 30 ♔g1 ♘e2+ 31 ♔f1 ♕f5 32 ♕xe2 ♕h3+ 0–1

Game No. 18
Belyavsky–Tukmakov
Odessa 1989

1 d4 ♘f6 2 c4 g6 3 ♘c3 d5 4 ♘f3 ♗g7 5 ♕b3 dc 6 ♕xc4 0–0 7 e4 ♘a6 8 ♗e2 c5 9 d5 e6 10 0–0 ed

11   ed   ♗f5

12   ♗f4   *(81)*

The more 'modest' bishop development with 12 ♗e3, which has been seen frequently of late, is examined in Game No. 19.

A standard position in this variation. The contemporary line **12 ... ♖e8** was examined in detail in Game No. 17 (where the move-order was 11 ... ♖e8 12 ♗f4 ♗f5). Before demonstrating the valuable novelty employed by Tukmakov in the present game, let us recall the 'classical' continuation **12 ... ♕b6**, which in our day has been undergoing further development. An entertaining

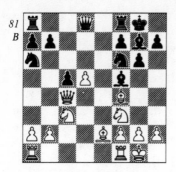

instance of this occurred in the 1987 USSR Championship in Minsk, where Grandmaster Gavrikov, one of the most noted specialists on the black side of the Grünfeld, employed this queen move three times.

Belyavsky–Gavrikov continued **13 h3?** (an unsuccessful innovation) 13 ... ♛xb2! 14 g4 ♝c2! 15 ♖ac1 ♘d7 16 ♘b5 ♝a4! 17 ♘d6 (Black also has the advantage after 17 ♖b1 ♘b6 18 ♖xb2 ♘xc4 19 ♖bb1, but now the White position becomes highly critical) 17 ... ♘b6 18 ♛e4 (18 ♛d3 ♘b4) 18 ... ♖ae8 etc.

A more logical plan was tried in Gurevich–Gavrikov from the same event: *13 ♝e5*.

This manoeuvre is the most dangerous to Black. 13 ♘a4 can be met by 13 ... ♛b4 or 13 ... ♛a5, and 13 ♖ad1 by 13 ... ♛xb2.

13 ... ♖ad8 (82)

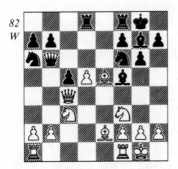

Alternatives are **13 ... ♖fe8** and **13 ... ♘e8**, but taking the b-pawn is risky; after **13 ... ♛xb2 14 ♘e4 ♛b6 15 ♘d6**, or **15 ♝xf6 ♝xf6 16 ♖ab1**, Black is in great danger. On the other hand, in Ivanchuk–Lputian, Irkutsk 1986, White played the mistaken **15**

♖ab1? ♘b4 16 ♗xf6, and now with 16 ... ♗xe4! 17 ♗xg7 (17 ♗e7 ♗xd5!) 17 ... ♗xb1 18 ♗xf8 ♗xa2 19 ♕xc5 ♖xf8, Black could have achieved a winning position.

14 ♖fd1

Perhaps 14 ♖ad1 was more exact.

14 ... ♖fe8

Against Lputian (this is the last in the trio of examples), Gavrikov played 14 ... ♘e8 15 ♘e4 ♕a5 16 ♗xg7 ♔xg7 17 ♖ac1 ♘d6 18 ♕b3 (it was better to play at once 18 ♕c3+ ♕xc3 19 ♘xc3, with equality) 18 ... ♗d7 19 ♕c3+ ♕xc3 20 ♘xc3, and now after the retreat of the knight to b8 or c7 Black would not be threatened with anything. Instead he continued with 20 ... ♖fe8?, when 21 ♗xa6 enabled White to obtain a big endgame advantage.

15 ♕h4

The immediate 15 b3 is more accurate.

15 ... ♘d7 16 ♗xg7 ♔xg7 17 b3 ♕a5 18 ♖ac1 ♘f6

Black has no problem whatsoever, and after **19 ♗b5 ♗d7 20 ♗xa6 ♕xa6 21 ♘d2 h6 22 ♕c4 ♕a5 23 f3 ♕b4 24 ♘de4 ♕xc4 25 bc ♘xe4 26 ♘xe4 b6 27 ♔f2 f5 28 ♘c3 f4 29 g3** the players agreed a draw.

After these three games by Gavrikov, the impression was formed that in the 12 ... ♕b6 line White has no particular prospects of gaining the initiative. An attempt to refute this opinion was undertaken in the game Vladimirov–Popović, Moscow 1989, which made a substantial contribution to theory. From diagram 82, play went: **14 d6!** ♕b4 (Black goes into a sharp endgame; 14 ... ♕xb2 loses to 15 ♘d5) 15 ♖ad1 ♕xc4 16 ♗xc4 ♘b4 (this game has been thoroughly annotated by the winner and by Grandmaster Makarichev and International Master N. Andrianov. I shall quote some of the interesting variations they give. At this point, Black could perhaps have got off with a slight scare by continuing 16 ... ♘e4 17 ♗xg7 ♔xg7 18 ♘xe4 ♗xe4 19 ♖fe1 ♗xf3 20 gf) 17 h3! (not prophylaxis, but preparation for an attack) 17 ... a6 (it is now too late for 17 ... ♘e4, in view of 18 g4! ♘xc3 19 bc ♗e4 20 ♗xg7, and White wins) 18 a3 ♘c6 19 g4 ♗d7 (19 ... ♗e6 is worse: 20 ♗xe6 fe 21 ♖fe1 ♘xg4 22 hg ♖xf3 23 ♗xg7 ♔xg7 24 ♘e4 ♖f4 25 ♘xc5 ♖xg4+ 26 ♔f1, with a solid advantage to White) 20 ♖fe1 b5 21 ♗d5! (Black has all the time been refraining from ... ♘c6xe5 in view of the dangerous pressure against f7. But his attempt to drive the bishop off its diagonal or block it in with 21 ♗a2 c4 does not succeed. White is prepared to exchange this bishop only if it can be replaced on its active square by a knight) 21 ... ♘xe5 (21 ... b4 would be answered by 22 ab cb 23 ♗xf6 ♗xf6 24 ♘a4 and 25 ♘c5, but 21 ... ♖fe8! was stronger) 22 ♘xe5 b4 23 ♘xd7! (the point of White's plan lies in the variation 23 ... ♖xd7 24 ♘a4 ♖fd8 25 ♘xc5 ♖xd6 26 ♘b7 ♘xd5 27 ♘xd8 ♖xd8 28 ♖d3 ♗xb2 29 ab followed by ♖ed1, winning. However, after 24 ... ♘xd5! 25 ♖xd5 ♖fd8 26 ♘xc5 ♖xd6 27 ♖xd6 ♖xd6 28 ♖e8+ ♗f8 29 ab ♔g7, Black would have every chance of holding on) 23 ... ♘xd7? (now Black has no counterplay at all) 24 ab cb 25 ♘a4 ♗f6 26 ♖e4 a5 27 ♗c6 ♘e5 28 ♗b5 ♖b8 29 ♖d5 (Black's extra pawn on the queenside has no significance and White wins the ending, creating quite a good textbook example in the process.) 29 ... ♘f3+ 30 ♔g2 ♘g5 31 ♖c4 ♘e6 32 d7 g5 33 ♔f1 ♔g7 34 ♗c6 ♗d8 35 ♖f5 b3 (35 ... f6 was more tenacious) 36 ♗d5 ♘f4 37 ♖c8 ♗f6 38 ♖xf8 ♖xf8 39 ♗xb3 ♖d8 40 ♘c5 ♖b8 41 ♘e4 ♗xb2 42 ♖xf7+ ♔g6 43 ♘d6 1–0.

Returning to diagram 81, we observe that the Odessa grandmaster excluded himself from the debate on the variation 12 ... ♕b6 13 ♗e5, and instead employed a very valuable novelty, which, it appears, he had prepared specially for this USSR Championship.

12   ...   ♘d7! (83)

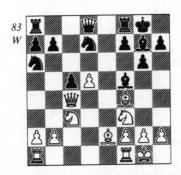

By this means (the rook on f8 and queen on d8 are both left where they are for now), Tukmakov succeeds in drawing his opponent into a tactical whirlpool.

13 d6

Although this advance fits into White's plans, in the present situation it is rather committal. It was worth considering 13 ♗g5, or 13 ♖fd1 ♘b6 14 ♕b3 ♘b4 15 ♖d2!

13	...	♘b6
14	♕b3	♘b4
15	♖ac1	

Perhaps the queen should have returned home with 15 ♕d1.

15	...	♗e6

Black has many possibilities – 15 ... a5, 15 ... ♘d3, 15 ... ♗d3 – but the move played is not bad either.

16 ♕a3

Again it was safer for the queen to return to its own camp: 16 ♕d1 ♘6d5 (16 ... ♗xc3 17 bc ♘xa2 18 ♖c2 ♘a4 19 ♕d2) 17 ♘xd5 ♘xd5 18 ♗g3 ♗xb2 19 ♖xc5 ♘c3 20 ♕c2 ♘xe2+ 21 ♕xe2 ♗a3 22 ♖c3 ♗b4 23 ♖c2, and White's chances are a little better (Tukmakov).

16	...	♘c4
17	♗xc4	♗xc4
18	♖fd1	b6

White's hope of 18 ... ♘d3 19 ♖xd3 ♗xd3 20 ♕xc5 is disappointed.

19 ♘e4

Here again, White had to play 19 ♕a4 a6 20 ♖d2, and then ♕a4–d1. It is becoming clear that the white queen is out of the action.

19	...	♗d5!
20	♘fg5	

Black also has a big advantage after 20 ♘c3 ♗xf3 21 gf ♕f6 22 ♗g3 ♕xf3 23 ♘d5 ♕xa3 24 ba ♘c6! 25 ♘e7+ ♘xe7 26 de ♖fe8 27 ♖d7 ♗d4. Now after 20 ... h6, White is counting on bringing his queen across to h3 (21 ♕h3 ♖e8! 22 d7 ♖e7).

20	...	♕d7! *(84)*

After this cool rejoinder, White's pieces turn out to be most precariously placed.

21 ♗d2

Against the piece sacrifice 21 ♘xc5 bc 22 ♖xc5, Black has the decisive 22 ... ♕b7!, since 23 ♖cxd5 ♘xd5 24 ♕f3 fails to 24 ... ♕b4!

21	...	♘xa2

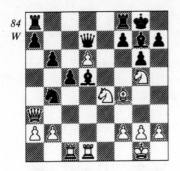

84
W

22	♖a1	h6
23	♘c3	♘xc3
24	♗xc3	♗xg2
25	♗xg7	♔xg7
26	♔xg2	hg

As well as two extra pawns Black has the better position, as the d-pawn presents no threat.

27	♕g3	♖fe8

Black could also calmly play 27 ... g4.

28	♕xg5	♖e4
29	h3	♖ae8
30	♖a3	♖8e5

30 ... a5 is simpler.

31	♕g3	♖e8
32	♖f3	a5
33	♖d5	♖4e6
34	♖f4	

This loses at once – the f7 point is invulnerable, and Black wins the d-pawn. 34 h4 was more stubborn.

34	...	♖d8!
35	♕b3	♕c6
36	♕f3	♖d7
37	♔g1	♖exd6

0–1

Game No. 19
Bareyev–Lputian
Lvov 1990

1 d4 ♘f6 2 c4 g6 3 ♘c3 d5 4 ♘f3 ♗g7 5 ♕b3 dc 6 ♕xc4 0–0 7 e4 ♘a6 8 ♗e2 c5 9 d5 e6 10 0–0 ed 11 ed ♗f5

12 ♗e3

The alternatives 12 ♗f4 and 12 ♖d1 were explained in the context of Game No. 17.

12 ♗g5 is also occasionally seen. An old game Brinck-Claussen–Jakobsen, Denmark 1970, continued 12 ... h6 13 ♗xf6 ♕xf6 14 ♖ad1 ♖ad8 15 ♗d3 ♖fe8 16 ♗xf5 ♕xf5, and White had no more than a minimal plus.

12 ... ♖e8 *(85)*

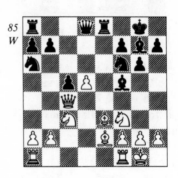

85
W

13 ♖ac1

The alternative is **13 ♖ad1**; let us look at a few interesting examples.

A game Ree–de Boer, played some time ago (Amsterdam 1983), went **13 ... ♘e4** 14 ♘xe4 ♖xe4 15 ♕c1 ♘b4 16 a3 ♘c2 17 ♗g5 f6 18 ♕xc2 fg 19 ♗d3 ♖f4 20 ♕xc5 g4 21 ♕e3, and White gained a clear advantage. An improvement is 15 ... ♕b6 16 b3 ♖ee8 17 ♘d2 ♘b4 18 ♘c4, with a minimal plus for White.

Farago–Kozul, Montpellier 1989, went **13 ... ♕b6** 14 b3 ♖xe3!? (14 ... ♕b4 leads to unclear play. In Ree–Chandler, Helsinki 1984, Black ended up in a difficult position after 14 ... ♘g4 15 ♗d2 ♖ad8 16 ♖fe1 ♘b4 17 ♘a4 ♕d6 18 ♗f4! ♕f8 19 ♗c7 ♖d7 20 d6. Black also stands worse after 14 ... ♘e4 15 ♘xe4 ♖xe4 16 ♕b5) 15 fe ♘g4 16 ♘a4 ♕d6 (16 ... ♕a5 17 e4 ♘e3 18 ♕d3 ♘xd1 19 ef ♘c3 20 ♘xc3 is in White's favour) 17 ♕f4! (better than 17 e4? ♗d7 18 ♕c1 b5 19 ♘b2 ♘b4, with sufficient compensation for the exchange, for example: 20 ♘d3 ♗d4+ 21 ♔h1 ♘xa2, with advantage to Black) 17 ... ♕xf4 18 ef ♘b4! (but not 18 ... ♘e3, in view of 19 ♗xa6 ba 20 ♘xc5) 19 ♖d2 ♘e3 20 ♖c1 ♘bxd5

21 ♗d3 ♘xf4 22 ♗xf5 ♘xf5 23 ♘xc5 ♗h6 24 ♖e1, and the sharp play eventually led to a peaceful conclusion.

In another game, the Yugoslav grandmaster Kozul played the white side, and had to contend with the novelty **13 ... h6**. There followed 14 h3 ♖c8 (better than 14 ... ♕b6 15 b3 ♕b4 16 ♘a4, or 14 ... ♘e4 15 ♘xe4 ♖xe4 16 ♕c1, hitting c5 and h6) 15 ♖d2 (15 ♕b3! is stronger) 15 ... ♘e4 16 ♘xe4 ♖xe4 17 ♕c1 c4! 18 ♘d4 ♗d7 19 ♘e6!? fe 20 de ♖xe6 21 ♗xc4 ♕e8 22 ♖fd1 ♗b5? (22 ... ♖xc4! is correct; Kozul gives the variation 25 ♕xc4 ♗b5 24 ♕b3 ♗a4 25 ♕xb7 ♗xd1 26 ♖xd1 ♖xe3! 27 fe ♕xe3+ 28 ♔h1 ♘c5 29 ♕xa7 ♔h7 30 ♖f1 ♕e2 31 ♖f7 ♕e1+, with a draw) 23 ♗xe6+ ♕xe6 24 ♕xc8+ ♕xc8 25 ♖d8+ ♕xd8 26 ♖xd8+ ♔f7 27 b3 ♘b4 28 a4 ♗c6 29 ♗xa7, and White won the ending; Kozul–Popović, Yugoslavia 1989.

Van der Sterren–Mirallès, Lyon 1990, went **13 ... ♖c8** (again Black innovates – this time successfully) 14 h3 ♘b4 15 ♘e1 ♘e4 16 ♘xe4 (better is 16 a3 ♘xc3 17 bc ♘c2 18 ♘xc2 ♗xc2 19 ♖d2 ♗e4, with unclear play – Mirallès) 16 ... ♖xe4 17 ♕b3 a5! 18 g4 ♗d7 19 ♖c1 a4 20 ♕d1 a3! 21 ba ♘xa2 22 ♗d3 ♖xe3 23 fe ♘xc1 24 ♕xc1 c4 25 ♗c2 (Black also has the advantage after 25 ♗e4 ♕e7 26 ♗f3 ♗h6 27 ♘c2 c3. Now the c-pawn settles matters) 25 ... ♕g5 26 ♕d2 c3 27 ♕d3 ♖c5 28 ♗b3 c2! etc.

13 ... ♘e4

The immediate 13 ... ♕b6 deserves attention.

14 ♕b3

Another possibility is 14 ♖fd1 ♘d6 (14 ... ♕b6 15 ♘a4) 15 ♕f4, with complex play.

14 ... ♕b6!
15 ♗b5

A level game results from **15 ♖fd1** ♕xb3 16 ab ♖ad8 17 ♘xe4 ♗xe4 18 ♗xa6 ba 19 ♖xc5. The chances are approximately equal after **15 ♗xa6** ba 16 ♘xe4 ♗xe4 17 ♖xc5 ♕xb3 18 ab ♗xb2.

15 ... ♖ed8
16 ♘h4 (86)

Rather a risky move; 16 ♖fd1, defending the central pawn, was safer.

16 ... ♘xc3
17 bc ♗e4
18 c4 ♘c7

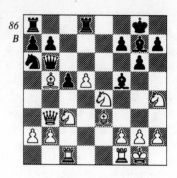

86
B

| 19 | ♗a4 | ♕f6! |

The awkward position of the knight on the edge of the board makes itself felt.

| 20 | ♘f3 |

Not 20 f3, on account of 20 ... ♗xd5!

20	...	♗xf3
21	gf	b6
22	♗d2

22 ♔g2 ♕h4, followed by ... ♗e5, is bad for White.

| 22 | ... | ♘e6?! |

This looks pretty, but now White extricates himself from a tricky situation. His defence would have been more difficult after 22 ... ♘e8! 23 ♗xe8 (otherwise 23 ... ♘d6) 23 ... ♖xe8 24 ♖fe1 ♕h4.

23	de	♖xd2
24	♕e3!	♖d6
25	♕e4	♖b8
26	ef+	♔xf7
27	♖cd1	♕g5+
28	♕g4!

More exact than 28 ♔h1 ♗d4 29 ♗c6 ♔g7 30 ♗d5 ♖f8. A level endgame now arises.

28 ... ♕xg4+ 29 fg ♖bd8 30 ♖xd6 ♖xd6 31 ♖d1 ♖xd1+ 32 ♗xd1 g5 33 ♔g2 ♔e6 34 ♔f3 ♗d4 35 ♔e4 ♗xf2 36 h3 ½–½.

5 4 ♗f4 System

Game No. 20
Lukacs–Ftačnik
Stara Zagora 1990

The reader will no doubt recall that for the eleventh game of the return World Championship Match in 1986, a brilliancy prize was awarded – to both players. Indeed, that game was one of the most fascinating played with the Grünfeld in recent years. We shall, of course, examine it here (in addition to other important games with the same variation) in the notes to the principal game.

1	d4	♘f6
2	c4	g6
3	♘c3	d5
4	♗f4	

Theory sometimes refers to this variation as the Classical Line.

4	...	♗g7
5	e3	c5

This system was used in the first game of the 1986 match, but with a different move-order (e2–e3 was postponed for three moves): 4 ♘f3 ♗g7 5 ♗f4 c5 6 dc ♕a5 7 ♖c1 (previously, 7 cd had been played; Kasparov responds to the novelty very precisely) 7 ... dc! 8 e3 ♕xc5 9 ♕a4+ ♘c6 10 ♗xc4 0–0 11 0–0 ♗d7 12 ♕b5 ♕xb5 13 ♗xb5 ♖ac8 14 ♖fd1 ♖fd8 15 h3 h6 16 ♔f1 a6 17 ♗e2 ♗e6 18 ♖xd8+ ♖xd8 19 ♘e5 ♘xe5 20 ♗xe5 ♖d2 ½–½.

| 6 | dc | |

Winning a pawn with 6 ♗xb8 ♖xb8 7 ♕a4+ ♗d7 8 ♕xa7 is too risky: 8 ... cd 9 ♕xd4 0–0 10 cd ♕a5 11 ♕d2 b5! 12 ♗d3 b4 13 ♘ce2 ♕xd5.

6	...	♕a5
7	♖c1	*(87)*

87
B

Here too, the pursuit of material gains brings trouble: 7 cd
♘xd5 8 ♕xd5 ♗xc3+ 9 bc ♕xc3+ 10 ♔e2 ♕xa1 11 ♗e5 ♕b1
12 ♗xh8 ♗e6 13 ♕d3 ♕xa2+, with a very strong initiative for
Black.

Instead, Timman–Kasparov, Belfort 1988, continued as follows:
7 ♕a4+ ♕xa4 8 ♘xa4 0-0!?

After 8 ... ♘e4 9 ♗xb8 ♗d7 10 f3 ♗xa4, the game is level.
But Kasparov is capable of finding new ideas even in seemingly
peaceful positions.

9 ♘f3

Salov–Korchnoi, Brussels 1988, went 9 ♖c1 ♗d7 10 ♘c3 dc
11 ♗xc4 ♘a6 12 ♘f3 ♘xc5 13 ♔e2 ♖ac8 14 ♗e5 a6 15 a3 ♘a4
16 ♘xa4 ♗xa4 17 ♘d4 ♘e4 18 ♗xg7 ♔xg7 ½-½.

9 ... ♘e4 10 ♗e5 ♗d7 11 ♘c3 ♘xc3 12 bc dc 13 ♗xc4 ♖c8
14 ♗d4 (88)

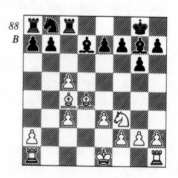

88
B

An improvement. In an earlier game between the same
opponents (Amsterdam 1988), White played the ineffective 14

♗d5? ♗c6 15 ♗xc6 ♖xc6 (15 ... ♘xc6! 16 ♗xg7 ♔xg7 17
0–0–0 ♘d8 18 ♖f8 19 ♖hd1 ♔e8 20 ♖7d5 ♘e6 would, in
Kasparov's view, have given Black a plus) 16 ♗xg7 ♔xg7 17
♖b1 ♖c7 18 ♘d4 ♘a6 19 c6 b6 20 f4 ♘b8 21 ♖b4 ♘xc6 22 ♖c4
♖ac8 23 ♘b5 ♖d7 24 ♘d4 ♖dc7 ½–½.

*14 ... e5! 15 ♗xe5 ♖xc5 16 ♗xg7 ♔xg7 17 ♗b3 ♖xc3 18
0–0*

White could have kept the game equal with 18 ♔d2 or 18 ♖d1.
Now Black seizes the initiative.

*18 ... ♘a6! 19 ♘e5 ♗e8 20 ♗d5 ♖c7 21 ♖ab1 ♘c5 22 e4
♖d8 23 ♖fc1 ♖dc8 24 g4 f6 25 ♘f3 b6 26 ♘d4 ♗d7 27 f3 ♘d3!
28 ♖xc7 ♖xc7 29 ♖d1 ♘f4 30 ♔f2 ♔f8 31 ♗b3 ♔e7 32 ♘e2
♘xe2 33 ♔xe2 ♖c3*

Black has an obvious endgame plus, and he quickly converts it
to a win.

*34 h4 h6 35 e5? ♗b5+ 36 ♔f2 fe 37 ♖d5 ♖c5 38 ♖xc5 bc 39
g5 hg 40 hg ♗d3 41 ♗g8 ♗f5 42 ♗b3 ♗e6 43 ♗c2 ♗xa2 44
♗xg6 a5 45 ♔e3 a4 0–1.*

7	**...**	**dc**
8	**♗xc4**	**0–0**
9	**♘f3**	**♕xc5**
10	**♗b3**	

10 ♘b5 will be mentioned in the notes to Game No. 21.

10	**...**	**♘c6**

Game 21 also introduces the idea of playing the knight to a6.

11	**0–0**	**♕a5** *(89)*

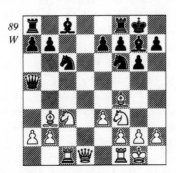

I should explain that the specific game which we are examining
reached the diagram position by way of 7 ♘f3 0–0 8 ♖c1 dc 9
♗xc4 ♕xc5 10 ♗b3 ♕a5 11 0–0 ♘c6. For convenience in the

layout of material, I have given the opening moves in a different order.

12   h3   ♗f5

12 ... ♕a6!? is also interesting. It was first played by Mecking against Ribli in Manila 1976. The idea is familiar – Black tries to exploit the weakness of the d3-square in the White camp. If **13 ♘d4**, Black should not play **13 ... ♖d8 14 ♗c7 ♖d7 15 ♗xf7+ ♔xf7 16 ♕b3+ ♔e8 17 ♘e6!** with the unanswerable threats of ♘c5 and ♘xg7+. In Farago–Gavrikov, Amsterdam 1987, Black replied correctly with **13 ... ♗d7**, and after **14 ♘db5** a draw was agreed; in the event of **14 ... ♖ac8**, the position is completely equal.

Another possibility (after 12 ... ♕a6) is **13 ♘a4 ♖d8 14 ♘c5 ♖xd1 15 ♘xa6 ♖xf1+ 16 ♔xf1 ♗f5 17 ♘c5**. In a game Schneider–Itkis, USSR 1987, White gained a big advantage after 17 ... b6? 18 g4! ♗c8 19 ♘e6!, but a new move 17 ... ♘a5! was played in Mikhalchishin–Gavrikov, Lvov 1987. There followed 18 ♗c2 ♗xc2 19 ♖xc2 ♘d5 20 ♗e5 ♘b4 21 ♖c3 b6 22 ♗xg7 ♔xg7 23 ♘d3 ♘xd3 24 ♖xd3 ½-½.

Finally, there is a third option for White: **13 ♘e5 ♘xe5 14 ♗xe5 ♗e6 15 ♗xe6 ♕xe6 16 ♗d4** (16 ♗h2 ♖ac8 17 ♕a4 a6 18 ♕a5 ♘e4 is good for Black; Sinkovics–Krasenkov, Budapest 1988) 16 ... ♖fc8 17 ♕f3 ♕c6 18 ♕xc6 ♖xc6 19 ♘b5 ♖xc1 20 ♖xc1 a6, with an equal game; Levitt–Gulko, St John 1988.

13   ♕e2

The ninth game of the 1986 match went **13 ♘d4 ♗d7 14 ♕e2 ♘xd4 15 ed e6 16 ♗d2 ♕b6**, resulting in equal chances. Another four moves – 17 ♖fd1 ♗c6 18 ♗e3 ♕a5 19 ♗d2 ♕b6 20 ♗e3 ♕a5 – and we agreed a draw.

An attempt at strengthening White's play was made in Petursson–Ivanchuk, Reggio Emilia 1989/90:

16 ♗e5 ♗c6 17 ♖fd1 ♖fd8 18 ♕e3 ♖d7 19 ♕g5

It is worth considering the sharp **19 d5 ♗xd5 20 ♗xf6 ♗xf6 21 ♘xd5 ed 22 ♕f3 ♗xb2 23 ♖xd5!** Ivanchuk examines two alternatives for Black: **19 ... ed 20 ♕d4 ♘e8 21 ♗xg7 ♘xg7 22 ♗xd5 ♖ad8 23 ♕e5 ♗xd5 24 ♖xd5 ♖xd5 25 ♘xd5**, and **19 ... ♘xd5 20 ♗xd5 ♗xd5 21 ♗xg7 ♔xg7 22 ♘e4! ♖e8 23 ♕f4 ♕d8 24 ♘c5 ♖de7** (but not 24 ... e5? 25 ♕d2 ♖d6 26 ♘xb7 ♗xb7 27 ♕xd6 ♕g5 28 f3! ♗xf3 29 ♕d2, with advantage to White) **25 ♘e4 ♖d7** – with equality in both cases.

19 ... ♕d8 20 ♘a4 h6 21 ♕g3 ♘h5 22 ♕e3 ♕h4 23 ♘c5 ♗xe5 24 de

The correct line was 24 ♕xe5 ♖e7 25 ♘xe6!? ♗xg2 26 ♔xg2 fe 27 ♗xe6+ ♔h7 28 ♖c7 ♘f4+ 29 ♔f1 ♖ae8 30 d5 ♘xh3 31 ♕g3 ♕xg3 32 ♖xe7+ ♖xe7 33 fg ♘g5, although Black's chances would still have been slightly better.

24 ... ♖xd1+ 25 ♗xd1 ♘f4 26 g3 ♕xh3 27 ♗f3 ♘d5

And Black went on to win.

13	...	♘e4
14	♘d5	e5 *(90)*

In Rizhkov–Epishin, Leningrad 1986, Black played 14 ... ♘c5 at once, which led to equality after 15 ♗c4 e6 16 b4 ♕a3 17 ♘e7+ ♘xe7 18 bc ♗e4.

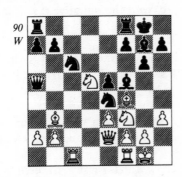

90
W

In the 'main' game which we are examining, the white queen's bishop calmly retreats to h2 – the familiar theoretical continuation. In the 'sensational' encounter in London (19th game, 1986), I played the unexpected 15 ♖xc6!? In the digression which now follows, we shall examine that game as well as the current theoretical verdict on White's exchange sacrifice.

15 ♖xc6 ef

So Kasparov decides to decline the sacrifice. Many commentators thought that accepting it would virtually lose outright: **15 ... bc 16 ♘e7+ ♔h8 17 ♘xe5 ♗xe5 18 ♘xc6**, but now after 18 ... ♕d2! 19 ♗xe5+ f6 it is White who suffers material loss. I was intending **17 ♘xc6**, and if **17 ... ♕b6** (17 ... ♕c5 18 ♘cxe5 ♕e7 19 ♘d4), then **18 ♘cxe5**. After **18 ... ♗e6**, White has three choices: **19 ♗xe6 ♕xe6 20 b3**, with two pawns for the exchange; **19 ♘c4**

♗xc4 20 ♗xc4 ♘c5, with unclear play; or **19 ♕c2 ♗xb3 20
♕xe4 ♗e6**, as in Gavrikov–Kochiev, Tallinn 1987.

16 ♖c7 ♗e6

If 16 ... fe 17 ♕xe3 ♗xb2, then 18 ♘d4 is strong; or if 17 ...
♘d6, White has 18 ♖d1, with mounting pressure.

17 ♕e1!

The natural-seeming **17 ♖xb7 ♗xd5** 18 ♖b5 would give Black
the better game after either 18 ... ♕a6 19 ♗xd5 ♖ae8 or 18 ...
♘c3 19 bc ♗xf3 20 gf ♕xc3. In a later game Szilágyi–Schmidt,
Hungary 1986, Black played the even stronger **17 ... ♘d6!**
(depriving the rook of the b5-square) 18 ♘e7+ ♔h8 19 ♘c6 ♕c5
20 ♗xe6 ♕xc6, and White came out a piece down.

The queen move to e1 was planned in my pre-game analysis,
but later it was established that **17 ♘e7+** is stronger: **17 ... ♔h8**
18 ♖fc1 ♗xb3 19 ab, with the initiative (19 ... fe 20 ♕xe3 ♘d6
21 ♕f4).

17 ... ♕b5!

The endgame after 17 ... ♕xe1 18 ♖xe1 ♗xb2 19 ♘e7+ ♔h8
20 ♗xe6 fe 21 ef ♖xf4 22 ♖xb7 ♗c3 23 ♖e2 is unattractive for
Black.

18 ♘e7+ ♔h8 19 ♗xe6 fe 20 ♕b1!

The white queen has made an unusual tour, ♕d1–e2–e1–b1,
and now unexpectedly aims at the opponent's kingside.

20 ... ♘g5!

The only move. 20 ... ♕b6 is simply answered by 21 ♖fc1, while
if the knight goes anywhere else, 21 ♘xg6+ is decisive.

21 ♘h4! (91)

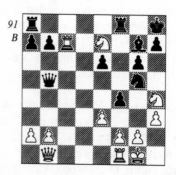

After 21 ♘xg5 (21 ♘d4 ♕e5) 21 ... ♕xg5 22 ef ♖xf4 23 ♖xb7
♖e8 24 ♘c6 ♕c5 25 ♘xa7 ♗d4, Black is dangerously active.

21 ... ♘xh3+!?

In this extremely sharp duel, each of us was hoping to outwit the other. No doubt for that reason, Kasparov refrains from 21 ... fe, after which I could have forced a draw with 22 ♘hxg6+ hg 23 ♘xg6+ ♔g8 24 ♘e7+.

22 ♔h2

Of course not 22 gh ♕g5+ 23 ♘g2 f3.

22 ... ♕h5?

A serious error. 22 ... ♘xf2! 23 ♖xf2 fe 24 ♖xf8+ ♖xf8 25 ♔h3 e2 26 ♕e4 ♕h5! 27 ♖c4 g5 28 ♕xe6 gh leads to a draw.

23 ♘exg6+

If **23 ♔xh3**, Black replies 23 ... g5.

Many observers thought that capturing with the other knight was stronger: **23 ♘hxg6+ hg 24 ♕xg6**. As we shall see, this variation is indeed unpleasant for Black, but it happens to be unimportant which knight takes on g6 first.

23 ... hg 24 ♕xg6

An inaccuracy throwing away the win! **24 ♘xg6+ ♔g8 25 ♘e7+ ♔h8 26 ♕g6!** (rejecting the perpetual check with 26 ♘g6+) would have given White a clear advantage; this is the same position that was arrived at in the previous note. I shall now quote the interesting variations given by Halifman: **26 ... ♕e5** (26 ... ♖f5 is met by 27 gh fe 28 ♕xh5+ ♖xh5 29 ♘g6+ ♔h7 30 fe!) 27 ♔xh3 fe (27 ... ♖f6 28 ♔g4!) 28 ♕g4! ♖f6 29 ♕h4+ ♗h6 30 f4! ♕xb2 31 ♖b1!, etc.; a more stubborn defence is **26 ... ♕h7**, but here again, after 27 gh ♖f6 (27 ... ♗e5 28 ♖c5!; or 27 ... fe 28 ♕xe6 ♖f6 29 ♕xe3 with two extra pawns) 28 ♕g4 (28 ♕xh7+ ♔xh7 29 ♖g1 is also good), Black is in a critical position since taking on e3 is no good: 28 ... fe 29 fe! ♖xf1 30 ♘g6+ ♔g8 31 ♕xe6+ ♖f7 32 ♕xf7 mate.

24 ... ♕e5!

An ingenious retort which gets Black out of danger. White cannot now play 25 ♔xh3, as the rook on c7 is *en prise* (whereas with the knight on e7, the capture 25 ... ♕xc7 would be unplayable: 26 ♕h5+ and mates).

25 ♖f7

Not **25 ♖xg7** fe+ 26 f4 ♕xg7 27 ♕h5+ ♔g8 28 gh ♕xb2+ 29 ♔h1 ♖f7!, or 26 ♕g3 ♕xg7 27 ♘g6+ ♔g8 28 ♘xf8 ♘g5! 29 ♘d7 ♖d8 30 ♘e5 e2 31 ♖e1 ♖d1 32 ♘d3 ♕h7+ 33 ♔g1 ♕xd3 34 ♕xg5+ ♔f7 etc. On the other hand, **25 ♕c2** would have forced a draw: 25 ... fe+ 26 ♔xh3 ♔g8 27 f4 e2 28 fe ef(♛ 29 ♖xg7+ ♔xg7 30 ♛g6+ etc.

25 ... ♖xf7! 26 ♛xf7 ♘g5!

After the game I discovered that the computer had indicated 26 ... ♛b5 here, but there would follow 27 ♘g6+ ♔h7 28 ♘e7 ♛e8 29 ♛xe6 ♘g5 30 ♛f5+ ♔h6 31 ♖h1! and in spite of his extra peice Black has no defence.

27 ♘g6+ ♔h7 28 ♘xe5 ♘xf7 29 ♘xf7 ♔g6 30 ♘d6 fe

The position has become simplified, the tension has abated, and Black has even emerged with a slight edge, though its significance is purely symbolic.

31 ♘c4 ef 32 ♖xf2 b5 33 ♘e3 a5 34 ♔g3 a4 35 ♖c2 ♖f8 36 ♔g4 ♗d4 37 ♖e2 ♗xe3 38 ♖xe3 ♖f2 39 b3 ♖xg2+ 40 ♔f3 ♖xa2 41 ba ½–½.

15   ♗h2   ♘c5

15 ... ♘f6 is very strongly answered by 16 ♖xc6! ♘xd5 17 ♖d6 ♘e7 18 e4, with a clear advantage; Pinter–Rogers, Szirak 1986. But a more popular continuation is **15 ... ♗e6 16 ♖fd1** *(92)*. Let us look at some interesting games with this line from recent years.

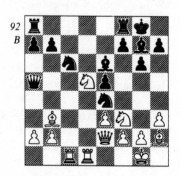

Farago–Smejkal, Baden-Baden 1985, went **16 ... ♔h8** 17 ♗c4 ♖ad8 18 b4 ♘xb4 19 ♘xb4 ♖xd1+ 20 ♖xd1 ♛xb4 21 ♗xe5, with a slight advantage to White.

Gleizerov–Vakhidov, Uzhgorod 1988, went **16 ... ♖fe8!?** 17 ♛c4 ♘f6 18 e4 ♖ac8 19 ♛c3 ♛xc3 20 ♘xf6+ ♗xf6 21 ♖xc3, and a draw was agreed.

Basin–Kozlov, Naberezhnie Chelny 1988, continued **16 ... ♖fd8** 17 ♛c4 (the exchanges with 17 ♛e1 ♖d7 18 ♛xa5 ♘xa5 19 ♘c7 ♘xb3 20 ♘xa8 ♘xc1 21 ♖xc1 f6 are to Black's liking; Rajna–

Nikoloff, St John 1988) 17 ... ♘d4? (the correct line is 17 ... ♘f6 18 e4 ♖ac8 19 ♘g5 ♘d4 20 ♘e7+ ♔f8 21 ♘xe6+ ♔xe7 22 ♘xd8 ♖xc4 23 ♗xc4 ♗h6, and Black's chances are no worse; Huzman–Dorfman, Lvov 1988) 18 ed ♗xd5 19 ♕e2 ♗h6 20 ♖c2 ♗f4 21 ♗xd5 ♕xd5 22 ♘xe5 ♗xe5 23 ♗xe5 ♘g5 24 ♕g4 ♘e6 25 ♕h4 g5 26 ♕h6 ♕e4 27 ♕f6 ♔f8 28 ♖cd2 ♕g6 29 d5 ♘c5 30 d6 1–0.

16 e4!?

An interesting novelty. After 16 ♗c4 ♖ad8? 17 b4! ♘xb4 18 ♘e7+ ♔h8 19 ♘xf5 gf 20 ♘xe5, White had a big advantage in Vainerman–Epishin, Norilsk 1987, but Black has the much better 16 ... e4!, with chances of seizing the initiative.

16 ...   ♖ad8! *(93)*

16 ... ♗xe4 loses to 17 ♖xc5 ♗xf3 18 ♕e3 ♗h6 19 ♕xh6. White also has the initiative after **16 ... ♗e6** 17 ♗c4, with a2–a3 to follow, or **16 ... ♘xb3** 17 ab ♗e6 18 ♖a1 ♕c5 19 ♖fc1 ♕d6 20 ♖d1 ♕b8 21 b4. But **16 ... ♘xe4!?** leads to sharp play.

93
W

17   ♕e3

An inaccuracy. In Ftačnik's view, an improvement is 17 ♖fd1 ♗xe4 18 ♖xc5 ♗xf3 19 ♕e3 ♗xd1 20 ♖xa5 ♗xb3 21 ab ♘xa5 22 ♘e7+ ♔h8 23 ♗xe5 ♘c6 24 ♗xg7+ ♔xg7 25 ♕c3+ f6 26 ♘xc6 bc 27 ♕xc6, with somewhat the better ending.

17	...	♘xb3
18	ab	♗xe4
19	♖c5	♕xc5
20	♕xc5	

20 ♘f6+ ♗xf6 21 ♕xc5 ♖d5 22 ♕e3 was more exact.

20	...	♖xd5
21	♕c4	♗xf3
22	gf	♖fd8
23	♗g3	♖d2
24	♕b5	♘d4
25	♕xb7	♘e2+

Black could have retained the better chances with 25 ... ♖xb2 26 ♕e7 ♖f8 27 ♕xa7 ♘xf3+ 28 ♔g2 ♖xb3.

26	♔g2	♘xg3
27	♔xg3	♗h6
28	♕xa7	♖xb2
29	♕b6	

The position has levelled out, and the game gradually heads towards a draw.

| 29 | ... | ♖d3 |
| 30 | ♖a1 | ♔g7! |

Precisely played. Not 30 ... e4? 31 ♕b8+ ♗f8 32 ♖a8 ♖xf3+ 33 ♔h4. Also 30 ... ♗f4+ 31 ♔g2 ♖dxb3 is dangerous in view of 32 ♖a8+ ♔g7 33 ♕d8, with an attack (Ftačnik).

31	♖a6	♗g5
32	♕c7	♗f4+
33	♔g2	♖d2
34	♕b6	

½–½

Game No. 21
Belyavsky–Gavrikov
Moscow 1988

1 d4 ♘f6 2 c4 g6 3 ♘c3 d5 4 ♗f4 ♗g7 5 e3 c5 6 dc ♕a5 7 ♖c1 dc

In the fifth game of the return World Championship Match, London 1986, Kasparov played 7 ... ♘e4 here. The game was quite interesting, so let us take this opportunity to give it in full:

7 ... ♘e4 8 cd ♘xc3 9 ♕d2 ♕xa2 10 bc

This variation came into use after the famous game Petrosian–Fischer, Candidates final 1971, which continued: **10 ... ♕a5 11 ♗c4 ♘d7 12 ♘e2 ♘e5 13 ♗a2 ♗f5 14 ♗xe5! ♗xe5 15 ♘d4 ♕xc5 16 ♘xf5 gf 17 0–0**, with a dangerous attack. Afterwards, various alternatives were proposed for Black; the most effective of them belongs to Mikhalchishin: **12 ... ♘xc5 13 0–0 0–0 14 f3** e5! 15 ♗g3 b5 16 ♗a2 ♕b6! 17 ♔h1 a5, with adequate counterplay.

Recently the investigations have switched to **12 ♘f3**, which so far has brought variable success. In Agzamov–Gulko, Frunze 1985, the interesting continuation was 12 ... ♘xc5 (12 ... 0–0 13 0–0 ♘xc5 14 ♗e5 ♗xe5 15 ♘xe5 f6 16 ♖a1 ♘e4 led to sharp play in Razuvayev–Mikhalchishin, Minsk 1985) 13 ♗e5 ♗xe5! (a game between the same opponents a few months earlier in Sochi had ended quickly with 13 ... 0–0 14 0–0 f6 15 ♖a1 ♕d8 16 ♗c7! ♕d7 17 d6+ e6 18 ♘d4 ♕f7 19 ♖a5 b6 20 ♖xc5! bc 21 ♘b3 ♕d7 22 ♕d3! ♖d8 23 ♕e4 1–0) 14 ♘xe5 f6 15 ♘f3 0–0 16 ♘d4 ♘e4 17 ♕b2 ♘d6 18 ♗a2 ♗d7 19 0–0 ♖ac8 20 e4! ♕c5 21 ♖fe1, with the initiative.

10 ... ♕xd2+ 11 ♔xd2 ♘d7 12 ♗b5

After 12 c6 bc 13 dc ♘b6 (or 13 ... ♘f6), White achieves nothing.

12 ... 0–0 13 ♗xd7

This time, 13 c6 would be met by 13 ... ♘c5. Now Black obtains the two bishops, but it soon becomes clear that they will both be constricted.

13 ... ♗xd7 14 e4 f5

The alternative 14 ... ♖ac8 is weaker: 15 ♗e3 f5 16 f3.

15 e5 e6!

A critical moment. The line that had previously been tested was 15 ... ♖ac8 16 c6 (16 e6 ♗a4 17 c4 ♖xc5 18 ♗e3 ♖c7 19 ♘f3 ♖fc8 20 ♔d3 b5! favours Black) 16 ... bc 17 d6 ed 18 ed ♖f6, with the advantage; Schmidt–Gross, Naleczow 1984. Why does Kasparov reject it? The answer is that after 15 ... ♖ac8 White has the much stronger 16 c4! ♖xc5 17 ♗e3. In Seirawan–Adorjan, New York 1987, there followed 17 ... ♖c7 (17 ... ♖a5 18 f4 e6 19 d6) 18 ♘f3 b6 19 c5 bc 20 ♖xc5 ♖xc5 21 ♗xc5 ♖c8 22 ♗xa7, and White won.

16 c4 ♖fc8

After 16 ... g5 17 ♗xg5 ♗xe5 18 ♘f3 ♗g7 19 ♖b1 and ♖he1, White would complete his development while maintaining powerful pressure.

17 c6!

The extra pawn cannot be retained, but in returning it White extracts the maximum profit: he creates a passed pawn and limits the scope of Black's rooks and light-squared bishop.

17 ... bc 18 d6 c5

Now the light-squared bishop acquires a little freedom, but the dark-squared one begins to suffocate. Perhaps the fate of the bishops should have been decided 'the other way round', with 18 ... g5 19 ♗xg5 ♗xe5 20 c5 ♖cb8, and Black has hopes of counterplay.

19 h4! h6 20 ♘h3! (94)

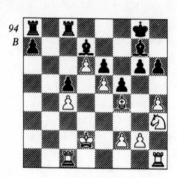

94
B

Kasparov must have been examining the more natural-seeming 20 ♘f3, which he could answer with 20 ... ♗c6!, leading to complex play with mutual chances. But I arrived at a solution to the position on mathematical lines. The white knight is heading for its ideal square, d3, by the only suitable route! Once the knight reaches its destination, the black bishop on g7 will be interned for good inside the cage formed by the pawns on d6 and e5 and the bishop on f4. At the present moment, White forestalls the freeing advance ... g6–g5.

20 ... a5 21 f3 a4 22 ♖he1!

Over-protecting the pawn on e5. The hasty 22 ♘f2 could be met by 22 ... g5! 23 hg hg 24 ♗h2 f4 25 ♘d3 ♗e8 26 ♗g1, when the situation is fairly obscure.

22 ... a3 23 ♘f2 a2 24 ♘d3 ♖a3 25 ♖a1 g5

The alternative 25 ... ♖b8 is inadequate on account of 26 ♖ec1 g5 27 hg hg 28 ♘xc5 (but not 28 ♗xg5 ♖bb3 29 ♘xc5 ♖b2+) 28 ... ♗a4 29 ♘xa4 ♖xa4 30 ♗xg5 ♗xe5 31 d7.

26 hg hg 27 ♗xg5 (95)

Now after 27 ... ♖b8, the contest could have ended in a study-like draw: 28 ♗f4 ♖bb3 29 ♘xc5 ♖b2+ 30 ♔c1 ♖xg2 31 ♗d2 ♗h6! 32 ♗xh6 ♖c3+ 33 ♔d1 ♖d3+! 34 ♘xd3 ♗a4+ 35 ♔c1 ♖c2+, with perpetual check. But there is quite a simple

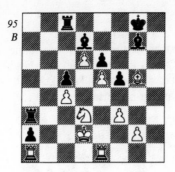

refutation of the 'study' in 28 ♔e2! ♖bb3 29 ♘xc5 ♖b2+ 30 ♔f1, and White wins.

27 ... ♔f7 28 ♗f4 ♖b8 29 ♖ec1 ♗c6 30 ♖c3 ♖a5 31 ♖c2 ♖ba8 32 ♘c1 1–0

8	♗xc4	0–0
9	♘f3	

A couple of years ago, when Black was achieving good results with this Grünfeld variation, the rare move 9 ♘e2 was tried out in a game Barlov–Gulko, New York 1988. There followed **9 ... ♕xc5 10 ♕b3 ♘c6 11 ♘b5 ♕h5 12 ♘c7**, and now after 12 ... ♕a5+ 13 ♕c3 ♕xc3+ 14 ♘xc3 Black equalised.

In *Informator 45*, Gulko considers **12 ... ♖b8**, and judges that White stands better on the basis of 13 ♗xf7+ ♖xf7 14 ♖xc6 ♕a5+ 15 ♘c3 ♘e4 16 ♘d5! e6 17 ♖c7. But this assessment was later refuted by Krasenkov in his game against Toth, Mazatlan 1988: 16 ... ♘xc3 17 ♘xc3 (17 ♖xc3 ♗xc3+ 18 bc ♗e6 19 ♗xb8 ♗xd5 20 ♕b2 ♗xg2 21 ♖g1 was more tenacious, although even then Black would be better) 17 ... bc 18 ♗xb8 (18 ♕xb8 ♗xc3+ 19 bc ♕xc3+ 20 ♔e2 ♕c4+ 21 ♔f3 ♕e6! 22 ♔e2 ♕xa2+, and White is in a bad way) 18 ... e6!, and in view of the threatened 19 ... ♖b7 and 20 ... ♖xb2, White loses his bishop on b8. A game Zlochevsky–Krasenkov varied with 17 ♘xe7+ ♔f8 18 ♖xc3 ♗xc3+ 19 bc ♖xf4! 20 ef ♔xe7 21 0–0 ♗e6 22 ♖e1 ♕b6, and White resigned after ten more moves.

A little later, Krasenkov ascertained that all these variations are redundant, as the simple 15 ... e5 (attacking the bishop and threatening 16 ... bc 17 ♕xb8 ♕xc7) settles matters at once. After 16 ♖xf6 ♗xf6 17 ♘d5 ef 18 ♘xf6+ ♔g7, White's position is completely hopeless.

9	...	♕xc5
10	♗b3	

10 ♘b5 looks like an active move, for example: **10 ... ♕b4+** 11 ♘d2 ♘a6 (11 ... ♘e4 is more precise) 12 a3 ♕a5 13 b4 ♕d8 14 ♗e5 with advantage; Huzman–Tseshkovsky, Tashkent 1987. However, Black has the powerful retort **10 ... ♗e6!** *(96)*.

96
W

11 ♘c7 (after this, Black seizes the initiative. Unclear play results from 11 ♗xe6 ♕xb5 12 ♗c4 ♕xb2 13 0–0; if 12 ♗b3, then 12 ... ♘e4) 11 ... ♗xc4 12 b3 (in Popchev–Lalić, Bosna 1988, White opted for 12 ♘d2, but after 12 ... b5 13 b3 ♘d5 14 ♘xa8 ♘c3 15 ♖xc3 ♗xc3 16 bc ♕xc4! 17 ♕e2 ♗xd2+ 18 ♕xd2 ♘c6 19 ♕e2 ♕b4+ his position was hopeless) 12 ... ♕a5+ 13 ♕d2 ♕xd2+ 14 ♘xd2 ♗d3 15 ♘xa8 ♘d5 16 ♘c7 ♖c8 17 ♘f3 ♘xf4 18 ef ♗b2 19 ♔d2 ♗xc1+ 20 ♖xc1 ♗e4 21 ♘b5 ♖xc1 22 ♔xc1 ♗xf3 23 gf ♘c6, and Black realised his advantage in the ending; Inkiov–Lputian, St John 1988.

10	...	♕a5
11	0–0	♘a6!?

A novel idea. The knight heads for c5, so as to eliminate the bishop on b3 in some variations. Instead, 11 ... ♘c6 12 h3 ♗f5 produces a position which we have already examined in Game No. 20. Gavrikov had introduced 11 ... ♘a6 a few months earlier, but in a less prominent tournament than the USSR Championship. Hence we have chosen Belyavsky–Gavrikov as the 'main' game.

12	♘e5

White utilises the fact that the e5-point is undefended. Stationing his knight there, he takes aim at f7. An equal game results from 12 ♗c4 (12 a3 ♗g4 13 h3 ♖ad8!) 12 ... ♘c5 13 a3 ♗e6 14

♗xe6 ♘xe6 15 ♗e5. In a later game Magerramov–Henkin,
Podolsk 1989, White played **12 ♕d4**, and there followed: 12 ...
♖d8 13 ♕e5 ♘d5 14 ♕g5 h6 15 ♕h4 ♘xf4 16 ef ♘c5 17 ♗c2
♗e6 (but not 17 ... e6? 18 b4, and White wins) 18 f5 gf 19 b4
♕c7? (a serious error; after 19 ... ♕a6! 20 bc ♗xc3 21 ♗xf5
♗g7! 22 ♗xe6 ♕xe6 23 ♖fe1, the game is about equal –
Magerramov. Now White obtains a strong attack) 20 bc ♗xc3
21 ♗xf5 ♗xf5 22 ♖xc3 ♔g7 23 ♖e1 ♖d7 24 ♖ce3 ♖ad8 25
♘e5 ♖d1 26 ♕g3+ ♗g6 27 h4 ♕a5 (more stubborn resistance
was offered by 27 ... ♖xe1+ 28 ♖xe1 h5 29 f4 ♕xc5+ 30 ♔h2
e6 31 ♘xg6 fg 32 ♖xe6) 28 ♖xd1 ♖xd1+ 29 ♔h2 ♕xc5 30 ♖f3!
(30 h5? ♕c1, and it is Black who wins) 30 ... ♔h8 31 ♘xg6+ fg
32 ♕b8+ 1–0.

12   ...   ♘c5 *(97)*

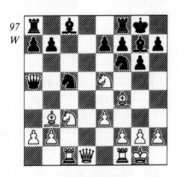

97
W

13   ♗xf7+!

From the material viewpoint this operation benefits Black, but
great complications now arise. A quieter move was 13 ♗c4.

13   ...   ♖xf7
14   ♘xf7   ♔xf7
15   b4!

The consistent follow-up to White's idea.

15   ...   ♕xb4
16   ♘d5   ♘xd5
17   ♕xd5+   ♘e6

Better than 17 ... ♗e6 18 ♕xc5 ♕xc5 19 ♖xc5 ♗xa2 20 ♗e5!
b6 21 ♖c2 ♗b3 22 ♖c3 ♗xe5 23 ♖xb3 a5 24 f4 ♗g7 25 ♖xb6
a4 26 ♖f2 a3 27 ♖a2 ♗b2, with advantage to White (Gavrikov).

18   ♖c4   ♕b2 *(98)*

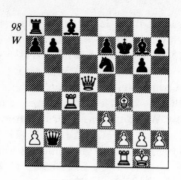

98
W

19 ♖fc1?

The black pieces are rather awkwardly placed, which compensates for White's material deficit. The position may be assessed as double-edged with approximately equal chances, for example: **19 ♖c7!** (threatening 20 ♕c4) **19 ... ♔f8 20 ♖xc8+ ♖xc8 21 ♕xe6 ♖c1 22 g4**, when the resulting situation is completely calm. **19 ♗g3** was also possible. The move played allows Black to extricate himself at once.

19 ... ♗d7!

The point is that after 20 ♕xd7 ♖d8 21 ♕a4 b5!, Black wins. If White had played 19 ♗g3, he could have answered 19 ... ♗d7 with 20 ♕xd7 ♖d8 21 ♖f4+. However, in that case Black has 19 ... ♗f6, and if 20 ♖fc1, only then 20 ... ♗d7!

20 h3

White loses not only after 20 ♕xd7, but also after 20 ♖4c2 ♗c6!

20 ... ♖d8

20 ... ♗c6 is even stronger; then 21 ♖xc6? bc 22 ♖xc6 fails to 22 ... ♕b1+ 23 ♔h2 ♕f5.

21 ♕a5

Interestingly enough, this very position arose in the first game that featured 11 ... ♘a6: Lukacs–Gavrikov, Debrecen 1988 (we come to it at last). In that game White chose a different queen move: 21 ♕f3, but after 21 ... ♔e8 22 ♖4c2 ♕b5 23 ♗g3 ♗c6 24 ♕g4 ♕f5 25 ♕b4 ♖d3 26 ♖c4 ♕d5 27 e4 ♕b5, he had to resign. Belyavsky presumably wasn't acquainted with that game; at any rate, the move he plays leads to the same result.

21 ... a6
22 ♗c7 ♖c8

23	♖4c2	♛b5
24	♛xb5	♗xb5
25	♗b6	♖c6
26	♖xc6	♗xc6

Black's endgame advantage is obvious, and he exploits it with no particular trouble – although it takes a full thirty moves.

27 f3 ♘f8 28 ♔f2 ♘d7 29 ♗a7 ♗e5 30 e4 ♗d6 31 ♔e3 e5 32 ♔d2 ♔e6 33 ♗e3 ♗e7 34 ♔c2 b6 35 ♔b2 ♔d6 36 ♖d1+ ♔c7 37 h4 a5 38 h5 g5 39 h6 ♘f8 40 ♗d2 ♘e6 41 ♗c3 ♗d6 42 ♔a1 ♘d4 43 ♔b1 ♘e2 44 ♗b2 b5 45 ♖d2 ♘f4 46 a3 ♘e6 47 ♗c3 b4

Slowly, but surely, Black accomplishes his task.

48 ab ab 49 ♖xd6 ♔xd6 50 ♗xb4+ ♔d7 51 ♔c2 ♘f4 52 g4 ♘e2 53 ♗c5 ♗b5 54 ♔d2 ♘f4 55 ♔e3 ♗e2 56 ♗b4 ♗d1 0–1

6 Fianchetto System

Game No. 22
Karpov–Timman
Candidates Final (2nd game)
Kuala Lumpur 1990

The King's Fianchetto System (g2–g3, ♗f1–g2) occurred twice in the London/Leningrad match and twice in Seville. The exchange in the centre (c4xd5 c6xd5) which took place in those games has recently become highly popular; it follows that this 'symmetrical variation' is worthy of close examination. In the present book I have included my three most recent games with it. Two of them were played in what may be considered the highest-calibre event in the interval between the last two contests for the world crown: my Candidates Final match with Jan Timman. In those two games I played White, yet in the third example I had the black pieces. With the large amount of supplementary material incorporated in the notes, what is offered here is the most up-to-date survey of the variation in question.

1	d4	♘f6
2	c4	g6
3	♘f3	♗g7
4	g3	c6

The advance ... d7–d5, which actually defines the Grünfeld Defence, is postponed by one move; in the event of an exchange in the centre, Black is preparing to recapture on d5 with the pawn. The other popular line, 4 ... d5 5cd ♘xd5, will be considered in Game No. 25.

5	♗g2	d5
6	cd	

On a previous occasion I decided to avoid exchanging in the centre. Here is what happened: 6 ♘c3 0–0 7 ♕b3 e6 8 0–0 ♘bd7 9 ♗f4 ♘b6?! (9 ... b6 is more appropriate) 10 c5 ♘c4 11 ♕c2

♘h5 12 b3 ♘xf4 13 gf ♘a3 14 ♕d2 b5 (on 14 ... b6, White has 15 ♕b2 bc 16 ♕xa3 cd 17 ♘a4 d3 18 ♖ac1 de 19 ♖fe1, or 15 ♘a4 b5 16 ♘c3, with the better chances) 15 ♖fe1 ♖b8 16 ♔h1 a5 17 e3 f5? (17 ... b4 18 ♘a4 ♘b5, or 17 ... ♕c7 followed by ... f6 and ... e5, was safer) 18 ♗f1 ♗d7 (now 18 ... b4 is less good: 19 ♘a4 ♘b5 20 ♘b6 ♘c7 21 a3) 19 ♗e2 ♗f6 20 ♖g1 ♔h8 21 ♖g3 ♕e7 22 ♖ag1 ♖g8 23 ♕c1! b4 24 ♘a4 ♖g7 25 ♕f1 ♖bg8 26 ♕h3 ♗e8 27 ♘b6 ♕d8 28 ♕h6 ♖c7 29 ♘e5 ♖cg7 30 ♗d3 ♘b5 31 ♗xb5 cb 32 f3 ♗h4 (he can't save himself with 32 ... ♗e7 33 ♘bd7! ♗xd7 34 ♖xg6 ♗f6 35 ♖xg7 ♖xg7 36 ♖xg7 ♗xg7 37 ♘f7+ ♔g8 38 ♕xg7+ ♔xg7 39 ♘xd8) 33 ♖h3 ♗f2 34 ♖xg6 ♗xe3 35 ♖xg7 ♖xg7 36 ♖g3 ♕e7 37 ♖xg7 ♕xg7 38 ♕xg7+ ♔xg7 39 c6 ♗xc6 40 ♘xc6 ♗xf4 41 ♘d7 1–0; Karpov–Kir. Georgiev, Wijk aan Zee 1988.

Notwithstanding my success in that game, I still believe that the immediate exchange on d5 promises White a more substantial initiative.

6	...	cd
7	♘c3	0–0
8	♘e5	e6 *(99)*

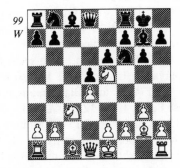

99
W

This book was virtually completed when one of the strongest tournaments in chess history took place: Linares, 1991. The game Karpov–Gelfand from that event is of interest for the theory of the line we are examining. Play proceeded: 8 ... ♗f5 (a rare move which 'almost' enabled Black to equalise) 9 0–0 ♘e4 10 ♗e3 ♘xc3 11 bc ♘c6 12 ♕b3 e6 13 ♘xc6 bc 14 ♕a3 ♖e8 15 ♗f4 e5 16 ♗xe5 ♗xe5 17 de ♖xe5 18 e3 ♗e4 19 ♖fd1 ♕f6 20 ♖d4 h5 21 h3 ♖b8 22 ♖ad1 ♗xg2 23 ♔xg2 ♕e7 24 ♕xe7 ♖xe7 25 ♖1d2

☗b6 26 c4 dc 27 ☗xc4 (for twenty moves we have been very close to a draw, but White has nonetheless extracted everything possible from the position; exchanging most of the pieces, he has obtained a superior rook ending. The remainder of the game provides a good illustration of 'exploitation technique') 27 ... ♔g7 28 ☗dc2 ☗c7 29 g4 hg 30 hg ♔f6 31 ♔g3 ♔e6 32 a4 ♔d7 33 g5 ☗a6 34 ☗d4+ ♔e8 35 ☗c5 ☗b6 36 ♔f4 ☗d7 37 ☗xd7 ♔xd7 38 ♔e5 ♔e7 39 f4 ☗b4 40 ☗a5 ☗b7 41 e4 ☗c7 42 ☗c5 ☗c8 43 ☗c3 ☗e8 44 ☗c4 ☗c8 45 ☗b4 ☗c7 46 a5 ♔d7 47 ☗b3 ♔e7 48 a6 ♔d7 49 ♔f6 ♔c8 50 ☗h3 ☗d7 51 f5 gf 52 ef c5 53 ☗c3 ☗c7 54 g6 fg 55 fg ♔d7 56 g7 ☗c8 57 ☗g3 1–0.

9 ♗g5

Postponing kingside castling for a while. For 9 0–0, see Game No. 23.

9 ... ♕b6

9 ... h6 weakens Black's position and wastes time. In Gutman–Zysk, Biel 1988, White acquired a big advantage after 10 ♗e3! ♕b6 11 ♕d2 ♘h7 12 0–0 ♘c6 13 ☗fc1 ♗d7 14 ♘a4 ♕c7 15 ♘c5 ☗ad8 16 b4! ♕b6 17 b5! ♘e7 18 a4.

10 ♕d2 ♘fd7

In Nikolić–Nunn, Amsterdam 1988, Black equalised after **10 ... ♘bd7 11 ♗e3 ♘e8!** 12 f4 ♘d6. Gutman recommends **11 h3!** h6 (11 ... ♘e8 12 ♗e7, or 11 ... ♘xe5 12 de ♘d7 13 ♗e3! and f4) 12 ♗e3, with the better chances for White.

The immediate **10 ... ♘c6** has also been seen: 11 ♘xc6 bc (11 ... ♕xc6 is also playable: 12 ☗c1 ♕d7 13 0–0 b6 14 ♗h6 ♗b7 15 ☗c2 ☗ac8 16 ☗fc1 ♘e4, and Black maintains the balance; Cvitan–Zysk, West Berlin 1988) 12 0–0 ♘d7 13 ☗fd1 ☗b8 14 b3 f6 (after 14 ... c5 15 dc, or 14 ... e5 15 de, White will play 16 ♗e3 and ♗d4, with obvious positional gains) 15 ♗h6 (here too 15 ♗e3 is not bad) 15 ... ♗xh6 16 ♕xh6 c5 17 ♘a4. This position arose in Haritonov–Ivanchuk, Frunze 1988. In Haritonov's opinion, after 17 ... ♕b4 or 17 ... ♕a5, White has a slight advantage. In the game, Black played 17 ... ♕d6?, which could have had severe consequences after 18 e4!. Instead, White replied 18 dc ♘xc5 19 ♘xc5 ♕xc5 20 ☗ac1 ♕d6 21 ♕d2 f5 22 ♕d4 ☗f7 23 e3, and still preserved some positional advantages. In the end, Ivanchuk was unable to hold the position, and lost.

11 ♗e3

I had already employed the manoeuvre ♗c1–g5 against the

Dutch grandmaster four years earlier, but at this point I withdrew my knight to f3.

Karpov–Timman, Bugojno 1986: 11 ♘f3 ♘c6 12 ♖d1 ♘f6 (12 ... ♛b4 is more precise) 13 0–0 ♗d7 (and here 13 ... ♘e4 was better; then 14 ♘xe4 de 15 ♘e5 ♘xe5 16 de ♗xe5 17 ♗xe4 ♛xb2 18 ♛xb2 ♗xb2 19 ♖b1 gives White no more than a minimal endgame advantage) 14 ♗xf6 ♗xf6 15 e4 ♛a5 16 ♛f4 (at this point 16 ed ed 17 ♘e5! ♘xe5 18 ♘xd5 ♛xd2 19 ♘xf6+ ♔g7 20 ♖xd2 ♘c4 21 ♘xd7 ♘xd2 22 ♖d1 ♖fd8 23 ♗xb7 would have given White a large plus) 16 ... ♗g7 17 ♖fe1 ♖ad8 18 ed ed 19 ♘e5 ♗e6. The chances are now equal; subsequently we both made plenty of mistakes. At first I landed in a difficult position, then Timman gave me the opportunity to restore equality and acquire a decisive initiative.

11 ... ♘c6

The exchange on e5 promises nothing good: 11 ... ♘xe5 12 de ♛a5 13 f4 ♘c6 14 0–0 ♖d8 (14 ... f6 15 ef ♗xf6 16 ♗f2) 15 ♗f2 ♗d7 16 a3! ♛a6 17 b4 ♘e7 18 ♖fd1, with a clear advantage to White; Nikolić–Nunn, Brussels 1988.

12 ♘xc6 bc *(100)*

Better than 12 ... ♛xc6 13 ♗h6 ♗xh6 14 ♛xh6 ♛d6 15 h4! and Black is in a dangerous position; Shpilker–A. Kuzmin, Moscow 1986.

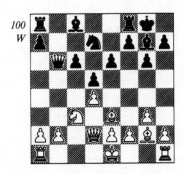

100
W

13 ♖c1

In Nikolić–Korchnoi, Amsterdam 1988, White played the hasty **13 h4?!**, when Black could have gained the better chances with **13 ... ♖b8 14 ♖b1 c5 15 ♘a4 ♛b5 16 ♘xc5 ♘xc5 17 dc d4**. But then, the game continuation **13 ... a5 14 h5 ♗a6 15 ♖d1 ♖fb8**

16 hg hg 17 b3 ♛b4 18 ♚f1 c5 also gave Korchnoi a plus. There followed 19 ♜h4 c4 20 ♝h6 ♝h8 21 bc ♛xc4 22 ♝f3 ♜c8 23 ♜c1 ♛b4 24 ♚g2 ♜c4 25 a3 ♛xa3 26 ♜ch1 ♛xc3 27 ♛xc3 ♜xc3 28 ♝d2 ♝xd4! and Black won.

13 ... ♛b4!

A good move. If at once 13 ... ♜b8, then 14 ♞a4 ♛b4 15 b3 ♛xd2+ 16 ♚xd2, and White's chances are better, for example: 16 ... ♜b4? 17 ♜xc6! ♝xd4 18 ♝xd4 ♜xd4+ 19 ♚c3 ♜g4 20 ♜c7 etc.

14 0–0

14 a3? would be premature: 14 ... ♛b3 15 ♛c2 ♜b8 16 ♞a4 ♝a6! with the initiative.

14 ... ♜b8
15 b3 c5

Ridding himself of the backward pawn while he still can. After 15 ... ♝a6 16 ♜fd1! ♜fc8 17 ♞a4, Black has difficulty freeing himself.

16 ♜fd1

Of course not 16 dc?, because of 16 ... d4!

16 ... cd
17 ♝xd4 ♝xd4

After 17 ... e5? 18 ♝xa7 ♜b7 19 ♝e3 d4 20 ♞d5!, or at once 19 ♞xd5!, Black would be left a pawn down.

18 ♛xd4 ♛xd4
19 ♜xd4 ♞b6
20 ♜dd1

Given White's chosen plan, this is indispensable. 20 e4? fails to 20 ... e5! 21 ♜dd1 d4, with good play for Black. If 20 e3, then after 20 ... ♝a6 21 ♞a4 ♜fc8 22 ♞c5 ♝c4! Black similarly has an easy game.

20 ... ♝b7
21 e4!

Seeing that White's 'heavy artillery' is better mobilised, his decision to open lines in the centre makes perfectly good sense.

21 ... de
22 ♞xe4 ♚g7
23 ♜c5

Invasion of the seventh rank would be illusory: 23 ♜c7 ♞d5 24 ♜d7 ♞b6.

23 ... ♜fd8

24	⃞xd8	⃞xd8
25	♘c3	♗xg2
26	♔xg2	⃞c8?

White's positional advantage lies in his queenside pawn majority, and Black has to play very accurately to avoid reaching a dangerous ending. The correct move here was **26 ... ⃞d2!**, and if **27 ⃞c7 ⃞c2 28 ♘b5?** ⃞xc7 29 ♘xc7 ♔f6, Black is not at all worse. A more precise line for White is **28 a4!** a5 29 ♘b5 ⃞xc7 30 ♘xc7 ♔f6 31 ♘a6 ♘d5 32 ♘c5 ♘b4! 33 f4 (33 ♔f3 ♔e5!) 33 ... ♘c6 34 ♔f3 ♔e7 35 ♔e4 ♔d6 36 ♘b7+ ♔c7 37 ♘c5 (37 ♘xa5 f5+!) 37 ... ♔d6, with a draw.

27 ⃞xc8 ♘xc8 *(101)*

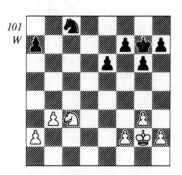

101
W

In this situation White could have utilised his active king position and obtained substantial winning chances by playing **28 ♔f3!** In view of the threat to penetrate to the queenside, Black's most natural course is: **28 ... f5 29 ♔e3 e5**, and now White has the very strong **30 ♘b5!**, preventing the stabilising manoeuvre ... ♘c8–d6. It is by no means simple for Black to defend. The variations I shall now quote were indicated by Holmov. **30 ... ♔f6 31 ♔d3 ♔g5!** (Black's best chance is to activate his king. He now threatens to advance by the route g4–h3 or g4–f3, so White has to take prophylactic measures; but this will lead to a weakening of his kingside, giving Black further possibilities for counterplay. Instead, the pawn endgame after 31 ... ♔e6 32 ♔c4 ♘d6+ 33 ♘xd6 ♔xd6 34 b4! is obviously lost for Black, and White can also count on success after 32 ... g5 33 a4) **32 h3! h5 33 ♔c4 h4 34 ♔d5 hg! 35 fg f4!** (after 35 ... e4 36 ♔e5! Black's defence would be incomparably more difficult) **36 gf+ ♔xf4! 37 ♘c3** (the straightforward 37 ♔c6 e4 38 ♔b7?

♘d6+! would even lose). Now Black has to play very precisely:
(a) **37 ... ♘b6+?** 38 ♔c6! (38 ♔e6? e4 39 ♔f6 e3! 40 ♔xg6? ♔f3 41 h4 ♘d5! etc.) 38 ... e4 (38 ... ♔g3 39 ♔b7 ♔xh3 40 ♔xa7 ♘d7 41 b4 g5 42 a4 g4 43 a5 g3 44 ♔b7 g2 45 ♘e2, and White wins) 39 ♔b7 g3 40 ♔xa7 ♘d7 41 b4! ♔f3 42 a4 e2 43 ♘xe3 ♔xe2 44 a5 ♔d3 45 ♔b7 ♔c4 46 a6 ♔b5 47 a7 ♘b6 48 h4! and wins.

(b) **37 ... g5!** enables Black to hold the position: 38 ♔c6 ♔e3! 39 ♔b7 ♘d6+ 40 ♔xa7 ♔d2 41 ♘d5 e4! (not 41 ... ♘b5+ 42 ♔b6 ♘c3 43 ♔c5! e4 44 ♔d4! ♘xd5 45 ♔xe4 ♘c3+ 46 ♔f5 and White wins but 43 ... ♘xa2! draws–G. Flear) 42 ♔b6! (less precise is 42 a4? ♔c2 43 b4 ♔b3 44 a5 ♔c4 45 ♘e3+ ♔xb4 46 ♔b6 ♘c4+ with a draw) 42 ... e3 43 ♘xe3 ♔xe3 44 ♔c6 ♘c8 45 ♔d7 ♘b6?! (45 ... ♘a7? is inferior: 46 a4 ♔d4 47 ♔e6 ♔c3 48 ♔f5! ♔xb3 49 ♔xg5 ♔xa4 50 h4 ♘c6 51 ♔f6! and wins; or 47 ... ♔e4 48 b4! ♘c6 49 b5 ♘a5 50 b6 ♔f4 51 ♔d5 ♔g3 52 ♔c5 ♔xh3 53 ♔b5, again winning for White) 46 ♔e6 ♔e4! 47 a4 ♘d5 48 a5 ♘b4 49 ♔d6 ♔d4!, or 49 ♔f6 ♔f4, with a draw in either case.

These variations show that although Black achieves a satisfactory result, it is only with immense difficulty.

	28	**f4?**

This throws away White's advantage, since the exchange of a pair of kingside pawns increases Black's chances of a peaceful outcome.

	28	...	**f5!**
	29	♘a4	

Having let my winning chances slip, I commit a further inaccuracy. 29 ♔f3 was simpler.

	29	...	**♔f6**
	30	♘c5	

Preventing 30 ... e5 on account of 31 ♘d7+.

	30	...	**♘b6**
	31	♘d3	**♘d7**
	32	♘b4	

I should have brought the king forward: 32 ♔f3 e5 33 fe+ ♘xe5+ 34 ♘xe5 ♔xe5 35 h4! with a draw.

	32	...	**e5**
	33	♘c6	**a6**
	34	fe+	**♘xe5**
	35	♘d4	

The pawn ending would be lost for White.

35	...	♚e7
36	♔f1	

36 ♔f2 is answered by 36 ... ♘g4+.

36	...	♚d6
37	♔e2	♚d5
38	♘c2	♚e4
39	a4	♘f3
40	b4	♘d4+

In the event of 40 ... ♘xh2!, White could maintain the balance with 41 b5 ab 42 ab ♚d5 43 ♘d4! ♘g4! 44 b6 ♚d6 45 ♘e6! ♚c6 46 ♘f8 ♘f6 47 ♔f3 ♚xb6 48 ♔f4 ♚c6 49 ♔g5 ♘e4+ (or 49 ... ♘h5 50 ♔h4 ♚d5 51 ♘xh7) 50 ♔f4 ♚d6 51 ♘xh7 ♚e7 52 g4; alternatively 42 ... ♘g4 43 b6 ♘e5 44 b7 ♘d7 45 ♘b4 ♘b8 46 ♘d3! and again White draws, as Black cannot win without the use of his knight.

41	♘xd4	♚xd4
42	b5	

½–½

After 42 ... ab 43 ab ♚c5 44 ♚e3 ♚xb5 45 ♔f4 ♚c4 46 ♔g5 ♚d3 47 ♔h6 ♚e3 48 h4! ♔f3 49 ♔xh7 ♚xg3 50 ♚xg6, both sides' resources are completely exhausted.

Game No. 23

Karpov–Timman

Candidates Final (4th game)

Kuala Lumpur 1990

1	d4	♘f6
2	c4	g6
3	♘f3	♗g7
4	g3	c6
5	♗g2	d5
6	cd	cd
7	♘c3	0–0
8	♘e5	e6
9	0–0	

In our discussion of this game, we shall scrutinise the fine points of the opening play arising from White's 9th move. The middlegame will proceed at a slow pace, yet the ending (after the adjournment) will be exceptionally interesting, and although this does not strictly

belong to the subject of the book, we shall give a large number
of entertaining endgame variations.

$$9 \quad \ldots \qquad \text{\textcircled{2}fd7}$$

The best move. After 9 ... ♘c6 10 ♘xc6 bc 11 ♘a4 ♘d7 12
♗f4 White has a clear positional advantage; Akhmilovskaya–
Chiburdanidze, Women's World Championship match 1986.

$$10 \quad \text{f4} \;\; (102)$$

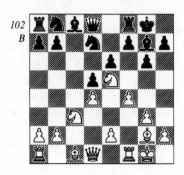

Karpov–Kasparov, 3rd game, London 1986, continued differently: 10 ♘f3 (the exchange 10 ♘xd7 ♗xd7 gives White nothing:
11 e3 ♘c6 12 b3 ♕e7 13 ♗b2 ♖fc8 ½–½; Portisch–Nunn, Budapest
1987) 10 ... ♘c6 11 ♗f4 ♘f6 12 ♘e5 ♗d7 (after 12 ... ♘xe5 13
♗xe5, White's chances are to be preferred) 13 ♕d2 ♘xe5 14
♗xe5 ♗c6 15 ♖fd1 (15 ♖ac1, with the prospect of f2–f3 and
e2–e4, would have preserved the initiative) 15 ... ♘d7 16 ♗xg7
♔xg7 17 ♖ac1 ♘f6 18 ♕f4 ♕b8 19 ♕xb8 ♖axb8 20 f3 ♖fd8 21
♔f2 ♖bc8 22 e3 ♘e8 23 ♖d2 ♘d6 24 ♖dc2 ♔f8 25 ♗f1 ♔e7
26 ♗d3 f5 27 h4 h6 28 b3 (in his notes to the game, Kasparov
states that after 28 g4 Black would be in quite a dangerous
position. But it seems to me that the continuation 28 ... ♖f8 29
g5 ♘e4+ 30 ♗xe4 fe 31 f4 h5, or 30 fe fe+ 31 ♔e2 ed+ 32
♔xd3 hg 33 hg ♖f5!, promises White nothing) 28 ... g5 29 ♘e2
♗d7 30 ♖c5 b6 31 ♖c7 ♖xc7 32 ♖xc7 ♖a8 33 ♘g1 ♘e8 34 ♖c1
♖c8 35 ♖xc8 ½–½.

$$10 \quad \ldots \qquad \text{\textcircled{2}c6}$$

In game 13 of the 1986 match, my opponent drove the knight
back with **10 ... f6**, but after **11 ♘f3 ♘c6 12 ♗e3 ♘b6 13 ♗f2**
f5 14 ♘e5 ♗d7 15 ♕d2 ♘c8 16 ♕e3 ♔h8 17 ♖fd1 (17 ♖fc1 was

stronger) White generated considerable pressure – although the game was eventually drawn after blunders by both sides.

White can retain the initiative by retreating his knight to d3. The game Hulak–H. Olafsson, Wijk aan Zee 1987, is instructive: (10 ... f6) **11 ♘d3 ♘c6 12 e3!** (more precise than 12 ♗e3 ♘b6 13 b3 ♗d7 14 ♘c5 ♖b8 15 ♕d2 f5 16 ♖fc1 ♘c8 17 ♗f2 ♘d6, with equality; Nikolić–Nunn, Linares 1988) 12 ... f5 (Andersson–Nunn, Brussels 1988, is worth mentioning: 12 ... ♘b6 13 b3 ♗d7 14 ♗a3 ♖e8 15 ♕d2 ♘e7 16 ♘c5 ♖b8 17 ♖fe1 f5 18 ♗f1 ♘ec8 19 ♖ac1 ♗c6 20 ♘d3 ♘d6 21 ♘e5 ♗f8 22 ♕b2! ♖e7 23 ♖c2 ♖c7 24 ♖ec1 ♖bc8, and now instead of 25 ♘b1, which led to approximate equality, White could have played 25 ♗c5!, when according to Nunn the threat of 26 ♕a3 gives him a noticeable plus) 13 ♗d2 (a good alternative is 13 ♘e5 ♘e7 14 b3 ♘f6 15 ♗a3 ♗d7 16 ♖c1 ♖e8 17 ♖f2 ♘e4 18 ♖fc2 ♘c6 19 ♗f1 a6 20 ♘xe4 fe 21 ♗d6 ♖c8 22 h4 ♘xe5 23 de ♕a5 24 h5; Dzhind-zhikhashvili–Mestel, Reykjavik 1990) 13 ... ♘f6 14 ♖c1 ♗d7 15 ♘e5 ♖e8 16 h3 ♘xe5 17 de ♘e4 18 ♘xe4 de 19 ♕b3 ♗c6 20 ♗b4, with advantage to White.

Shortly after the London/Leningrad match, Kasparov played this variation himself with White, against Nunn (Brussels 1986). The exchange on e5 unexpectedly led to a crushing defeat for Black: **10 ... ♘xe5 11 fe ♘c6 12 e4!** de 13 ♗e3 *(103)*

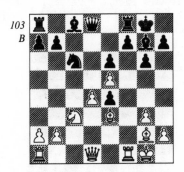

103
B

With Black at the moment a pawn up and not having made any noticeable mistake, it is hard to imagine that he will resign after six (!) more moves. 13 ... f5 14 ef ♖xf6 (the play up to here was still on familiar lines. For example, this position had arisen by transposition in Sveshnikov–Mikhalchishin, Lvov 1983; after

15 ♖xf6 ♗xf6 16 ♘e2 ♘b4, White's advantage evaporated. Kasparov doesn't waste time exchanging rooks) 15 ♘xe4 ♖xf1+ 16 ♕xf1 ♘xd4? 17 ♖d1 e5 18 ♘g5, and Black stopped the clock. The following beautiful variation is possible: 18 ... ♕e7 19 ♗d5+ ♗e6 20 ♖xd4 ed 21 ♗xe6+ ♔h8 22 ♘f7+ ♔g8 23 ♘d8+ ♔h8 24 ♗g5! ♕b4 25 ♘f7+ ♔g8 26 ♘e5+ ♔h8 27 ♘xg6+ hg 28 ♕h3+. Incidentally, all this actually happened in a correspondence game Hjorth–M. Andersson (1986), and at this point Black resigned.

Instead of 16 ... ♘xd4, Black might play 16 ... ♗xd4 17 ♗xd4 ♘xd4 18 ♖e1 e5 19 ♕f6. Kasparov judged this position to be in White's favour, in view of 19 ... ♕xf6 20 ♘xf6+ ♔g7 21 ♘e8+ ♔f8 22 ♖xe5 with the better ending, but Gutman has suggested 19 ... ♕b6 20 ♔h1 ♗d7 21 ♕xe5 ♖f8 22 ♘g5 ♗c6. However, after 23 ♗d5+! (G. Flear) Black can resign!

12 e4, then, seems quite strong but White can also play the solid 12 ♗e3!?. This position arose in Karpov–Timman, Amsterdam 1986, though by a different move-order (10 ... ♘c6 11 ♗e3 ♘xe5 12 fe). Let us look at a few moves of that important encounter.

12 ♗e3 f6 13 ef ♖xf6

Better than 13 ... ♗xf6 14 ♕d2 ♗d7 15 ♔h1 ♖f7 16 ♗g1 ♗e8 17 ♖ad1 ♗g7 18 ♖xf7 ♗xf7 19 e4, with the advantage; Makarov–Glek, Moscow 1986.

14 ♕d2 ♗d7 15 ♔h1 ♖xf1+ 16 ♖xf1 ♕e7 (104)

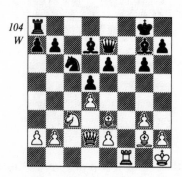

This is a safer post for the queen than a5 (16 ... ♕a5 17 a3 ♖f8 18 ♖xf8+ ♗xf8 19 ♗g1) or b6 (16 ... ♕b6 17 ♗g1 ♘xd4? 18 ♖f4).

17 ♖d1

Over-protecting the d-pawn and preparing ♗e3–g1 and e2–e4. But White can also withdraw his bishop to g1 at once. Ribli–Nunn, Dortmund 1987, went 17 ♗g1 ♖d8 18 a3 ♔h8? (18 ... ♗c8 19 ♗e3 ♖f8 is safer) 19 e4! (the fiasco against Kasparov has not put Nunn off this variation, but once again the advance of the centre pawn puts him in a difficult position) 19 ... de 20 ♘xe4 ♗c8 21 ♗e3 (21 ♘g5 ♗f6) 21 ... ♖f8 22 ♖xf8+ ♕xf8 23 b4, with a clear advantage.

17 ... ♖c8

In Karpov–Chiburdanidze, Bilbao 1987, the Women's World Champion played 17 ... ♔h8 18 a3, and only then 18 ... ♖c8. After 19 ♗g5 ♕f8 20 ♖f1 ♕g8 21 e3 h6 22 ♗f6 ♗xf6 23 ♖xf6 ♖f8 24 ♖f2 ♕g7 25 ♖xf8+ ♕xf8 26 e4 de 27 ♘xe4 b6 28 ♔g1 ♕g7 29 d5 ed 30 ♕xd5 ♕d4+ 31 ♕xd4+ ♘xd4, the game had turned from an opening into an ending, with White retaining a minimal edge. But Maya defended precisely, and obtained a draw in spite of all my efforts.

18 a3!

White's intention is to retreat his bishop to g1 and seize the centre. But in reply to the immediate 18 ♗g1, Timman had prepared 18 ... ♕b4!. Then after 19 e4 de 20 ♗xe4 ♗e8, Black can secure his position with ... ♗e8–f7 (21 d5? ♗xc3!). If instead 20 ♘xe4 ♕xd2 21 ♖xd2, Black has the tactical device 21 ... ♘xd4 22 ♖xd4 (22 ♗xd4 ♗xd4 23 ♖xd4 ♖c1+ 24 ♗f1 ♗b5) 22 ... ♗xd4 23 ♗xd4 ♖c1+ 24 ♗g1 ♗c6, with counterplay in a complex endgame.

18 ... ♗f6

White easily refutes 18 ... ♘a5 with 19 ♘xd5 ed 20 ♗g5 ♘c4 21 ♗xe7 ♘xd2 22 ♗xd5+ ♔h8 25 ♖xd2.

19 ♗g1 ♗g5?

A more precise move was 19 ... ♕g7, hindering e2–e4 for the moment, on account of 20 e4 de 21 ♘xe4 ♗xd4 22 ♗xd4 ♘xd4 23 ♕xd4 ♕xd4 24 ♖xd4 ♖c1+ 25 ♗f1 ♗b5!.

20 ♕e1 ♘d8 21 e4 de 22 ♕xe4 b6 23 d5

Black could not prevent this breakthrough, and has to go over to wholly passive defence. The results of the opening can now be summed up as miserable for Black. The game, however, lasted another 35 moves and ended in a draw.

11   ♗e3

At this point the exchange on e5 leads to variations we have looked at already (11 ... ♘dxe5 12 fe f6 etc.). In the main game we are examining, Black drives back the centralised knight and follows with ... ♘b6. I should mention that on two occasions in Seville, Kasparov played 11 ... ♘b6 at once, and equalised easily in both cases. We shall thoroughly discuss the immediate knight move in the notes to Game No. 24.

11	...	f6
12	♘d3	♘b6
13	b3	♕e7

13 ... ♗d7 would transpose into the Nikolić–Nunn game that we have already seen. So it may be said that we are only now breaking new ground.

14	a4	♗d7
15	♗c1	♖fd8
16	e3	♗e8
17	♗a3	♕f7
18	♖c1	♗f8
19	♗xf8	♕xf8 *(105)*

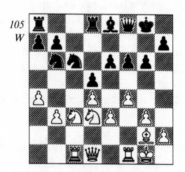

As the result of some complex manoeuvres, a certain advantage for White has emerged on the queenside.

20	g4	♕e7
21	♕d2	♖ac8
22	♘e2	♖c7
23	♖c5	♘c8
24	f5	g5

White is slightly better after 24 ... ♘d6 25 ♘df4 (25 fe? ♘e4 26 ♗xe4 de 27 ♘df4 ♕xc5, and Black wins) 25 ... gf 26 gf ♘xf5 27 ♘xd5 ed 28 ♖xf5.

25   ♘g3

25 fe ♕xe6 26 ♘c3 (26 ♘g3 ♗g6 27 ♘f5 ♘8e7) 26 ... ♘8e7 27 e4 is less clear.

Now the threat of bringing the knight to f5 is more dangerous: 25 ... ♗f7 26 fe ♕xe6 (26 ... ♗xe6 27 ♘h5 ♖f8 28 ♘b4!) 27 ♘f5. To avoid this, Black sacrifices a pawn.

25   ...   e5!? *(106)*

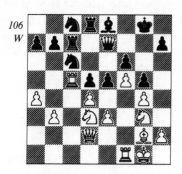

26   ♕c1

An inaccuracy, committed after much thought. The sheer variety of possibilities put me in rather a quandary, and I decided to decline the pawn sacrifice although Black's position would almost have become critical if I had calmly accepted it. After **26 ♗xd5+** (26 ♖xd5 ed 27 ed ♗f7! 28 ♖xd8+ ♕xd8 gives Black counterplay for the pawn) **26 ... ♔h8**, White has a wide choice:

(a) **27 ♗xc6 ♗xc6 28 ♕c1 ed 29 e4!**, or

(b) **27 ♖fc1 ed 28 e4!**. This strategic operation involving the return of the pawn and the inevitable break with e4–e5 secures White a considerable plus.

(c) **27 de ♘xe5 28 ♖xc7 ♕xc7 29 ♖c1 ♕e7 30 ♘xe5 ♕xe5 31 ♕d4!** is also good.

(d) **27 ♕c1 ♖xd5 28 ♖xd5 b6** (28 ... ♘b4 29 ♖c5!) **29 de ♘b4 30 ♘xb4 ♖xc1 31 ♖xc1**, or 27 ... b6 28 ♖xc6 ♗xc6 29 ♗xc6 ed (29 ... ♖d6 30 d5 ♖xd5 31 ♗xd5) 30 ed ♖xd4 (30 ... ♖d6 31 d5 ♖xd5 32 ♖e1!) 31 ♖e1 ♕d6 (31 ... ♖xd3 32 ♖xe7 ♘xe7 33 ♕e1 ♘xc6 34 ♕e8+ ♔g7 35 ♘h5+ ♔h6 36 ♕f8+ and mates) 32 ♖e8+ ♔g7 33 ♖e6 – with a very strong initiative for White in either case.

(e) **27 ♗g2** (in some of the foregoing variations the white king's bishop departs from the board, but it is also possible to bring it home before anything else) 27 ... ed 28 e4!, followed by e4–e5 (if necessary supported by a rook – ♖fe1). If 28 ... ♘e5, then 29 ♖xe5! fe 30 f6 and 31 ♕xg5 is crushing.

The queen move to c1 allows the centre to be blocked; if I had been playing for that, I should have continued 26 ♖fc1! e4 27 ♘b4! – possession of the c-file is not without significance. The trouble is that I had 'too many irons in the fire' (trying to control the c-file and f-file at once). Now Black nullifies the danger in the centre and obtains a fully viable game. The ensuing phase, as I have said already, is a trifle dull; the most interesting events occur only after the adjournment.

26	...	b6
27	♖c2	e4
28	♘f2	♘d6
29	♕d2	♖dc8
30	♖fc1	a5

Black also stands quite well after 30 ... ♘a5 31 ♖xc7 ♖xc7 32 ♖c3 ♕d8 33 ♕c2 ♖xc3 34 ♕xc3 ♕c8!

31	♗f1

If White hadn't made the superfluous queen moves, this bishop manoeuvre would now be extremely dangerous for Black.

The attempt to build up with 31 ♕c3 would be countered by 31 ... ♗d7 and 32 ... ♘e8.

31	...	♘b4

31 ... ♘xd4! looked inviting, but after 32 ed e3 33 ♕d3 ef+ 34 ♔xf2 ♖xc2+ 35 ♖xc2 ♘e4+ 36 ♔f3, the draw is not far away (the exchange of the good knight on c6 for the bad one on f2 is not advantageous to Black). The match situation compelled Timman to maintain the tension in the hope of seizing the initiative.

32	♖c3	♕d7
33	♘d1	♖c6
34	♖xc6	♖xc6
35	♖xc6	♕xc6
36	♘c3	♔f8
37	♔f2	♔e7
38	♔e1	♔f8
39	♔d1	♕c8
40	♔e1	♔g7

Under pressure from the clock, we have both been marking time with our kings a little, and I should mention that Black missed quite a good opportunity: 40 ... h5! 41 gh (41 h3 with equality) 41 ... ♘xf5 42 ♗h3 ♗d7!

	41	♘a2	♘xa2
	42	♕xa2	♕c7

A possibility was 42 ... ♕c3+ 43 ♔f2 b5 44 ab ♘xb5 (but not 44 ... ♗xb5 45 ♘h5+ ♔f7 46 ♗xb5 ♘xb5 47 b4!).

	43	♔f2	♔f8
	44	♕b2	♔e7
	45	♗e2	♔d8
	46	♔e1	♔c8

46 ... b5!? is sharper.

	47	♔d2	♔b7
	48	♕c1	♕e7

For drawing purposes, 48 ... ♕xc1+ was simpler.

	49	♔e1	♗d7
	50	♔f2	♘e8
	51	♕h1!	*(107)*

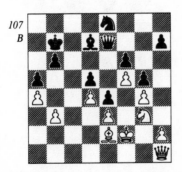

107
B

I didn't feel like settling for a draw, and decided to provoke mind-bending complications by abandoning my queenside to its fate while going ahead on the kingside. Obviously there could be no question of calculating the variations to the end.

	51	...	♕b4
	52	h4!	♕xb3
	53	hg	fg
	54	♕xh7	♕xa4
	55	♕e7	♕c6

56	♕xg5	a4
57	♕e7	♕d6
58	♕xd6	♘xd6
59	♗d1	♗b5?!

It was hardly a good idea to block the path of his pawn. After 59 ... b5, it is most likely that the game would soon have been drawn; at any rate Black would not be risking anything. Here are some sample variations: 59 ... b5 60 f6 (60 ♘e2? b4 61 ♘c1 ♔c7) 60 ... ♗xg4 61 ♗xg4! a3 62 ♗e6 ♔c6 63 ♘e2 (not 63 f7 ♘xf7 64 ♘xe4 ♘g5! 65 ♘xg5 a2, and Black wins) 63 ... a2 (63 ... b4 64 ♘c1) 64 ♗xd5+ ♔xd5 65 ♘c3+ ♔c4 66 ♘xa2 b4 (nor does he gain anything from 66 ... ♔b3 67 ♘c1+ ♔b2 68 ♘e2 b4 69 d5 b3 70 ♔g3 ♔c2 71 ♘d4+ ♔c3 72 ♘xb3 ♔xb3 73 ♔f4 ♔c4 74 ♔e5) 67 ♘xb4 ♔xb4 68 ♔g3 ♔c4 69 ♔f4 ♔d3 (69 ... ♔d5 70 ♔g5 ♔e6 71 ♔g6) 70 ♔e5 ♘f7+ 71 ♔e6 ♘g5+, with a draw.

60	♘e2	a3
61	♘c1 *(108)*	

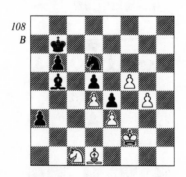

108
B

In this position Timman sealed his move after nearly half an hour's thought. Many commentators were misled by Black's queenside activity, and in the local newspapers the following day there were even headlines like "Can Karpov survive?" In actual fact, adjournment analysis revealed that the only winning chances lie with White, whose pawns are much more dangerous than his opponent's. All the same, we shall see that the rightful outcome of this tense struggle would have been a draw.

61	...	♔c7

A good sealed move, but of course we had analysed others too.

Let us look at the main variations discovered by Zaitsev and myself:

(a) **61 ...** ♗d7 62 ♗b3! ♔c6 63 ♔g3 ♘c4 64 ♔f4 ♘b2 (threatening the deadly ... ♘d3+) 65 ♔g5! ♘c4 66 ♗xc4 (given White's active king, the creation of another black passed pawn is not dangerous) 66 ... dc 67 ♔f6 b5 68 ♘a2 b4 69 ♘xb4 ♔b5 70 ♘a2 ♔a4 71 ♘c1 a2 72 ♘xa2 ♔b3 73 ♘c1+ ♔c2 74 ♔e7 ♔xc1 75 f6 c3 76 f7 ♗xg4 77 f8(♕) c2 78 ♕f4 ♗f3 79 d5 ♔d2 80 d6 c1(♕) 81 d7, and Black is defenceless.

(b) **61 ...** ♗e8 62 ♘a2 (after the careless 62 ♔g3, the black knight performs the same nimble triangulation that we have seen before: 62 ... ♘c4! 63 ♔f4 ♘b2, and wherever the bishop goes, Black plays 64 ... ♘d3+) 62 ... ♔c6 63 ♗b3 ♘c4 64 g5 ♘d6 65 f6 ♗f7 66 ♔g3 ♘c4 67 ♔f4 ♔d6 68 ♘c3 ♗g6 69 ♗xc4 dc 70 ♘b5+ ♔c6 71 ♘xa3 ♔d5 (71 ... b5? 72 ♔e5 c3 73 ♘c2 ♗f7 74 d5+! ♗xd5 75 g6) 72 ♘b5 ♔c6 73 ♘c3 b5 74 ♔e5 b4 75 d5+ ♔d7 76 ♘a2 b3 77 ♘c3 b2 78 ♔d4, with a decisive advantage.

(c) **61 ...** ♔c6 62 ♔g3 ♘c4 (if 62 ... ♗c4 63 ♔f4 ♔d7 64 g5 a2 65 ♘xa2 ♗xa2 66 g6, Black is mated after either 66 ... ♘e8 67 ♗a4+ ♔e7 68 ♗xe8 ♔xe8 69 ♔g5 b5 70 ♔h6 b4 71 g7 ♔f7 72 ♔h7 b3 73 g8(♕)+, or 66 ... ♔e7 67 g7 ♔f7 68 f6 ♗c4 69 ♗h5+ ♔g8 70 ♗g4 ♗b5 71 ♗e6+ ♘f7 72 ♔f5 ♗e8 73 ♔g6 b5 74 ♗xd5) 63 ♗e2 ♔d6 (if 63 ... ♘xe3?, then 64 ♗xb5+ ♔xb5 65 f6, and the pawn goes on to queen. Other variations are also unacceptable: 63 ... ♘d6 64 ♗xb5+ ♔xb5 65 ♔f4 ♔b4 66 g5 ♔c3 67 g6 ♘e8 68 ♔e5 ♔b2 69 g7 ♘xg7 70 f6 ♔xc1 71 fg a2 72 g8(♕) a1(♕) 73 ♕g1+ ♔b2 74 ♕xa1+ ♔xa1 75 ♔xd5, or 63 ... ♘d6 64 ♗xb5+ ♘xb5 65 ♘a2! ♔d6 66 ♔f4 ♘c7 67 g5 ♘e8 68 g6 ♘f6 69 ♔g5 ♔e7 70 ♘b4 b5 71 ♘c6+! ♔d6 72 ♔xf6 a2 73 g7 a1(♕) 74 g8(♕) ♔xc6 75 ♕e6+) 64 ♔f4 ♗a4 65 g5 ♘b2 66 g6 ♘d3+ 67 ♘xd3! ed 68 ♗xd3 ♔e7 69 g7 ♔f7 70 f6 ♔g8 (70 ... a2 71 ♗h7 a1(♕) 72 g8(♕)+ ♔xf6 73 ♕f8+ ♔e6 73 ♗f5 mate) 71 ♔g5 a2 72 ♔h6 a1(♕), and a familiar mate follows: 73 ♗h7+ ♔f7 74 g8(♕)+ ♔xf6 75 ♕f8+ etc.

Now let us see what happened in the game.

62   ♔g3   ♘c4

62 ... ♔d7? loses in a way which we have seen before: 63 ♔f4 ♗c4 64 g5 a2 65 ♘xa2 ♗xa2 66 g6 ♔e7 (66 ... ♘e8 67 ♗a4+)

67 g7 ♔f7 68 f6 ♗c4 69 ♗g4 ♔g8 70 ♗e6+ ♘f7 71 ♔f5 ♗b5 72 ♔g6 ♗e8 73 ♗xd5 b5 74 ♗a2 b4 75 ♗b3.

63   ♗e2

But not 63 ♔f4? ♘b2! threatening ... ♘d3+.

63   ...   ♗e8!

The strongest defence. 63 ... ♘xe3 is inadequate: 64 ♗xb5 ♘c2 65 g5 ♘xd4 66 f6 ♔d6 67 g6 ♔e6 68 g7 ♔f7 69 ♗e8+ ♔g8 70 ♔f4, and wins.

64   ♔f4

Podgayets revealed a striking variation culminating in a problem-like mate: 64 g5 ♘xe3 65 ♔f4 ♘c2 66 ♔e5 ♘b4 67 ♔f6 ♔d6 68 g6 ♘c6 69 ♗b5 e3 70 g7 ♘e7 71 ♗xe8! e2 72 ♘xe2 a2 73 ♘c3! ♔g8+ 74 ♔f7 ♘h6+ 75 ♔f8 a1(♕) 76 ♘b5 mate *(109)*.

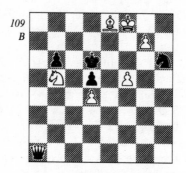

109
B

It would indeed be pleasant to finish the game like this, but unfortunately Black has a defence: 64 ... ♔d6 65 ♗xc4 dc 66 ♘a2 ♗a4 67 ♘c3 ♗b3 68 ♘b5+ ♔e7 69 ♘xa3 c3 70 ♔f4 b5! 71 ♔xe4 b4 72 ♔d3 ba 73 ♔xc3 ♗d5 with a draw.

64   ...   ♘b2

In my adjournment analysis I considered 64 ... b5 to be more precise: 65 ♘a2 ♘b2 (but not 65 ... ♔d6 66 g5 ♘b2 67 g6 b4 68 ♔g5! b3 69 ♘c1 ♗a4 70 g7 a2 71 g8(♕) a1(♕), as White obtains an irresistible attack with 72 ♕b8+ ♔d7 73 f6! ♕xc1 74 ♗g4+ ♔c6 75 ♕c8+) 66 f6 ♘d3+ 67 ♔f5 b4 68 ♗d1. But the move played is not yet the cause of a catastrophe, either.

65   ♔g5

The sole winning attempt. It is true that after 65 ♘a2, the following long variation gives White good prospects: 65 ... ♔d6

66 ♔g5 ♔e7 (66 ... ♘c4 is a mistake in view of 67 ♗xc4 dc 68 ♔f6 ♗a4 69 ♔g7 ♗b3 70 f6 c3 71 ♘xc3 a2 72 ♘xa2 ♗xa2 73 g5) 67 ♔h6 ♔f6 68 ♘b4 ♗f7 (inadequate alternatives are 68 ... ♘d3 69 ♘xd5+ ♔f7 70 g5 a2 71 g6+ ♔f8 72 g7+ ♔f7 73 ♗h5+ ♔g8 74 ♘e7 mate, and 68 ... ♗c6 69 ♗f1! ♘d1 70 g5+ ♔f7 – 70 ... ♔xf5 71 ♗h3 mate, is pretty – 71 g6+ etc.) 69 ♗f1! ♘d1 (it is too late for counterplay with 69 ... ♘d3 70 g5+ ♔e7 71 ♘c2 a2 72 ♔g7) 70 g5+ ♔e7 71 ♔g7 ♘xe3 72 f6+ ♔e6 73 ♗h3+ ♘f5+ 74 ♗xf5+ ♔xf5 75 ♔xf7 e3 76 ♔g7! e2 77 ♘c2 a2 78 f7 e1(♛) 79 ♘xe1 a1(♛) 80 f8(♛)+. However, after the correct 65 ... b5!, nothing can be found for White.

65	...	**♘d3**

65 ... ♘c4 comes too late: 66 ♔f6 ♘xe3 67 ♔e7.

66	**♘b3!?**	**a2**
67	**♘a1**	**b5**
68	**♗d1**	**b4** *(110)*

Bringing the king a little closer to the pawns does not work: 68 ... ♔d6? 69 ♗b3 ♘c1 70 ♔h6 b4 71 f6 ♔e6 72 ♔g7 ♘xb3 73 ♘xb3 ♗a4 74 ♘c5+! ♔d6 75 f7 a1(♛) 76 f8(♛)+ ♔c6 77 ♛c8+ ♔d6 78 ♛d8+ ♔c6 79 ♛d7+ ♔b6 80 ♛b7+ ♔a5 81 ♛a6 mate.

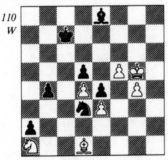

110
W

69	**♗b3**	**♘c1**

After 69 ... ♔d6 70 ♔f6, the g-pawn cannot be stopped.

70	**♗xd5**	**♔d6**
71	**♗c4**	**♗b5**

Not 41 ... ♔e7 42 f6+ ♔f8 43 ♔h6 ♗f7 44 d5 b3 75 d6!, or 71 ... ♗a4 72 f6 b3 73 ♔h6! b2 74 f7 b1(♛) 75 f8 (♛)+ ♔d7 76 ♛f5+ ♔c7 77 ♛a5+, but here 74 ... ba (♛) leads to a completely unclear position – G. Flear.

An interesting possibility is 71 ... b3 72 ♗xb3 ♘xb3 73 ♘xb3

♔d5 74 ♘a1 ♔c4 75 ♔f6 ♔c3 76 ♔e7 ♔b2 77 ♔xe8 ♔xa1 78 f6 ♔b2 79 f7 a1(♕) 80 f8(♕) ♕a4+ 81 ♔f7 ♔b3+. We had reached this position in our analysis, and Zaitsev suggested 82 ♔f6 ♕xe3 83 ♔e5 ♔c2 84 ♕f4 ♔d3 85 d5 with chances of success. But in the post-mortem, Timman pointed out the more effective 82 d5! ♕xe3 (82 ... ♕xd5+ 83 ♔g6 with a technically won ending) 83 ♕b4+ ♔c2 84 g5 ♕f3+ 85 ♔g7 e3 86 ♕c4+ ♔b2 87 ♕b5+ ♔c1 88 d6 e2 89 ♕c5+ ♔b2 90 ♕b6+ ♔c1 91 d7 e1(♕) 92 d8(♕) ♕ec3+ 93 ♕df6 etc. According to computer analyses, this ending is a win for White.

72	**♗g8**	**♔e7**
73	**♔h6**	

After 73 f6+ ♔f8 74 ♗e6 b3 (74 ... ♗a4 leads to the same result as in the game) 75 ♗xb3 ♘xb3 76 ♘xb3 ♗c4 77 ♘a1 ♔f7 78 ♔f5, White wins. However, Black has the saving move 74 ... ♗d7!, and if 75 ♗xd7 (it is more sensible to settle for a draw) 75 ... b3 76 ♔f5 b2 77 g5 ♘e2! 78 g6 ♘g3+! 79 ♔g5 ♘h5! 80 ♔xh5 ba(♕) 81 g7+ ♔f7 82 ♗e8+ (82 ♗e6+ ♔xf6 83 g8(♕) ♕h1+) 82 ... ♔xf6, it is Black who unexpectedly wins.

73	**...**	**♔f8?**

It is only now that Timman commits the decisive error. He could have drawn with 73 ... b3! 74 ♗xb3 ♘xb3 75 ♘xb3 ♗c4 76 ♘a1 ♔f6!, as pointed out by his second, the Hungarian grandmaster Sax.

74	**♗e6!**	**♗d7**
75	**g5**	**b3**
76	**g6**	

1–0

Black resigned rather than be mated: 76 ... ♗xe6 77 fe b2 78 g7+ ♔e7 (78 ... ♔g8 79 e7 ♔f7 80 g8(♕)+ ♔xe7 81 ♕g5+ ♔f7 82 ♕d5+ ♔f6 83 ♕c6+) 79 g8(♕) ba(♕) 80 ♕f7+ ♔d6 81 ♕d7 mate.

After this victory, it became clear that another duel for the world crown between Kasparov and myself was inevitable.

Game No. 24
Wojtkiewicz–Karpov
Haninge 1990

I have played the White side of the Grünfeld so often, especially the g2–g3 system, that when the symmetrical variation arose in the present game, it was with some interest that I handled it for the other colour.

1	♘f3	♘f6
2	c4	g6
3	g3	♗g7
4	♗g2	0–0
5	d4	c6

I have rarely played either the King's Indian or the Grünfeld with Black. But given the choice between them, I prefer the latter.

6	♘c3	d5
7	cd	cd
8	♘e5	e6
9	0–0	♘fd7
10	f4	♘c6
11	♗e3	♘b6 *(111)*

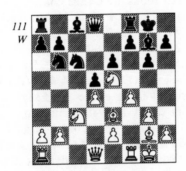

111
W

Kasparov had played this knight move against me in the first and third match game in Seville, and now I decided to use it myself. An alternative of equal value is 11 ... f6 (see Game No. 23). In the present game, you might say that I combined the two ideas.

Before proceeding with the main game, in which White played 12 b3, let us look at the two encounters from Seville, where I preferred 12 ♗f2. The first match game went as follows:

12 ♗f2 ♗d7 13 e4 ♘e7 14 ♘xd7

In the game Drasko–Nikolić, Vrnjacka Banja 1987, where it appears this position occurred for the first time, White opted for **14 ed** ♘bxd5 15 ♘xd5 ♘xd5 16 ♕b3 ♗c6 17 ♖ac1 ♕a5 18 ♖c5 ♕a6, and a draw was agreed.

Another possibilty is **14 a4! de 15 a5 ♘bd5 16 ♘xe4 ♖b8 17 ♕b3 ♗e8** 18 ♖fc1 ♘c6 19 ♕a3 ♘cb4. Nikolić–Hulak, Zagreb 1987, continued 20 ♖c4? ♘a6 21 ♘d6 ♘ac7 22 ♖ac1 ♘b5 23 ♘xb5 ♗xb5 24 ♖c5 ♗e8 25 b4 b6, and White achieved nothing; but Gutman's suggestion 20 ♘c3! gives him the advantage. At move 17, an alternative is **17 ... ♗c6** 18 ♘c5 ♘c7 19 ♗xc6! with the initiative; this is stronger than 18 ♖fc1 a6 (18 ... ♘c7! at once is more precise) 19 ♖c4 (19 ♘c5! is correct) 19 ... ♘c7 20 ♘c3 ♗xg2 21 ♔xg2 ♘cd5, with equality; Andersson–Hulak, Wijk aan Zee 1987.

14 ... ♕xd7 15 e5 ♖fc8 16 ♖c1 ♗f8 17 ♗f3 ♖c7

An accurate move which equalises. I would have answered the incautious 17 ... a6 with 18 ♗e2 ♖c7 19 g4! ♗h6 20 ♕d2, and if 20 ... ♘c4, then 21 ♗xc4 ♖xc4 22 ♘e4!. But now this idea doesn't work: 18 ♗e2 ♖ac8 19 g4 ♗h6 20 ♕d2 ♘c4 21 ♗xc4 ♖xc4, and both black rooks are on the c-file.

18 b3 ♖ac8 19 ♕d2 ♘c6 20 ♕b2 a6 21 ♗e2 ♕e7! 22 ♘b1 ♘b4 23 ♘c3 ♘c6 24 ♘b1 ♘b4 25 ♖c5 ♘d7 26 ♖xc7 ♖xc7 27 ♘c3 ♘c6 28 ♘b1 ♘b4 29 ♘c3 ♘c6 30 ♘b1 ½–½.

In the third game, Kasparov varied with **12... ♘e7!** (a refinement on 12 ... ♗d7 of the first game) 13 a4 a5 14 ♕b3 (Black would have had more problems after 14 e4 de 15 ♗xe4 ♘bd5 16 ♕b3. Greenfeld–Birnboim, Tel-Aviv 1988, continued 16 ... f6 17 ♘c4 ♔h8 18 ♖fe1 ♘b4 19 ♖ad1 ♘ed5 20 ♘e3 ♖a6 21 ♗xd5 ed 22 ♘exd5 ♗g4 23 ♖d2 ♖e6 24 ♘xb4 ♖xe1+ 25 ♗xe1 ab 26 ♕xb4 ♖e8 27 ♗f2, and White gained the advantage) 14 ... ♗d7 15 ♖fc1 ♗c6 16 ♘b5 ♘bc8! 17 e3 ♘d6 18 ♘xd6 ♕xd6 19 ♗e1 ♖fb8 20 ♗f1 f6 21 ♘f3 ♕d7 22 ♕c2 ♘f5 23 ♗d2 ♘d6 24 b3 ♖c8 25 ♕d1 h6 26 ♗e1 g5 27 ♖a2 ♕e8 28 ♖ac2 ♗f8 29 ♗d3 g4 ½–½.

12   b3

This move was played for the first time in Portisch–Korchnoi, Reggio Emilia 1987/8. It seems to me that if White is seeking the initiative, it is worth trying 12 ♘xc6 bc 13 ♗f2.

12   ...   ♗d7
13   ♕d2   f6

In Portisch–Korchnoi, Black first played 13 ... ♖e8 14 ♖fc1, and only then 14 ... f6. After 15 ♘d3 ♖e7 16 ♔h1 ♗e8, the players agreed a draw. Evidently on that day they were just not in the mood for a fight; the result has nothing to do with the position. In the present game, I carry out a regrouping in the centre as Black, without wasting time on rook manoeuvres.

14	♘d3	♘c8
15	♖ac1	♘d6
16	♗f2	*(112)*

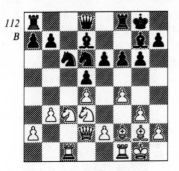

The position is characterised by so-called dynamic equilibrium. The pawn chains are closed, and the forces cannot clash for some time yet. Some precise and none-too-obvious manipulation of the pieces is called for, and of course such operations are not to everyone's taste. But I personally have always liked this kind of game, based as it is on a wealth of subtle points. I had previously encountered such situations with White, but was also ready to try them with Black, especially since the configuration of pieces is nearly symmetrical.

Here, by the way, is an illustration of the subtleties inherent in the position. Black just needs to play one careless move, 16 ... ♗e8?, and White immediately seizes the initiative: 17 ♘c5! ♗f7 (17 ... ♕e7 18 ♘xe6!) 18 e4 de 19 ♘3xe4 ♘xe4 20 ♗xe4 ♕e7 21 ♘xb7!

16	...	f5
17	♘e5	♕e7
18	♔h1	♖fc8
19	g4!?	

19 ♘a4 or 19 a3 would have preserved equality, but White is trying for more.

19	...	♘e4
20	♘xe4	fe
21	♘xd7	

The knight cannot hold out on e5 for long, but perhaps it was worth exchanging it for the black one: 21 ♖c3 ♘xe5 22 de ♖xc3 23 ♕xc3 ♖c8 24 ♕d2 b6 25 ♗g3, intending f4–f5.

21 ♗g3!? at once is also interesting: 21 ... ♘xe5 22 de ♖xc1 23 ♖xc1 ♖c8 24 ♖xc8+ ♗xc8 25 ♕c3 (White's aim is to carry out f4–f5, but the situation does not yet call for it: 25 f5? ef 26 gf gf 27 ♕xd5+ ♗e6, or 25 ♕d4 b6 26 f5 ef 27 gf gf 28 ♕xd5+ ♗e6 29 ♕a8+ ♔f7, with a good game for Black in either case) 25 ... ♕d7 (but not 25 ... ♕d8 26 ♗h4!, or 25 ... ♗d7 26 ♕c7) 26 e3 b6 27 a4 ♗b7, and again the chances are about equal.

21	...	♕xd7
22	a3 *(113)*	

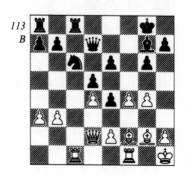

113
B

One thoughtless move, made on general grounds – and already Black has a chance to seize the initiative. 22 e3 was correct, avoiding weakening the queenside.

22	...	a5!
23	♗h3	♕e7

Forcing the rook to abandon the c-file.

| 24 | ♖a1 | ♘d8 |

Black could have prevented the f4–f5 break by playing 24 ... ♗h6 25 g5 ♗g7. After 26 ♖fc1, followed by e2–e3 and ♗h3–f1, it would be hard for either side to play for a win. Instead, I attempt to bring my knight over to the kingside, where the decisive events will shortly take place.

| 25 | f5 | g5 |

The sharp 25 ... ♘f7!? is also interesting.

| 26 | ♗g3 | ♘c6 |

At this point I convinced myself that after 26 ... ♘f7 27 fe! ♛xe6 28 ♖f5 h6 29 ♖af1 ♘d6 30 ♗e5! ♘xf5 31 gf ♛d7 32 ♗xg7 ♛xg7 33 f6 the initiative is with White, so I decided to bring the knight back again.

27	e3	♖d8
28	fe	♛xe6
29	♖f5	h6
30	♛e2	

30 ♖af1 looks more consistent, yet White cannot successfully exploit his domination of the f-file: 30 ... ♘e7 31 ♗c7 ♖dc8! (but not 30 ... ♖e8 31 ♗e5 ♘xf5 32 gf ♛a6 33 ♗xg7 ♔xg7 34 f6+, with an attack for the exchange), and now 32 ♗e5 is not so effective: 32 ... ♘xf5 33 gf ♛a6! 34 ♗xg7 (34 f5 ♖f8!) 34 ... ♔xg7 35 f6+ ♔h8! 36 ♛f2 ♖c7 37 ♗d7 ♖d6 38 f7 ♖f8 39 ♛f5 ♔g7 40 ♛e5+ ♖f6 41 ♗b5 ♛d6, and White's attack is spent. On the other hand after 32 ♗xa5 Black takes the exchange, and his chances must be preferable.

30	...	♘e7
31	♖f1	♖dc8
32	♖ac1	♖c6
33	♖xc6	♛xc6
34	♖b1	

Rather a passive move. It was worth considering 34 ♖f2!?, and if 34 ... ♛c1+ 35 ♗f1 ♛xa3, then after 36 ♛b5 ♛b4 (36 ... a4? 37 ♛xb7 ab 38 ♗d6) 37 ♛d7 White has a dangerous initiative for the pawn. Instead, 34 ... a4! leads to unclear play: 35 ba (better than 35 b4 ♛c1+ 36 ♛f1 ♛xa3 37 ♗d6 ♘g6 38 ♛b5 ♛c1+ 39 ♗f1 ♛c6 with advantage to Black, or 36 ♗f1 ♛xa3 37 ♛b5 ♛xe3 38 ♛xb7 ♖f8 etc.) 35 ... ♖xa4 36 ♛b2.

34	...	♗f8
35	♗f1	♘c8
36	♛b2	♛d7
37	♗e2	♗d6
38	♗e1	

The advantage of the bishop pair is illusory – it was better to eliminate the bishop on d6. After 38 ♖f1 (more precise than 38 ♗xd6 ♘xd6) 38 ... ♗xg3 39 hg, it would be difficult to breach White's fortress.

| 38 | ... | ♘e7 |
| 39 | ♖c1 | ♖f8! |

40 &g2

Not 40 &xa5?, on account of 40 ... &f2. But 40 &g1, followed by &e2–d1, was more tenacious.

40 ... &g6
41 b4 a4
42 &c2 &f7!

The threats on the f-file are becoming formidable.

43 &d1

The black a-pawn is immune: 43 &xa4 &f4+! 44 ef &xf4 45 &g3 &xc1 46 &xd6 &e1! 47 &xf8 &xe2+ 48 &g1 e3 49 h3 &f2+ 50 &h1 e2, and wins.

43 ... &h8!

Preparing to open the g-file.

44 &c3 (114)

44 &g1 would likewise be answered by 44 ... h5!, intending to take the g-pawn; after 45 gh &f5! 46 hg (46 &g2 &h4+ 47 &xh4 gh is crushing) 46 ... &h3 47 &g3 &xg3 48 hg &xg3+ 49 &h1 &f2 50 &c8+ &g7, it is all over.

Nor does 44 &c2 help: 44 ... h5! 45 gh &e7 (45 ... &h4+ is premature because of 46 &xh4 gh 47 &g4) 46 h3 (46 &c3 g4! and ... &xh5) 46 ... &f5 47 &c3 &h4+ 48 &xh4 gh 49 &e1 (49 &g1 &g8+ 50 &g4 &f3 mate) 49 ... &g3 50 &f1 &f2+, and Black wins.

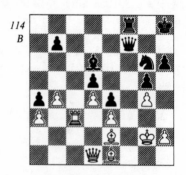

114
B

44 ... h5!
45 gh &h4+!
46 &xh4

If 46 &g1 (46 &h1 &f1+), then 46 ... &f5, followed by ... &f5–h3, is decisive.

46	...	gh
47	♕e1	h3+!
48	♔h1	

Other continuations are less stubborn: 48 ♔g1 ♕g7+, or 48 ♔xh3 ♖g8 49 ♗g4 ♖xg4 50 ♔xg4 ♕f3+ 51 ♔g5 ♗e7+ 52 ♔h6 ♕f6 mate.

48	...	♕f2
49	♕xf2	♖xf2
50	♖c2	♖xh2+
51	♔g1	♖g2+
52	♔h1	♖f2
53	♔g1	

55 ♗d3 is met by 53 ... ♖f3.

53	...	♗g3
54	♔h1	♔h7
55	♔g1	♔h6
56	♔h1	♖h2+
57	♔g1	♖f2
58	♔h1	♗d6
59	♔g1	♖g2+
60	♔f1	♖g8
61	♖c1	♖g3

61 ... ♗h2 was immediately decisive; so was 61 ... ♗xb4 62 ab h2 63 ♔f2 ♖g1 64 ♖xg1 hg(♕)+ 65 ♔xg1 a3.

The game was now adjourned. Realising that Black's threats were unanswerable, White resigned without playing on.

0–1

Game No. 25
Vaganian–Kasparov
Barcelona 1989

1	♘f3	♘f6
2	c4	g6
3	g3	♗g7
4	♗g2	0–0
5	♘c3	d5
6	cd	♘xd5

The reader will recall that in the World Championship matches of 1986–7, Kasparov preferred the symmetrical system, in which Black prepares ... d7–d5 with ... c7–c6 and recaptures on d5 with the pawn. In a game we played later (and which I shall examine further on), he chose ... ♘xd5. In the last two or three years, Kasparov has played a number of quite interesting games with this line, and the one I have selected here as the 'principal' game is among the most fascinating of all. In the notes, as usual, I shall also mention other important examples from recent practice.

$$\begin{array}{llll} \textbf{7} & \textbf{0–0} & & \textbf{♘c6} \\ \textbf{8} & \textbf{d4} & & \textbf{♘b6} \;(115) \end{array}$$

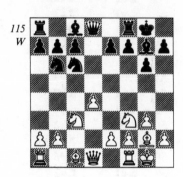

Here White has the choice between the slow e2–e3, as in the actual game, and the more committal d4–d5 and e2–e4. Let us first consider the latter.

9 d5

Another possibility, seen more rarely, is 9 ♗f4.

9 ... ♘a5 10 e4

The modest **10 ♕c2** quickly leads to equality; here are two examples:

Tukmakov–Halifman, Simferopol 1988, went **10 ... c6 11 dc ♘xc6 12 ♖d1 ♗f5** 13 e4 ♗d7 14 ♗f4 ♖c8 15 ♕e2 ♕e8 16 h3 ♗e6 17 ♘d5 ♗xd5 18 ed ♘b4 19 ♘e1 ♕d7 20 ♕d2 ♘a6 ½–½.

Plachetka–Smejkal, Trnava 1989, varied with **12 ... ♕c7** 13 ♘b5 ♕b8 14 ♗f4 e5 15 ♗e3 ♗f5 16 ♕c5 ♖c8 17 ♘xa7 ♘a4 18 ♘xc6 bc 19 ♕e7 ½–½.

In Nikolić–Kasparov, Skelleftea 1989, White played instead **10 ♗f4**, and there followed 10 ... c6 11 dc ♕xd1 12 ♖axd1 ♘xc6 13 ♘b5 ♗g4! 14 b3 e5! 15 ♗e3 e4! 16 ♘fd4 ♘xd4 17 ♘xd4 ♘d5 18 h3 ♘xe3 19 fe ♗d7. Black's position is the more pleasant, though the game was eventually drawn.

10 ... c6 11 ♗g5

An inadequate alternative is 11 ♖e1 ♘ac4! 12 ♕e2 ♗g4 13 dc (13 ♗g5 h6) 13 ... bc 14 h3 ♗xf3 15 ♗xf3; Yurtayev–Belov, Podolsk 1989. At this point, 15 ... ♕d6 (instead of 15 ... a5), with the idea of 16 ... ♕c5 or 16 ... ♕b4, would have given Black a good game.

11 ... h6

Black failed to justify 11 ... ♗g4 in Hansen–Kasparov, Thessaloniki Ol 1988: 12 h3 ♗xf3 13 ♕xf3 cd 14 ♘xd5 ♘xd5 15 ♖ad1 ♕c7 16 ed ♗xb2 (16 ... ♘c4 17 ♕e2 ♖fe8 18 ♖c1 b5 19 b3 ♕e5 20 ♕xe5 ♘xe5 21 d6, and Black is in a bad way) 17 ♖fe1 ♖fe8 18 ♖xe7! ♖xe7 19 d6 ♖e1+ 20 ♖xe1 ♕xd6 21 ♖e7 ♖f8 22 ♕d5, and although Black did manage to save himself, his position does not inspire much confidence.

12 ♗f4 cd 13 ed

13 ♘xd5 is strongly answered by **13 ... ♘ac4!**. In Pastircak–Hort, Czechoslovakia 1984, White continued with the straightforward **14 ♘c7?**, and ended up in a difficult position after 14 ... ♖b8 15 ♕xd8 ♖xd8 16 ♖ad1 (16 ♘a6 e5!) 16 ... ♗g4 17 ♘d5 e5 18 ♘xb6 ♖xd1 19 ♖xd1 ♘xb2! 20 ♖d2 ef. Instead **14 ♕b3** might appear dangerous for Black, but with 14 ... e5! 15 ♘xb6 ♕xb6! 16 ♗xh6 (16 ♕xc4 ef) 16 ... ♗xh6 17 ♕xc4 ♕xb2 18 ♖ab1 ♕a3 19 ♘xe5 ♗e6, he obtained the bishop pair and plenty of chances for the pawn in Shpilker–Krasenkov, Moscow 1987.

13 ... ♘ac4 14 ♕e2 g5

If 14 ... ♘xb2, then 15 ♘e5!.

15 ♗c1 e6! 16 de

Better 16 ♖d1, although 16 ... ed 17 ♘xd5 ♘xd5 18 ♕xc4 ♘b6! 19 ♕b3 ♕f6 gives Black slightly the better game (Popović).

16 ... ♗xe6 17 ♖d1 ♕c8 18 ♘d4

A sounder line is 18 h4 ♗g4 19 hg.

18 ... ♗g4! 19 ♗f3 ♗h3! 20 ♘d5 ♘xd5 21 ♗xd5 ♖d8 22 ♘c6 bc 23 ♗xc4 ♕f5 24 ♗d3 ♕e5 25 ♕xe5 ♗xe5

Black has a clear endgame advantage, and went on to win in Hjartarson–Popović, Belgrade 1989.

9   e3   e5

9 ... ♖e8 is also seen. Kasparov, for example, played it twice against Portisch in 1988. Both games continued **10 d5 ♘a5 11 ♘d4 ♗d7**. In Saloniki, Portisch played **12 ♕e2**, which led to equality after 12 ... c6 13 dc ♘xc6 14 ♘xc6 ♗xc6 15 ♗xc6 bc

16 ♖d1 ♕c8 17 ♗d2 ♕e6 18 ♗e1 a5. In Reykjavik, he innovated with **12 b4?!**, but after 12 ... ♘ac4 13 a4 a5 14 b5 ♕c8 15 ♖e1 ♗h3 16 ♗h1 ♕g4 17 ♘ce2 ♖ad8 18 ♕b3 ♕d7 19 ♘f4 ♗g4 20 ♖a2 ♕d6, Black had some initiative in the complexities. All the same, this game too ended in a draw.

In Ljubojević–Kasparov, Barcelona 1989, White introduced a different novelty, though he moved the same pawn: **12 b3**. However, after five more moves – 12 ... c5 13 dc ♘xc6 14 ♘xc6 ♗xc6 15 ♗xc6 ♕xd1 16 ♖xd1 bc 17 ♗d2 a5 – a draw, once again, was agreed.

Finally, another game by Kasparov went **12 e4** c5 13 dc ♘xc6 14 ♘xc6 ♗xc6 15 ♕b3 ♕d3 16 ♗e3 ♖ac8 17 ♖fd1 ♕a6 18 ♗d4 ♕a5, with equality; Hjartarson–Kasparov, Reykjavik 1989.

| | **10** | **d5** | **♘a5** |

Practice has shown that retreating with 10 ... ♘e7 is too passive.

| | **11** | **e4** | **c6** |
| | **12** | **♗g5** | |

At this point we shall digress to examine the game Karpov–Kasparov, Amsterdam 1988, in which the same position arose, only with the rooks on the e-file instead of the f-file. The order of the opening moves was 1 d4 ♘f6 2 c4 g6 3 ♘f3 ♗g7 4 g3 d5 5 cd ♘xd5 6 ♗g2 ♘b6 7 ♘c3 ♘c6 8 e3 0–0 9 0–0 ♖e8 10 ♖e1 e5 11 d5 ♘a5 12 e4 c6 13 ♗g5 *(116)*.

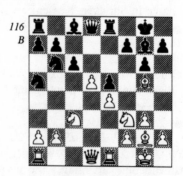

Play continued 13 ... f6 14 ♗e3 ♘ac4! 15 dc ♘xe3 (Black is willing to give up a small amount of material rather than accept defects in his pawn structure. At the same time he activates his forces) 16 ♕xd8 ♖xd8 17 cb ♗xb7 (if 17 ... ♘xg2, then 18 ba(♕) ♘xe1 19 ♕xa7 destroys all Black's illusions) 18 ♖xe3 ♗h6 19

♖ee1 ♘c4 20 ♖ad1 ♔f8 21 h4 ♖ac8 22 ♗h3 (White appears to have seized the initiative, but this is purely temporary) 22 ... ♖xd1 23 ♖xd1 ♘xb2 24 ♖d7 ♖xc3 25 ♖xb7 (it was worth testing Black by first playing 25 ♖d8+ ♔e7 26 ♖d7+ ♔f8; the point is that 26 ... ♔e8 is risky, since the king needs to guard g7 as a retreat square for the bishop) 25 ... ♘c4 (the opposite bishop ending after 25 ... ♖xf3 26 ♖xb2 is unpleasant for Black) 26 ♘h2 (not 26 ♖c7?, in view of 26 ... ♖c1+ 27 ♗f1 ♘d2 28 ♖xc1 ♘xf3+ 29 ♔g2 ♘xh4+ 30 gh ♗xc1, and now it is White who has to hold an opposite bishop ending a pawn down. On the other hand, a draw results from 26 ♗e6 ♘d6) 26 ... ♘d6 27 ♖xh7 (or 27 ♖xa7 ♖xg3+! 28 fg ♗e3+ with equality) 27 ... ♗g7 28 h5 gh 29 ♖xh5 ♖c1+ 30 ♔g2 ♖c2 31 ♗e6 ♘xe4 32 ♘g4 ♖d2 33 ♗b3 (the last chance was 33 ♔f3 ♘g5+ 34 ♔e3 ♖b2 35 ♗b3, but 33 ... ♘c5 34 ♗c4 maintains the balance) 33 ... a5 34 ♖f5 ♘d6 35 ♖h5 ♘e4 36 ♖f5 ♘d6 37 ♖h5 ♘e4 ½-½.

12	...	f6
13	♗e3	cd
14	ed	

After 14 ♗xb6 ♕xb6 15 ♘xd5 ♕d8 16 b4 ♘c6, the chances are approximately equal.

| 14 | ... | ♗g4 |

Black's plans involve the advance ... f6–f5, which may be carried out with the bishop on either g4 or c8.

Mikhalchishin–Gavrikov, Budapest 1989, went 14 ... ♖f7 15 ♗c5 f5 16 ♕c1! (16 ♘d2 e4 17 ♘b3 ♘ac4 18 ♕e2 ♘e5 19 ♖ad1 ♘bc4 20 ♘d4 b6 21 ♘c6 ♕e8 led to equality in Gligorić–Gavrikov, Moscow 1989) 16 ... e4 17 ♘g5 ♖c7 18 b4 ♘bc4 (other continuations are worse, for example 18 ... ♘xd5 19 ♘xd5 ♕xd5 20 ♖d1, with a won position) 19 ♖d1 ♗xc3 20 ♕xc3 ♕xg5 21 ♗e3! (peace was quickly concluded in Mikhalchishin–Ftačnik, Palma de Mallorca 1989: 21 ♗d4 ♗d7 22 ba ♕e7! 23 ♗b6 ♖cc8 24 ♗c7 ♘d6 25 ♗xd6 ♕xd6 26 ♕d4 ½-½. On the other hand, 21 ♕d4? b6 22 d6 ♖xc5 23 bc ♗e6 is good for Black) 21 ... ♕d8! (better than 21 ... ♘xe3 22 ♕xc7 ♘xd1 23 ♖xd1) 22 ba ♘xe3 23 ♕xe3 ♕d6 24 f3 ef 25 ♗xf3 ♗d7 26 ♖ac1 (better 26 ♖ab1. Now the game is level) 26 ... ♖xc1 27 ♖xc1 b6 28 ♕f4 ♕xf4 29 gf ♖c8 30 ♖xc8+ ♗xc8 31 ab ab 32 ♔f2 ♔f7 33 ♔e3 ♔e7 34 ♔d4 ♔d6 ½-½.

15 ♗c5

Practice has also seen 15 h3 ♗xf3 16 ♗xf3 f5 17 ♗e2, with complex play.

15	...	♖f7
16	b3	f5
17	♗b4	*(117)*

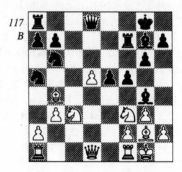

117
B

A well-known position. Black normally used to play 17 ... ♘c8, whereupon White has the strong move 18 ♕e1. This occurred, incidentally, in Vaganian–Thorsteins, Copenhagen 1988. The idea is that Black no longer has the important tempo-gaining move ... ♕d8–b6 (it would be met by ♘c3–a4), his knight on a5 is indirectly attacked, and the position is very difficult for him. After 18 ... ♗xf3 19 ♗xf3 ♘d6 20 ♗e2 b6 (better 20 ... e4) 21 ♗a6, White gained the advantage and won.

But Kasparov has a remarkable surprise in store for his opponent.

17	...	♘ac4!

An unexpected piece sacrifice, although admittedly the material is quickly regained. Kasparov had, of course, prepared this novelty in his pre-game analysis, knowing that Vaganian regularly plays this variation.

18	bc	e4

White's pawn-couple looks strong, but Black has ample resources. A notable point is that as long as the black knight was on a5, the white bishop on b4 was splendidly placed, both attacking and defending; but once the knight has sacrificed itself, the bishop is constantly exposed to the threat of ... a7–a5. Vaganian himself commented on this paradox of the instant transformation of this bishop.

| 19 | ♖c1 |

If 19 c5, Black has the very strong counter-blow 19 ... a5!

| 19 | ... | ♕d7?! |

The situation is extremely tense, and Black fails to choose the correct path. Evidently Kasparov underestimated his opponent's retort. After the game, he demonstrated the following variations: **19 ... ♘xc4** 20 ♘xe4 fe 21 ♖xc4 ♗xf3 22 ♕d2 ♕d7, with equality; or **19 ... ef** 20 ♗xf3 ♗xf3 21 ♕xf32 ♘xc4. The latter, however, was played in Ionov–Urban, Katowice 1991, and after 22 ♘b5 ♘e5 23 ♕b3 a5 24 ♗d6 a4 25 ♕e3 f4 26 gf ♘g4 27 ♕e6 ♕h4 28 f5 ♕g5 29 fg ♘e5+ 30 ♔h1 ♘xg6 31 ♖c7 White neutralised his opponent's initiative and went on to win.

20	♘b1!	ef
21	♗xf3	♗xf3
22	♕xf3	f4
23	g4	♕a4
24	♕b3	

This time it is White who plays inaccurately. After 24 ♗c3! ♗xc3 25 ♘xc3 ♕xc4 26 ♖fd1 ♖d8 27 d6, he could feel fairly confident.

| 24 | ... | ♕d7 |

The players are committing errors alternately. Black should have played 24 ... f3, with a good game for the pawn; White's king is badly placed, and his pieces are rather passive.

| 25 | f3 | h5 *(118)* |

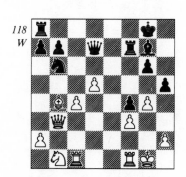

118 W

| 26 | h3 | ♖e8 |
| 27 | ♕d3 | |

It was not worth chasing after a second pawn. After 27 ♗c5! ♕c7 28 ♗f2 ♖e3 29 ♕d1, White would have set up a solid protective wall while keeping a material advantage. Now the mutual turmoil subsides, and the game quickly heads towards a peaceful result.

27 ... hg 28 hg ♖e3! 29 ♕xg6 ♖f6 30 ♕g5 ♕f7 31 ♗c3 ♖g6 32 ♕d8+ ♖e8 33 ♕h4 ♗xc3 34 ♖xc3 ♕g7 35 ♖e1 ♕d4+ 36 ♔g2 ♖xe1 37 ♕xe1 ♘xc4 38 ♕e8+ ♔g7 39 ♕e7+ ♔h6 40 ♕h4+ ♔g7 41 ♕e7+ ♔h6 42 ♕f8+ ♔h7 43 ♕f7+ ♔h6 ½–½

Index of Variations

Exchange Variation with 7 ♗c4 – other systems

3	♘c3	d5
4	cd	♘xd5
5	e4	♘xc3
6	bc	♗g7
7	♗c4	c5
8	♘e2	♘c6
9	♗e3	0–0
10	0–0	

Modern Exchange Variation